WHEN
BAD THINGS
HAPPEN TO
GOOD
WOMEN

WHEN
BAD THINGS
HAPPEN TO
GOOD
WOMEN

Getting You
(or Someone You Love)
Through the Toughest Times

CAROLE BRODY FLEET

Published in the United States by Cleis Press, an imprint of Start Midnight, LLC, 101 Hudson Street, Thirty-Seventh Floor, Suite 3705, Jersey City, NJ 07302.

Printed in the United States.
Cover design: Scott Idleman/Blink
Text design: Frank Wiedemann
First Edition.
10 9 8 7 6 5 4 3 2 1

Trade paper ISBN: 978-1-63228-016-9
E-book ISBN: 978-1-63228-030-5

Author's Note

All suggestions regarding medical, financial and legal subject matter are based upon the information, belief and personal opinions of Carole Brody Fleet and non-compensated contributors only and should not be construed as directed advice. The ideas, suggestions and procedures contained in this book are not intended as a substitute for expert assistance. Any application of the recommendations set forth in this book is at the reader's discretion and sole risk.

The third-person stories, anecdotes and quotations contained in the book are authored by non-compensated contributors, and permission has been granted to reprint their contributions. Stories have been edited in the interest of space, grammar, continuity and privacy. Bracketed additions have been made for the sole purposes of privacy protection, continuity, grammar and/or subject matter clarification.

Actual names have been used, except where otherwise indicated by an* that a pseudonym selected by a contributor has been used at the contributor's request in the interest of privacy protection and/or for safety and security reasons. With the exception of well-known public figures or those who have otherwise given specific permission, last names have been excluded in the interest of privacy and for safety reasons.

All stories contained herein are the exclusive property of the author, the publisher and the various contributors who have consented to the use of their stories and are subject to all copyright protections therein.

dedication

This book is lovingly dedicated to:

All of the inspiring women who so bravely and generously shared their stories of adversity, determination and courage. Your spirit of sharing in an effort to help others is to be greatly admired.

Rabbi Harold Kushner
Your vision has helped millions and continues to do so today. Thank you for helping to inspire this book and for lighting the path of healing for so many who have suffered their own bad things—including yours truly.

Eilene Clinkenbeard
For being Mama to a writer-chick, and for allowing me to share your Mom-isms with a smile (and a few out-loud laughs).

Kendall Leah Brody, Michelle Louise Stansbury and Natasha Tillett Slayton
You are each my light and my inspiration, my joy and my reason. Mommy loves you very much.

Dave Stansbury
To my partner in life and in love—thank you for proving that no bad thing is forever, that good things are always just around the corner, and for "Drive How *You* Drive"…the wisest words ever spoken. I love you very much.

Elvin "Clink" Clinkenbeard (1923-2001) and Michael Fleet, Sr. (1945-2000)
You both give me strength and fill me with warm memories every day.
I honor you both, and I love you forever.

table of contents

prologue

Let's face it—as women of the twenty-first century, our collective plates are pretty full.

We are movers, shakers and possibility-makers in a world that would be lost without our influence and contributions, both large and small. Most of us work, be it out in the world, for ourselves or in our households as wives and/ or mothers. We have relationships of all manner. We volunteer in an effort to make the world a better place. We see suffering and we strive to fix it, whether it is skinned knees or starving populations. We live abundantly and love without condition. We are breadwinners, parents, partners, girlfriends…

All in all, we are pretty awesome.

Unfortunately though, all the awesomeness in the world does not prevent one very stark reality: Bad things happen to women.

Really bad things happen to *really* good women doing *really* good things in an ever-more-challenging world.

Chances are excellent that at some point in your life, you or someone you know has experienced some kind of misfortune. Perhaps you lost a loved one.

Maybe you lost a job, a home or are going through a divorce. And what about the some of the other "core-shakers"—such as you or someone you love being diagnosed with a life-threatening illness, your financial security being threatened or destroyed, becoming a victim of a violent crime or discovering that you have been cheated on or otherwise betrayed.

Yes, bad things indeed happen to good women...things that no one deserves to experience. The question is, what do you do when those bad things invade your life or the lives of those you love? How do you move forward? Where do you start? How do you even *begin* to recover? What does your future look like, especially when it is likely not the future that you originally planned?

You are about to get the answers to all of these questions and a whole lot more.

The purpose of this book is actually two-fold. The book is first intended for those who are experiencing, or have experienced, their own bad-thing challenge(s) of a lifetime. As you read, you will discover a wide variety of some of the most common life challenges and situations with which women cope. You will be reading actual stories shared by real women who were faced with challenges that forever changed their lives. You will be taken through very common thought and reaction processes that we all tend to go through when presented with adversity. Best of all, you will learn how all of these women eventually overcame their respective bad things, and you will gain fantastic insight as to what to do should you find yourself in the same or similar situations.

The second purpose of the book is for those who know someone who has been touched by serious challenge or adversity. In my many years as a grief recovery expert, I have heard the phrase "I just don't know what to say/ what to do/how to act" over and over again,. Since direction for the "I-Just-Don't-Knows" is almost as important as it is for those directly affected by bad things, you are going to find wonderful ideas and suggestions as to what to say and do—and perhaps even more importantly, what *never* to say or do—when someone you know and love is dealing with a bad thing. **"Definite Do's"** are packed full of suggestions and action items to help your mother, daughter, sister, cousin, girlfriend, best friend and any and all women in your life deal with their personal bad things in positive and uplifting ways. The "**Without a Doubt...Don't**" quotes that you see within each chapter are all actual quotes that should never be used to anyone going through that particular bad thing.

Naturally, it is impossible to include every single bad thing that may cross our paths throughout our lives in one book. As one radio show host noted during an interview, "This book could easily become another World Book Encyclopedia"[1]— and he was not wrong in his observation. While it is impossible to include every bad thing, what is included are real-life situations and scenarios for which women are seeking help, advice, guidance and—most importantly—hope for a promising future.

You will be amazed and inspired by the stories of courage and perseverance shared by over forty women who will each touch your heart. If you are going through what feels like the challenge of a lifetime, *or* if you know someone who is facing or has faced a life-altering set of circumstances, get ready to have your questions answered, your mind eased and a positive pathway of healing set out before you.

The journey begins...

---

1 Encyclopedia (n.): A book-looking thing packed full of information that we used before Wikipedia took over our lives.

introduction

December 22, 2000: It was the day after my late husband's funeral. Two years and three months after ALS (Lou Gehrig's Disease) invaded and eventually took the life of a one-time healthy, robust, hard-working, fun-loving husband and father, I was newly widowed and sitting alone in the living room, staring off into Nowhere-in-Particular Land with the blinds drawn tightly shut.

Permit me to share exactly what was going through my mind at that horrible moment in time:

It's all over.

The doctors and the hospitals and the insurance companies and the commotion and the *constant* parades of people (well-meaning and otherwise).

The exercise in survival into which a heinous illness turned a once-happy home.

Over.

I can't quite believe it actually happened.

He is really gone.

And the excruciating pain of anticipating the inevitability of his death for over two years?

Also gone.

And now?

Quiet.

But not a peaceful quiet.

The quiet that emptiness brings.

Calm is supposed to be peaceful, right?

This is *not* calm.

Over and over, the same question frenetically whirled in my mind: "Is *this* really *it?*"

And at that moment in time…it *was*. I remember being convinced that *"this"* was indeed *"it."*

Uneasy silence. A bone-chillingly cold loneliness.

This…is…*it.*

No bright future. No laughter. No shining light in the darkness.

No love.

This is what everyone keeps referring to as my "New Normal."

I *hate* that phrase.

No one *ever* uses that phrase when they are talking about something good or happy or positive.

No one ever wins a lottery and shrieks, "This is my New Normal!"

New normal?

There is *nothing* "normal" about this.

All of these feelings felt as permanent as if they had been tattooed onto my heart with a jackhammer. I could not see any future from where I was sitting: on that couch in a dark living room, surrounded by the complete physical, financial and emotional wreckage that was once a wonderful life.

Then…I made a decision.

A conscious choice: A bad thing has happened. A *really* bad thing.

But it is not about to define who I am…and it is certainly not going to define who I will *become.*

Bad things happen.

Really bad things.

Things bad enough that they have the capability to stop our carefully crafted worlds from turning, and to bring us to our knees.

Bad things can cause us to doubt that life ever can or will be wonderful again.

Bad things can hold us back from experiencing everything that is in our heart to experience.

Bad things can keep us from healing.

Bad things can do all that and more…but it doesn't *have* to be that way.

A wretched illness has already claimed my husband's life. It's destroyed our family.

It does *not* get to take my life too.

It also does *not* get to destroy the life of a little girl then on the cusp of adolescence, who had already experienced so much loss in her young life.

My spirit is definitely damaged.

By illness, by death, by people who seemingly meant well… and as it turns out, did not mean so well.

I am damaged…but I will *not* be broken.

Healing didn't happen overnight.

It all began with a choice.

One tiny step.

chapter one

"How Can I Help?"

Beginning a book of this sort with a chapter intended for people not directly affected by a bad thing is kind of like trying to frost a cake that has not been baked—you just don't do it that way. However, I also believe that the more urgent a message, the sooner it needs to be heard. So as I am wont to do, I am breaking from convention by beginning with a chapter dedicated to the people who surround the "warriors"; the survivors of bad things…loss, life-challenges, adversity and situations that we all dread ever having to face.

We begin with the "Don'ts":

The Biggest "Don't-Say"

The absolute, no-doubt-about-it, definitive, number-one thing that you should never say to anyone who has just shared any kind of bad-thing news with you is:

"I know how you feel"
(also occasionally disguised as *"I know what you're going through"*)

Little does more harm to a person in need of compassion, sympathy or actual support and help than hearing "I know how you feel" or "I know what you're going through" from the people around them. A seemingly innocuous phrase, and commonly used in an attempt to relate to the pain of another person, this sentiment has the capacity to create very hard feelings. *No one* knows how someone else feels, and to say otherwise is presumptuous at best and can be devastatingly hurtful at worst.

Let's explore the reasons why this phrase needs to be immediately eliminated from our sympathy lingo and blasted off of the planet (along with phrases like, "Aren't you over it yet?" and "Everything happens for a reason," both of which you will see recurring many times throughout this book).

REASON # 1

It is not your turn. Leave the spotlight where it belongs.

I have spent many years in service to the bereaved. I have written about, been interviewed regarding and spoken about a wide variety of loss and life-challenge experiences at great length. The stories that I have heard are countless. Moreover, when it comes to loss and life-challenge, I unfortunately also have a great deal of personal insight and experience (that includes widowhood); far too much overall for my liking.

It might then surprise you to learn that not once have I *ever* looked at anyone who shares their story of loss or challenge and responded with, "I know how you feel."

Why?

Regardless of whatever news has just been shared, whether you have been through the same or similar experience or not, the minute you say, "I know how you feel," you will inevitably follow those words with, "because I..." and then you are then likely to fill in the blank with your own tale(s) of woe. There is then an unspoken and automatic shift in the focus of the conversation and the person who has just come to you in need of sympathy, compassion, advice or perhaps just a shoulder to lean on is now being forced to focus on *your* story, *your* feelings and how *you* were affected by *your* situation. Whether intended or not, the emphasis is now on you and at this particular moment in time, the emphasis is misplaced. It is not about you right now.

The focus needs to remain on the person who has opened a conversation with bad-thing news and is looking to you for compassion and reassurance. They should not have to be in the position of consoling you. Leave the spotlight where it belongs—on the person in immediate need.

REASON #2

**You really *can't* compare apples to oranges
(...or one situation to another situation)**

Most of us have experienced at least one traumatic or challenging situation in our lives. While you may think that you are compassionately empathizing with someone by letting them know that you have had what you *perceive* to be a similar experience, what you may be unintentionally doing is trivializing their loss experience by making impossible comparisons. For example, imagine the horror of a mother who had recently lost her young child and in the guise of consolation, was told, "I know exactly how you feel because that's how I felt when my [105-year-old] great-aunt died." While the loss of a 105-year-old great-aunt is sad and the loss should be mourned, this is not only a violation of the spotlight-shifting rule, you cannot and should not compare loss experiences—particularly those that are simply incomparable.

REASON #3

You are *you*

As stated earlier, I will never, *ever* look another widow in the eye and say, "I know how you feel," even if that widow lost her husband to the same illness as the one that claimed my husband's life. I will never look at someone who has lost their father and say, "I know how you feel," even if they lost their father to cancer mere months after they lost their husband, as I did. I will never look at someone who had to euthanize a beloved pet and say, "I know how you feel," even though, like so many, I too have taken part in this very sad good-bye process with our own furry family members. I have had every single one of these experiences (and then some), yet I refuse to utter that phrase. Why?

Because I am not the other person who is sharing their life challenge or loss experience. I am me. I am individual. I am unique.

(…And the world breathes a collective sigh of relief.)

If I am unique, it then follows that everything surrounding my experiences is unique. Even if I have lost a loved one, a job, a relationship or anything else in what appears to be the exact same manner as another person, the fact is that my circumstances, the people who surround me, my reactions and my relationships to what has been lost or challenged are each unique. So how can anyone else know how I feel? How can I know how someone else feels during their time of loss, when their own loss experience is unique and individual to *them*?

It's impossible.

Now, if someone directly asks you, "How did *you* feel when this happened to you?" or "How did *you* handle this situation?" your input has been actively solicited and you can then respond with honest answers: how you felt, what you did to cope and so forth. However, to simply respond to bad news with "I know how you feel," and follow with sorrowful tales of your own, is effectively sweeping someone else's experience and feelings under the carpet.

Vow that you will never again tell someone that you know how they feel or you know what they are going through, because quite frankly, you *don't* know how they feel…and you never will.

The Three "Never-Dos"

There are three big "Never-Dos" during a time of loss, trouble or crisis. Let's start our Never-Do Hit Parade Countdown in fine Top-Forty-countdown fashion with the number three Never Do:

Never Do "The Dance"

Mike was diagnosed with ALS in September of 1998. Within just one year, the illness had tragically progressed quite rapidly and by then, Mike was rarely able to leave the house. In that short period of time, the illness had attacked his respiratory system, making it very dangerous for him to be away from the emergency medical equipment that we had in our home. He had also become wheelchair-bound and his speech was very difficult to understand.[2]

We naturally welcomed visitors to our home—some more regularly than others, and regrettably, fewer and fewer as the illness progressed. I recall two visitors in particular with whom Mike was eagerly anticipating spending a real "boys' afternoon"; longtime colleagues from the police department with whom he had logged twenty-eight years of award-winning service.

When the visitors arrived, they sat with Mike and talked about absolutely *everything*...the "good ol' days" that they had shared in the department, the parties attended, the endless number of beers partaken, the rounds of golf played on days off, the pranks played, the patrol calls gone hilariously awry— the stories and memories went on for hours. I had remained on hand to translate Mike's compromised speech to his friends and from my vantage point, it appeared that a good time was being had by all.

After the visitors had left, Mike quietly remarked, "They never asked me how I was feeling or what's going on with my health. I felt like saying *I* know I'm sick so they don't have to pretend I'm not. But I guess I can't blame them because almost everyone else does the same thing."

Wow.

My eyes stung with tears at Mike's observation, for he had spoken the absolute truth. Not once did these friends—or most people, come to that— acknowledge the fact that Mike was terminally ill. Worse yet, I never took any notice.

---

2 ALS can affect a patient's ability to speak, as this ability is also muscle-driven. As Mike's speech had become unintelligible except to those who spent continuous time with him, I remained with him to translate his speech to others who might not have otherwise been able to understand him.

To disregard whatever challenging circumstance has befallen the person with whom you are spending time is to ignore the proverbial "elephant in the room." In Mike's case, there was a great, big, ugly, rotten elephant in the room named ALS—and absolutely no one was talking about it.

Except for Joel and Rob.

Joel and Rob are two of our family's dearest friends—the kind of people who actually transcend the word "friend" and plop themselves right down in the "We Are Family" column. Every Thursday evening without fail, Joel and Rob would appear on our doorstep for a visit, always bearing a six-pack of beer. Wives were left at home on these precious evenings and, upon the boys' arrival, I myself was always politely but firmly excused from the living room. For them, there was never any need for me to translate Mike's worsening speech; they would either figure out what Mike was saying or make him repeat himself until they did understand. This was "boy time" and no girls were invited or necessary.

If Mike was having a bad day physically or was feeling depressed (and under the circumstances, who wouldn't?), he knew that he could talk about it without causing discomfort or awkwardness. On those bad days, Joel and Rob simply sat quietly with him and listened. If it was a good day, I would hear ribald jokes, good-natured insults and loud laughter echoing down the hallway. But whatever the sort of day that Mike was having, whatever his mood was when Joel and Rob arrived for their visit, they *never* failed to ask, "How ya *really* doin' buddy?" or "What's the latest from the doctor?" Or even just, "You know, this whole thing really sucks."

Joel and Rob always recognized and discussed the awful elephant named ALS that had taken unwelcome residence in our home, and instinctively knew that refusing to talk about it would not make that elephant disappear into thin air. Most importantly, they never failed to create an atmosphere where Mike could just relax and talk about being sick. Whether it was fear, anger or just plain frustration, Joel and Rob acknowledged (occasionally with very colorful language) what was going on, that it did indeed suck and that they were there to listen, commiserate and be afraid, angry or frustrated right along with Mike. I know that along with the rest of us, on the inside, they were feeling all of those things and then some; however, the difference between Joel and Rob and the majority of people who came to visit (or worse, chose to stay away) is that they *said* so. Furthermore, regardless of how distressing it certainly must have been for them, they allowed Mike to discuss not just his physical health, but his emotional health as well. What an incredible gift.

The fact is that people who are victims of illness, loss or life-altering circumstances of *any* kind are completely aware of what is going on in their lives. Ignoring the circumstances or "dancing" around whatever issue exists (whether out of personal discomfort or out of fear of creating upset) does not help matters at all. People are cognizant of their situation. People *know* when they have lost a loved one. People *know* when they (or someone they love) are seriously or terminally ill. People *know* when they are having financial difficulties. People *know* when they have lost a job or a home or a relationship. Ignoring the elephant in the room doesn't get rid of the elephant, and the person who is coping with that elephant can feel your avoidance.

Does it mean that you focus exclusively on the negative? Of course not. People who are in the midst of life-altering challenge absolutely *do* want to talk about the weather and the good ol' days and what's going on with the kids— and they want to hear about what is going on in your life as well. However, you must also recognize that the person with whom you are spending time is going through trial and tribulation—perhaps the worst that they have ever experienced—and you need to get outside of yourself and past your own discomfort to a place where you can really be "there" for them as a source of support.

Remember earlier when we said it was not about you right now? The same applies here. Put your discomfort away until a time when you are away from the person. Take a vital lesson from Joel and Rob, who were willing and able to momentarily put their feelings of anger, deep sadness and fear aside to be there for another person who was so badly in need of exactly the kind of support they gave.

We continue our countdown with our first runner-up:

Never Ask Someone to Call You If They Need Anything

"When a friend is in trouble,
don't annoy him by asking if there is anything
you can do. Think up something appropriate...and do it."

—Edgar Watson Howe[3]

On its face, asking someone to call you if they need something sounds lovely and no doubt, you are being quite sincere in your gesture. That's great—but there is one small problem with that gesture.

The call will never come.

It does not matter what the situation is or what challenge has befallen someone you know and care about. No one is going to pick up the telephone and call you to say, "I need you to pick up my kids, run an errand, take me out for a coffee, hold me while I cry..." It just doesn't happen, for a number of reasons. Chief among those reasons are:

- Burden 'n' Bother: Whether it is asking a favor or needing a compassionate ear, people who have suffered a loss or life-challenge inevitably feel like a burden if they initiate a phone call to say "I need..." No one wants to feel like they are bothering someone with their troubles—that is just human nature. People in a position of need know that you have a life too, and they do not want to be the ones to upset your carefully balanced apple cart.

- The "Fog Factor": Loss or serious challenge throws you headlong into a fog of sorts. You are generally not thinking straight, which is part of the phenomenon of shock. Especially within the first days and weeks after a trauma, your mind tends to muddle, and with

---

3 Excerpted from Inspiration for a Lifetime: Words of Wisdom, Delight and Possibility by Allen Klein (Viva Editions). Reprinted with permission.

everything else that is swimming around in your head, picking up a phone and asking for help is not on the list.

- The Power of Pride: As a society, we have collectively gotten it into our heads that it is a sign of weakness to reach out for help. If the situation at hand includes something like losing a job or being left by a spouse or partner, add an additional scoop of self-esteem battering with a side of humiliation. No one wants to feel weak or like a "loser" or a "downer" to other people, and that makes reaching out much more difficult.

With the rarest of exceptions, a person suffering through loss or trial is generally not going to call you. It is up to *you* to pick up the phone and tell *them* what you plan to do to help—and then follow through with it.

The Number One "Never-Do" is:

Never Do...Nothing!

Lest you think that the English major has tripped up by using a double-negative, allow me to explain.

Many people truly do not know what to do or how to react during times of trouble or turmoil. They do not know what to say, they do not know how to behave and they do not know what actions to take—it's an affliction also known as "I-Can't-Stand-to-See-Them-that-Way Syndrome." These people choose to do nothing rather than putting their own uneasiness aside to be a part of the sufferer's dynamic by rolling up their sleeves and pitching in to help in whatever way they are able. They instead choose to do nothing and stay away, blissfully unaware that ignoring the situation will not make it disappear.

Sadly, Mike saw this very thing happen with many people who had once counted themselves as friends. The further along in the disease that Mike progressed, the fewer people came to visit or call to find out how he was doing. The big problem? Since ALS does not affect cognitive abilities in any way, he was one hundred percent, completely aware of the fact that many people were choosing to avoid him. He knew it, he voiced it, I saw the pain on his face... and it broke my heart.

Once Mike passed away, my daughter Kendall and I unknowingly graduated to Avoidance 2.0—except this time, the people who were being avoided or outright abandoned were the two of us. Some of those people eventually came back into our lives with apologies aplenty, explaining that they simply did not know what to say or do because the situation was so sad. They had instead chosen to do the worst thing in the world:

Nothing

People who are suffering through loss or life-challenges are not mind-readers. They are not sitting at home thinking, "Well, So-and-So really *does* feel badly for me; they just don't know what to do with me right now." They are instead sitting at home thinking that no one cares or that they have been forgotten altogether. Can you imagine how that feels on *top* of what they are already going through?

It is not up to a person who is going through a life-challenge or who has suffered a devastating loss to put *you* at ease or make *you* feel better. You are an adult. It is therefore up to you to get out of your own way, momentarily put your own feelings aside and get into the game.

"How CAN I Help?"

By now, you may be thinking, "Okay, Carole, I'm not supposed to tell someone that I know how they feel, I'm not supposed to tell them to call me if they need me, I can't skirt the situation, and ignoring the circumstances apparently isn't an option either. What *am* I supposed to say or do?"

I am so happy you asked.

The reason for starting with the bottom line—the things that you should never say or do, regardless of the situation at hand—is so that you will have learned the most important lessons in dealing with (or helping someone else deal with) some of the more difficult life situations that most of us have or will encounter.

If you know someone who is going through a bad-thing life experience, before you say or do anything, ask yourself:

1. *"If I were her, would I want to hear what I am about to say?"*
2. *"Will what I am about to say help someone in facing their bad thing?"*
3. *"Will what I am about to say bring comfort and reassurance?"*
4. *"Will what I am about to say be to anyone's advantage?"*

Now that you know the absolute bottom-line "Don'ts," we'll begin our journey with the most common difficulties and challenges that women encounter throughout life (either firsthand or as witness to family, loved ones and friends), how to best cope if any of these situations do happen to you, and if someone you know is affected by a bad thing, how *you* can be the best source of encouragement and support possible.

chapter two

Home No More: The Loss of a Home

Home.

There aren't many words that convey comfort, goal-achievement and dreams-come-true in only four letters. It does not matter if home to you is a mansion on a hill or a one-bedroom, walk-up apartment—the very word "home" is gentle to the ear and warm to the spirit.

Home instantly conjures up so many memories, be they recent or from many years ago. Your memories might include those of your own Declaration of Independence when you moved into your very first apartment, or the first home you purchased on your own or as a couple. Home represents the many gatherings for which we decorated, the holidays that we celebrated and the occasions that we've commemorated.

Home is always the place that we want to "get to." Whether we have just left work after a tough day, we are arriving back from vacation or itching to get out of a hospital, all we ever *really* want to do…is go home.

Home is our respite and our sanctuary. It is the very reflection of who we are, right down to the colors of the interior decor. It is being surrounded by that which makes us smile. It is putting nails in walls and pictures in halls. You can put your hair up or let your hair down. You can take off your makeup and put your feet up. It is where you can be still and quiet or preside over a beehive of activity.

Home is where we entertain. We entertain friends and relatives; we entertain our girlfriends without whom we would be lost. We surprise children with ice-cream sundaes and our romantic partners with candlelit dinners. We make wishes while we blow out candles and clink glasses. It is where we build memories to last a lifetime.

Best of all, home is…*home.*

Then one terrible day, your home is gone.

Losing a home is an incredible devastation, and the way in which a home is lost determines much of the practical and emotional paths that are taken in recovery. We look at the primary ways that a home can be lost, as well as how to battle back from this terrible loss.

Losing a Home to Disaster

The thought of losing a home is indeed fearsome. The actual loss of a home is a worst fear realized—and certainly compounded when the loss circumstances were complete beyond your control. Such is the case when a home is lost to fire (be it wild or due to a criminal act, household accident or systemic failure within the house) or to other natural disasters, such as a hurricane, a tornado, flash flooding, snowstorm, rock slide, mudslide or earthquake.

Meet Kristen Moeller, author of *What Are You Waiting For? Learn How to Rise to the Occasion of Your Life,*[4] who lost her home and her possessions to a fire and eventually—and quite literally—rose from the ashes.

Kristen's story

I will never forget the first time we found our home. After getting used

---

4   To learn more about Kristen and *What Are You Waiting For?…* (Viva Editions), please visit www.kristen-moeller.com.

to mountain living, we craved even more adventure [and] the ad in the paper sounded too good to be true: thirty-seven acres, two bedrooms, one bath, far-ranging views, and an exciting bonus: completely "off-the-grid," meaning solar power only.

As we walked to the property down the mile-long Jeep trail of a road, through groves of shimmering aspen trees, the view began to emerge. When we rounded the last corner, we glanced at each other as the sweetest profile of a house I had ever seen greeted us. Set against towering pines and perched on the side of the hill, this sanctuary looked out over a vast expanse of mountain ranges, including Pikes Peak.

Each time I pulled in my driveway, I would take a moment to admire that sweet profile of our magical home and breathe a sigh of relief. I never took it for granted. We had found our forever home, and I was glad to be home forever.

A day that began like many others—with me sitting in my favorite chair by the window, gazing at our vast view, sipping coffee and beginning my routine—ended in chaos and confusion. My home burned to the ground in a raging wildfire that left three of my neighbors dead and twenty-one families homeless. During our last-minute evacuation, I fled with a handful of precious items, as well as my computer and my animals. When I drove out of my driveway, I had no idea that it would be the last time that I saw my house. My world was rocked the day my house burned to the ground.

Walking Through Fire

At this point in my life, I had walked through many metaphorical "fires": addiction, cancer, miscarriage and the deaths of dear friends. On some level I knew I would walk through this one as well; [however], I did want to know that I would grow. I was well aware of the rich symbolism surrounding fire, and I committed to rise like a Phoenix from the ashes—but not one minute before I was ready and my grief had run its course.

The Other Side

I spent a long time in the metaphorical hallway wondering who I would be on the other side. I am not who I was on that day, and some days I still don't quite know who I will be. I wanted to be deeper, stronger and wiser on the other side. I wanted to be more willing to let go and to dance in the unknown.

On a practical level, we didn't know where we were going to live, if we were going to rebuild [the house] or what we wanted. We lived in friends' basements, in hotel rooms and for a short while, in an Airstream trailer on our burned-out land. We finally we bought a new house in a completely different setting.

We have now put up a Yurt on our land, and when we are there, we still love the quiet and the vast views. We still get covered in ash and soot, we still fry in the heat due to the lack of shade on our south-facing lot and it still breaks our hearts to see the splintered forest where once stood lush and towering pines.

THE FREEDOM TO BE...

In the transitory period after I lost my home and all my possessions, grief became my teacher. While struggling to live a still-vibrant life, I developed a new respect for both jumping into action and what it means to wait. After writing an entire book on the concept of why we wait in life instead of living our dreams, you might think I had it mastered. Yet, after the fire, I learned the difference between waiting as a way of avoidance and malcontent, and the type of patient waiting required for going through a grieving process. As I peered into my old behaviors, I saw the truth of how deeply I was still waiting to get somewhere, be someone other than I was—to arrive. Slowly, I began to relax my grip on the idea that life would go the way I thought it should, and I let my desire for perfection be burned away.

Where once I had celebrated my intense push to succeed, that now felt as barren as the smoldering remains of my home. Instead of my "driven-ness," what began to emerge as the smoke cleared and the ashes settled was a newfound freedom to simply be.

ENJOY THE RIDE

We walk through the fires of life one step at a time, one day at a time and sometimes one minute at a time. There is no "right" way to do grief. Let yourself have your own process and journey, and allow others to have theirs as well.

Great gifts came from this tremendous loss. I realized that life is a simply a string of moments. Some of them will be good and some not so much. Some that we judge as "not good" end up being our greatest teachers. After the fire, I finally embraced my messy humanity, as well as my beautiful strengths. I finally let go of the concept of perfection and never doubting again. I made friends with my darkness. I found that I am able to dance on the brink of the abyss because deep down in my bones, I know I will be okay. And the knowing doesn't mean I always know. There are many moments when I forget. Yet the knowing remains. It's a quiet voice, or simply a sensation. I now know I can and will walk through anything.

Who knows what the future will hold? I certainly hope that we may have "smooth waters" for a bit. I have buckled my seatbelt for this wild ride called life, and I am enjoying the journey. And just as my burned-out land continues to transform, so do I. I don't know who I am, yet I do know. I am a Phoenix emerging from the fire.

HOW YOU CAN HELP

Someone who has just lost their home to fire or natural disaster is in an understandable amount of shock, which effectively eliminates an ability to know in what direction to turn first or next. Your immediate proactivity in such a situation will be welcome with a tremendous amount of grief and gratitude.

Definite Do's

- **Remain calm:** Someone who has lost their home to a disaster needs a calming presence and a cool head. Choose to be both.

- **Ensure that her physical condition is sound (as well as that of her family if applicable):** Those who are victims of home loss and perhaps had to make an emergency escape or otherwise take refuge may be injured and not even realize it. Though first responders obviously check thoroughly, a victim may unwittingly decline going to a hospital for further examination, believing that their injuries are "no big deal." Oftentimes this reaction is part of the shock factor. After things calm a bit, quietly double-check to make sure that she (and her loved ones if applicable) are physically okay, and if anyone has any complaints of physical injury, strongly encourage them to call their doctor or go to an emergency room (and accompany her/them if possible).

- **Help her with necessities:** Provide whatever necessities that you can in the immediate: clothing, toiletries and cosmetic items (including things like feminine products, toothbrush and tooth-paste, underwear and other things that people tend to overlook).

- **If you are able, gift her several comfort items:** These might include a few magazines, a gift card to her favorite coffee house or yogurt shop, inexpensive bath accessories…in other words, items that will help comfort her and that she likely will not provide for herself.

- **If you are not in a position to provide temporary shelter, help her locate shelter:** If her loss was as the result of widespread disaster, there will likely be a shelter (or several) available nearby, courtesy of the American Red Cross[5] or another disaster relief agency. If hers is an isolated situation (e.g., a house fire that did not affect any other homes in her area) and you are able to do so, offer to house her for a night or two. If you are unable to accommodate her (or her along with her family), do what you can to help secure accommodations: offer to drive her to a friend or relatives home, or help her locate a local hotel or motel—they might even be willing to donate a stay for a night or two.

---

5   To contact the American Red Cross, please visit www.redcross.org.

- **Help her compile a list of what needs to be accomplished immediately:** She will need to contact the insurance agent who manages her homeowner (or renter's) insurance policy in order to immediately file a claim and begin the appropriate financial processes. You may get resistance from her, as financial entanglement is the last thing that anyone wants to deal with after a disaster. However, the sooner that paperwork begins its sometimes slow churn through the system, the sooner she will receive relief.

  She will also want to contact her bank, credit card companies, mortgage company[6] and anyone else to whom she writes a check to let them know what has happened and to see what relief they may have to offer. She will also want to contact the post office to let them know what has happened and to provide information as to where mail can either be held for her or forwarded to an alternate address.

  If applicable, you can also help her contact the various state and government agencies that provide assistance in times of disaster. For example, once a state governor and/or the President of the United States declares a state of emergency or that a geographic area is a disaster area, she will be eligible to receive state and/or federal aid. You can help her with filing for this kind of aid.

- **Listen:** The greatest gift that you can provide right now are your two ears. She will need to talk. She will need to cry. She will need to reminisce. She will need to process. Most of all, she will need you to give her a hug and reassure her that you are going to be there for her, no matter what.

Without a Doubt...Don't

- **Don't play down the loss of personal possessions and mementos:**

---

6   Her mortgage company may also be able to assist in working with the insurance company.

"It's just 'stuff—at least you're alive"; "You can always buy another [whatever has been lost]*"; "Even if you don't have photos, you still have the memories in your head"; "It must be so freeing not to have so much stuff to worry about."*

Treasured keepsakes and mementos aren't "stuff." Keepsakes and mementos represent a life lived, a life in progress and a future planned. Take a moment and think about what is inside your house and garage that you would be devastated to lose. Prom pictures. Wedding photographs. Baby books. Yearbooks. Photographs of relatives and ancestors that date back generations. Trophies. Children's report cards. *Your* report cards. Family holiday decorations lovingly passed down. Silly souvenirs and reminders that would mean nothing to anyone other than you. Would the "memories in your head" bring you any comfort whatsoever or make you feel any better? Probably not.

As to being able to buy another fill-in-the-blank, while that may be true, the object itself is only one small part of the loss equation. It is the sentimentality *behind* that fill-in-the-blank that can never be replaced. For example, I could run down to any toy store tomorrow and purchase a new stuffed gorilla; however, that new stuffed gorilla wouldn't be "Barf,"[7] gifted to Kendall by her now-late grandfather on the day she was born.

This is just one silly-sweet example of an irreplaceable memento— what about things like the tri-folded American flag that gently draped Mike's coffin at his funeral? Or my late grandmother's china, saved and meant for her only great-grandchild?

The reality is that much of what is inside our homes truly is irreplaceable. Do not reduce that enormous loss to another pile of rubble in her mind.

---

7   When Kendall was four years old, she named the gorilla "Barf." I asked her why she chose the name "Barf." She looked at me as if I were a moron and replied, *"Because that's his name. Why is your name Mommy?"* This was one of the few times in my life where I had no words.

- **Don't make her feel guilty, intentionally or otherwise:** *"Your neighbors had it so much worse"; "You're so lucky to be alive"; "God must have been watching out for you."*

  I can promise you that no one is standing amongst the wreckage of a home thinking about how fortunate they are. Even if they are noble enough to feel grateful at that moment in time (and if such is the case, they are a better person than I), to imply that someone is somehow "lucky" in that moment is ill timed at best. Further, the most spiritual among us may not necessarily want to hear about how God was watching out for them; many are indeed angry at their God for allowing such a tragedy to happen. Let *her* bring up the faith aspect of her tragedy—if she wants to imbue her faith as part of her coping and recovery, she will do so, and she will be vocal about it.

- **Unless you are prepared to offer financial assistance or you are an expert in property loss matters, financial questions are completely inappropriate:** *"How much are you insured for?"; "How much did you* [monetarily] *lose?"; "How can you afford to rebuild?"*

  Inquiries of a financial nature are absolutely improper, unless you are either standing ready to write a check to help out or you are her insurance agent. If she wishes to ask questions or comes to you for direction, let *her* initiate that conversation. Otherwise, financial questions of any kind are far too personal.

Loss of a Home Due to Financial Challenge

Recent years have seen historic economic times in our country—and not in a good way. As the economy imploded, millions of jobs disappeared, millions of homes were considered "underwater"[8], banks refused to work with millions

---

8   Owing more to the bank than the home was worth.

of homeowners to help them keep their homes which were subsequently lost as a result and one-time attractively packaged mortgage eventually became known as "toxic mortgages" that swallowed both dreams of home ownership and financial security.

Then too are the "everyday" reasons for financial loss of a home; most commonly the result of divorce, the death of a loved one whose inheriting relatives cannot afford to maintain the home or the inability to sell the home.

The devastation of losing a home to financial hardship oftentimes leaves the homeowner feeling embarrassed and ashamed. Amy Zellmer,[9] a talented professional photographer and activist on behalf of those living with TBI (traumatic brain injury), shares how financial challenge borne of divorce and the subsequent loss of her home to that financial challenge eventually led way to both triumph over financial difficulties and achieving peace of mind.

Amy's story

I had divorced my husband. My business was doing well; however, I found that covering all of my expenses without the support of a spouse extremely challenging. There were days where I didn't know how I was going to pay for gas to get to my next appointment.

I filed for bankruptcy and made the decision to let my home foreclose. I owed more than the value of the home and had made several attempts to work with the bank—but the bank refused to work with me. After filing for bankruptcy, I was approved for a loan on a live/work studio loft. It was the answer to my prayers, and I am very blessed.

THE "SNOWBALL" EFFECT

Once I divorced, things felt amazing for a bit. Then everything started to snowball away from me. I couldn't understand how I had let this happen. I was a responsible person, I had a business and a home, and suddenly it was all in question. It was a very dark, lonely and miserable place to be. As the burden

---

9   For more information about Amy, visit www.amyzellmer.net.

of [the photography studio] rent became an issue, I couldn't figure out how to fix the situation. I needed the studio to run my business, yet I needed a home to live in. It was a vicious cycle of thinking that I could not stop.

Finally, a good friend suggested that I should file for bankruptcy. I was shocked at his suggestion as I didn't have any [major] debt. When my friend explained to me that bankruptcy would get me out of my [studio] lease obligations, I knew what my next step should be.

Seeing the Light at the End of the Tunnel

Once I made the decision to meet with a lawyer, I knew that I was on the right path. Since the bank wasn't willing to work with me, he encouraged me to let my house go. It was an incredible relief to know that my landlord could no longer intimidate me, the bank would no longer be calling me and all of the other outstanding expenses I had were also forgiven. I got over the initial embarrassment and started feeling relief. There really *was* a light at the end of the tunnel.

Throughout everything, only a very small handful of friends knew what was going on in my life. Some were judgmental and didn't approve, and others were amazingly supportive. I don't know what I would have done without those friends and their encouragement.

Never Give Up on Your Dreams

I am at a place where everything amazing is starting to happen. Business is better than ever, I have been traveling a lot, I have been making new friends (who know my story) and I live in an amazing community. There were dark times when I didn't ever think there was going to be a light at the end of the tunnel. I am so glad I didn't give up, because it is only the beginning.

My advice to anyone going through a similar situation would be to find someone to confide in. I confided in the right friend, who had been through all of this and was able to guide me in the right direction. I know it seems scary to take these big steps, but once you take those first steps, you will feel lighter and brighter than you have in a long time. It's like a giant exhale.

While the road might get bumpy and rough along the way, it really will all work out. Believe in yourself and never, *ever* give up on your dreams!

HOW YOU CAN HELP

Losing a home for financial reasons is incredibly discouraging. It is watching a dream fade away, generally through no fault of the homeowner. Do what you can to soothe her worries and boost her spirit with a positive eye to the future.

Definite Do's

- **Offer assistance in locating another place to live:** Has she found another home? If so, offer to help her pack and move…the pizza and Chardonnay is on you. If not, ask her where she thinks she wants to live, if she is planning to rent, lease or buy, etc., and then help her scout locations. Go with her to view apartments, or join her with a realtor and then go out for lunch afterward. Your support will help to soften her reality.

- **Once she has relocated, purchase a small housewarming gift:** Start her off in her new place with something that will make her smile: a small print for a blank wall, a decorative vase, two beautiful wine glasses or coffee mugs—even something like a cute picture frame holding a photograph of a fun memory. You do not have to spend a lot of money, and you can help start her off with a smile.

- **If she is compelled to move in with relatives, you can still do all of the above:** Being forced to move in with relatives or friends makes us feel burdensome. Her self-esteem is already flagging and a small gift to let her know that you care will lift a wilting spirit.

Without a Doubt…Don't

- **Don't treat the loss as though she has just received a financial windfall:** *"Now you'll have more money to spend"; "No more mortgage*

*to worry about!"; "When are we going to celebrate?"; "Woo-hoo! When
are we going shopping?"*

No one who has lost a home to financial challenge is thinking
about a shopping spree. If the person did not want a mortgage, they
would not have bought a home. No one loses a home to financial
challenge and immediately thinks, "Look out mall, here I come!"

- **Don't pretend that this is a wonderful opportunity:** *"This is a
  great time for you to downsize"; "Now you have a chance for a fresh
  start"; "Moving is an adventure!"*

  If someone who has lost her home outwardly expresses these
  sentiments, by all means encourage that thought process—if she
  is putting an optimistic spin on the situation, it is wonderful to
  support it. However, most in this position are not intentionally
  looking to downsize, otherwise she would have sold the home of
  her own volition. The same thing applies to people who are looking
  for a "fresh start." If we want a fresh start, we also want to control
  where, when and how that fresh start happens—and having a home
  forcibly taken away is not within our control.

  Incidentally, for most of us, moving is *not* an "adventure"… it is a
  royal pain in the ass.

- **Don't play character assassin:** Amy says, "One friend who knew I
  was struggling complained about how a family member was letting
  their house foreclose. They went on about how irresponsible that
  was and said, 'How could you do that? It was just wrong.' It made
  me feel awful. When I confided to this friend that I was going to a
  local food drive to get groceries and was on state health care assistance, they said, 'I didn't think you were that type of person.' What
  does that even mean? If you've never been in a situation where you
  couldn't afford gas or groceries, you have no idea what it's like. You
  should never ever judge."

  I could not have said it any better myself.

- **Don't compare her situation to those of other people**: *"Everyone else is going through financial difficulty too"; "You're not the only one in the world this has happened to"; "So many people have it much worse than you do."*

Since these particular statements pop up often in so many bad-thing situations, let's spend some publishing real estate on this last one.

When I was young, one of the meals that my mother used to regularly serve to our family consisted of macaroni and cheese (*the* dish of champions), peas…and fish sticks.

I *hate* fish sticks.

I remember those evenings when I would come into the kitchen and if I smelled macaroni and cheese baking, I was instantly filled with dread. Even though, to this day, I believe that macaroni and cheese should be its own major food group, I knew then that if macaroni and cheese was in the oven, fish sticks were lurking closely behind. Perhaps the macaroni and cheese was a bribe to get me to eat those damn fish sticks…I don't know.

Now in all fairness to Mom, I have never in my life liked anything that once swam or walked sideways before winding up on a plate. I can also guarantee that the genius who decided that slapping beige-hued breading all over chopped-up mystery fish, coaxing it into stick-form[10] and flash-freezing it (thereby guaranteeing a life span that would survive a nuclear winter) didn't help foster my taste for any food with oceanic origins.

Nevertheless, Mom insisted on putting this meal in front of me over and over again, in the vain hope that one day I would see the light and gobble up the fish sticks.

It never happened…because I *hate* fish sticks.

Seriously.

As was ritual, I would eagerly devour the macaroni and cheese, followed quickly by the peas and then sit and stare at the fish sticks, willing them to

---

10 Though they may well exist, I have never seen a rectangular-shaped fish that was meant for eating.

disappear. As the fish sticks grew cold and my frustration increased, one of my parents would offer the inevitable phrase that most of us have heard at least one hundred times growing up:

"*There are people starving in*
[fill in the blank with the name of a famine-ravaged country]
who would be thrilled to have this food"

Meaning no disrespect to those in the world who are hungry, and understanding that I support charities who endeavor to eradicate hunger worldwide, please remember that at the time, I was just a kid who had to restrain myself from inviting my parents to wrap up the fish sticks and send them off to whomsoever wished to partake.

(Exercising verbal restraint was necessary since, in those days, you didn't talk back to your parents without suffering serious consequences—and at the tender age of single-digits, I was not ready to take a gamble on whether or not my parents would appreciate my rapier wit.)

It may be simplistic to compare a childhood hatred of fish sticks to the sad event of losing a home to financial difficulty; however, it does illustrate a point. I was not interested in hearing about the multitudes of people in other countries. I was concerned with my situation alone. Similarly, while in the midst of the trauma of being financially forced from their home, people are not interested in hearing what the rest of the world is going through. It does not help. It is not a source of comfort.

When someone is in need of compassion and they are greeted instead with statistics, not only are they looking at you thinking, "I'm not really concerned with other people; I'm concerned with myself, my family (if applicable) and my/our displacement," they are highly unlikely to confide in you again.

FROM BAD THING TO BRIGHTER DAYS AHEAD

Stay proactive and continue to investigate any and all resources that will enable you to rebuild or re-house as soon as possible. If losing your home involves working with an insurance company, calendar regular follow up with them until all claims are paid. If you are dealing with banks and mortgage companies, the same rule applies—calendar regular follow up with them until your home ownership situation is resolved to your satisfaction.

No matter the circumstances, losing a home is incredibly difficult and extremely traumatic. Do your very best to retrain your focus on you and the loved ones (including pets) with whom you share your life. Draw close to one another and know that wherever all of you reside together in love will indeed truly be "home."

chapter three

FROM "DAY-TO-DAY" TO "GETTING THE DOOR": THE LOSS OF A JOB

FOR MOST OF US, A JOB ISN'T SIMPLY A "JOB." IT IS MORE THAN JUST A PAYCHECK or a means to an end. It is usually the second thing about which people meeting us for the first time will inquire (right after "What's your name?"). If we are very fortunate, it is also our passion.

Oh yeah…a job pays the bills, and keeps a roof over our heads, clothes on our backs and food in our stomachs.

A job is financial security, both present and future. We spend more time at our jobs than anywhere else, at least until retirement. A job is linked closely to our identity, be it for the short-term or the long haul. With rare exception, the great majority of us need a job to provide for our very existence, and in this day and age, even those of us who are lucky enough to choose whether or not to work are oftentimes working at *something*. The very activity gives us a feeling of accomplishment, of being worthwhile and contributing to society.

For all of these reasons and more, losing a job is incredibly difficult. Losing a job can demoralize us—and even if it does not demoralize us entirely, it can certainly knock us back on our heels (if not flat on our asses).

Guess what? *Almost every single one of us* who has ever been in the workforce has been there.

We have been invited into *that* office or *that* conference room or *that* room in the back for "the talk." We have emerged from that office or those rooms with a final paycheck and a box in which to pack the personal belongings that litter our desks or workplace space, while likely either blinking back tears or holding back four-letter words.

"BECAUSE WE CAN"

The reasons for job loss are as varied as there are jobs on the planet. Downsizing, outsourcing, going "in-house" (or any other description beginning with a foreboding preposition) are common reasons for dismissal, as are the "Re's": *re*locating, *re*structuring, *re*distributing, *re*directing, *re*inventing—and *re*ally lousy for those affected. Further, unless there is blatant discrimination involved or an airtight contract is in place, you can also be summarily dismissed for just about any reason that might move a superior to dismiss you. In fact, one recent State Supreme Court decision held that an employer could fire an employee for being *too* attractive.[11]

A TRUE STORY

Many years ago, I held a senior paralegal/settlement negotiator position at a firm in one of the tonier areas of Southern California, complete with a corner office and gorgeous view of the Pacific Ocean. Although no one had any argument with the quality of my work, I struggled with the win-at-any-cost, not-always-ethical attitude of a few of the managing partners at the firm—so much so that it kept me up at night and gave me headaches and heartburn during daylight hours. I also knew that in addition to being frustrated with my annoyingly pesky integrity, the partnership was less than impressed with my occasional need to telecommute, a term that was all but unheard of at

---

11 That was not a misprint. This was an *actual* court decision made by *actual* State Supreme Court justices because apparently, you *can* be "too attractive"—a devastating piece of news for the multi-multi-multi-billion-dollar fashion, beauty, cosmetics, plastic surgery, diet and physical fitness industries.

the time yet fundamentally necessary to those of us with school-aged children who also tend to be periodically afflicted with school-aged illnesses and school-aged injuries. No matter that the work was being accomplished on time and above standard—to the minds of the senior partnership, if you were not sitting in your office, your work simply did not count.

It was on a Friday afternoon that I was summoned into the senior-most partner's office and, after listening to a soliloquy about the supposed Wonder That Is Carole (which automatically sent my BS radar into overdrive), I was informed that I was being let go because—and these were his exact words...

"You're a great quarterback, but unfortunately, we're a baseball team."

This may have been code for, "Your work is fine; however, the fact that you are a working mother with a child who gets sick every so often is not—and we also don't care for your sanctimonious, can't-we-just-be-honest attitude." However, to have said as much would have been toeing a legal line. Better to cloak the firing of a competent employee in a cutesy fish-out-of-water metaphor.

As unfair as it may be, the fact is that the firm was within their rights to let me go, no matter how moronic the reason (or metaphor). Stories like these are literally without end and yet the conclusions are identical: we all wind up in the parking lot where we stuff the box of desk paraphernalia into the trunks of our cars, disconsolately pull out of the parking lot for the last time and likely head for the nearest store that sells either chocolate or vodka.

(...Or perhaps both. I understand that there is now such a thing as chocolate-infused vodka).

However, unless you are either walking out the door with the petty cash, or you are seriously incompetent at your job, layoffs and even firing oftentimes have little to do with you personally and everything to do with the company itself. Do not beat yourself up when the situation may have nothing directly to do with you.

Grieving the Loss and Facing the Fear

No matter the reason, the loss of your job is just that—a *loss*. I have long held that anyone who has suffered a loss of any kind has the absolute right to mourn that loss however they choose, as long as it is not destructive to themselves or anyone around them.

Even if you had suspected that the proverbial pink slip might be coming your way (due to other employee layoffs, a superior's dissatisfaction with your performance, personality conflicts, etc.), the *reality* of job loss is every bit as shocking as if you had no idea it was coming. Your reality is that tomorrow morning you will not be going to work. It feels empty, it feels lonely, but most of all, it feels *scary*. Envelopes with windows still show up in your mailbox, and banks, creditors, landlords and mortgage companies still expect their payments in full and on time.

The One Thing that Absolutely Should Not Wait

I always advise taking time for yourself after any kind of loss, and a job loss is certainly included. However, there is one thing that I always insist upon that cannot wait —and it is the same advice that I give to millions of bereaved right after a loss.

**You cannot wait on anything that will generate
income to your household.**

You must file for unemployment benefits immediately. The good news is that most of the fifty United States (as well as many countries) permit the filing for unemployment benefits online, which greatly expedites the process. However, laws differ widely from state to state (or country to country) and there may be a waiting period before you will begin receiving benefits. There may also be an interview process to determine your eligibility. The important thing is to take care of the initial filing without delay; even if you find a new job right after you've lost your previous job, you may still be entitled to unemployment. This is money that is due you—do not simply throw it away because your unemployment period was brief.

SPRINGING INTO ACTION

As appealing as it might seem to take off work for an indefinite period of time, your financial situation likely dictates otherwise. Once you have filed for unemployment and your personally allotted "Me Time" has passed, it's time to get proactive about re-employment:

- Update your resumé immediately, and prepare copies for interviews. Yes, I know that you can email a resumé and many prospective employers request that you do so, but you will still want to arrive at an interview with a resumé in hand. Remember, emails get lost or wind up in spam folders, and computer systems can crash. I have never once had a piece of paper "crash" on me.

- If you have a personal website or *professional* social media page of any kind, ensure that it is up-to-date. However, do not simply refer a prospective employer to your website to find out more about you—they do not have that kind of time. Be prepared to turn in a hard-copy resumé, and allow your personal website to be an extension of the resumé.

- Begin networking in every way you can. Who else do you know in your industry? With whom have you made professional acquaintanceship at other companies, organizations or institutions similar to yours? Who do you know in your circle that might know someone who might know someone else? Do you belong to a professional organization? Do you have a local Chamber of Commerce or other business networking organization at your disposal? Remember, there is no shame in letting others know that you're in the job market, and your greatest marketing tool will always be *you!*

Take a Breath and a Beat

If at all possible, take a day or two after the loss to absorb what has happened to you. Enjoy the temporary extra time that you have to yourself. Sleep in if you are able. Have an extra cup of your favorite wake-you-up beverage in the morning, and perhaps even a real breakfast to go with it. Indulge yourself in inexpensive ways—an at-home pampering; a coffee or glass of wine with a friend; a leisurely walk through your neighborhood (when you might otherwise be sitting in traffic); an extra-long yoga class—whatever activity speaks to your calm.

If you have children, relish the temporary extra time that you have to enjoy them. Go to the park, take them on the neighborhood walk, go out for an ice cream or slice of pizza…they will see it as extra-special Treat Time with Mom. (…And that goes for older kids too!)

HOW YOU CAN HELP

Someone who has lost her job needs real, practical help, as well as support and encouragement. Be the support that she needs right now.

Definite Do's

- **Brainstorm:** Invite her to coffee and brainstorm with her as to what her next steps might be. Even if you have no experience in her field, just the fact that you are sitting down and trying to come up with positive ideas shows that you care and that you're interested in helping her move in a positive direction.

- **Network:** Do you know anyone in her industry? What is your familiarity with Internet job searching? Have her give you a copy of her resumé and keep it handy, in case you meet someone who expresses interest.

- **Pick up the phone:** Your friend needs you right now. Call her. Ask, "How are you *really* doing?" If she is up for it, ask her to coffee, lunch or cocktails. Get her out of the house, and offer your ready ear and a shoulder to lean on.

Without a Doubt…Don't:

- **Don't deprive her of the need to be sad:** *"You need to get right back out there* [interviewing] *tomorrow"; "Moping isn't going to do any good"; "It was just a job."*

  My mother tells a story that goes back farther than my memory. In our days as a young family, my father worked part-time to both support our family and put himself through optometry school. Mom was a stay-at-home parent and with two young children. There was not much money to be had—and certainly no money for any "luxuries."

  My father came home one day and informed my mother that he had lost his part-time job. Keep in mind that this job was the only source of income for a family of four. Not known for over-the-top spending at any time in her life, upon hearing this news, my mother took their last twenty-five dollars (all the money in the world in those days) and bought the best steaks that she could find. She prepared their small but extravagant meal and in her words, they "spit in the eye of the devil" by enjoying their "decadent" steak dinner.

  While an interesting phrase for my Jewish mother to turn, she unknowingly began a tradition that exists in our family to this day. Whenever any misfortune befalls a member of our family, we go out to dinner and spit in the eye of that imaginary devil, as if to say, "Take *that*, Cruel World! You can knock us down, but we're not going to *stay* down."

  Lesson: It is absolutely okay to be sad (or angry or fearful) after having lost a job. She does not have to "get back out there" tomorrow. She can wait a day or two before planning her next move and during that time, if she wants to cry, get angry, feel lousy or go devil-spitting while enjoying a steak, that's okay too.

- **Don't trivialize her loss:** *"There are plenty of other jobs out there"*; *"You didn't need that job anyway"*; *"That job was beneath you."*

  First of all, if she was working, it's a reasonable assumption that she actually *needed* the job. I am also unsure as to how a job could be "beneath" someone, especially if they were at that job voluntarily and it enabled them to take care of themselves (and their family if applicable).

  Further, there may indeed be "plenty of other jobs out there," but are there plenty of jobs for *her* out there? For example, there may be a surplus of jobs available in the nursing field, but if she is not a nurse, those available jobs are not going to be especially helpful to her.

  Treat her job loss as the challenge that it is, as well as the challenge that it presents to her immediate future and to both her financial and emotional well-being.

- **Don't diminish her skills, her worth in the marketplace or her self-worth:** *"Just get any job you can"*; *"Go flip burgers someplace"*; *"There's no such thing as a 'bad job.'"*

  With much gratitude and respect paid to those who flip burgers (especially because I consume more than my fair share), unless burger-flipping is an occupation that she chose, this sort of comment is not seen as encouraging and supportive. From a practical standpoint, taking "just any job" may not be in her best interest—a job that pays less than what will pay her bills (or less than what unemployment pays while she searches for a job) is economic foolishness. It would literally *cost* her money to go to work.

  Generally speaking, comments such as these are usually said in a last-resort tone, as if to say, "It doesn't matter what the job pays, or even if it suits you financially, educationally or otherwise—just take it." Remember, when you lose a job, your self-esteem takes a huge hit. Do not compound that hit by diminishing a person's self-esteem even further.

FROM BAD THING TO BRIGHTER DAYS AHEAD

Treat your job search as a full-time job: get up every morning, put yourself together as if you are going to work and then get busy. Schedule interviews, follow up on previous interviews, send thank-you notes to those with whom you have already interviewed...searching for a job really *is* a full-time job, and you indeed have work to do.

The most important mantra to remember during your job search is to never give up and never give in. Sometimes a job hunt elicits results very quickly and other times, it can take longer to find suitable employment. Most importantly, remember that each "no" you hear is taking you one step closer to the "yes" that is in your future.

Chapter Four

BIDDING GOODBYE TO A BUSINESS

THOSE WHO OWN THEIR OWN BUSINESSES ARE OFTEN THE SUBJECTS OF ENVY of those around them. After all, you are The Boss.[12] You can work whenever you want. You can take vacations whenever you want. You are rolling in dough. You are in complete control. No worries or cares in the world, right?

Not exactly.

Having been self-employed for many years, I can absolutely attest to the fact that there can be many perks to being the first name on the company letterhead. However, being in business for yourself really is not about work-whenever-you-want and three-martini lunches. I suppose it *could* be, but then again, I do not foresee much success with that kind of work ethic.

(…And I don't even want to imagine the quality of work that I would produce after three martinis!)

The truth is that being The Boss means working when you are sick,

---

12   ..as in The One In Charge, not as in Springsteen.

working when you would really rather be doing something else, taking a vacation every couple of years if you are lucky, putting family time and friendships on hold in favor of deadlines, being open for business on weekends and holidays, and occasionally planning your personal schedule around the demands of the job—and for the first few years at least, you generally are not rolling in dough…unless you happen to own a bakery.

I would not have it any other way.

Being in business for oneself does take tremendous personal sacrifice, a strict work ethic, incredible discipline—and more sacrifice. Furthermore, you are not the *only* one making the sacrifices. I am quite sure that my family would like to see me outside of my office more than a few minutes each day, and pulling continuous all-nighters in front of a computer or constantly being on the road takes a toll on everyone.

Your business is sweat, more than a few tears, serious financial expenditure and obligation, very little in the way of measurable income for a *very* long time and an emotional commitment on a level rivaling a marriage.

I *still* would not have it any other way.

Being in business for yourself is a labor of love. Your business is your "baby." So, with all that is involved in starting, running and sustaining a business for any length of time, you can well imagine the devastation when that business is forced to end.

Whether due to economic hardship, personal financial challenge, health issues or anything else, closure of a business for reasons beyond your control is far more than simply the loss of a job or loss of income. It is the loss of a dream. It is a crisis of identity. It is the loss of an achieved goal for which you have worked hard to accomplish, perhaps for many years. It is a serious blow to self-esteem. It is being compelled to either reinvent yourself or find another dream to chase.

Teddie is one of the best friends that I have ever known, the person to whom Kendall refers to as her second mother, and whose daughter is like my own as well. Looking twenty years younger than her actual age, and with a figure that makes me want to just give up and run to Taco Bell and down fourteen bean-and-cheese burritos with extra sour cream,[13] Teddie has the gift of effortless chic in just about every way. A touch of lipstick, a little mascara, a quick fluff of the hair and she is ready for a night on the town. Her immaculate home would do *Architectural Digest* proud as a study in cool, relaxed elegance: turquoises and teals with unexpected pops in design and color (a mirror behind the stove; a warm pumpkin color in an office) and she designed all of it herself. Her wardrobe is so incredibly fashion forward, she's wearing pieces anywhere from six months to a year before it occurs to the rest of the world to follow suit.

(Just for the record, my getting-ready regimen takes a *minimum* of an hour and a half; I would look ridiculous in the outfits that she wears; my house is in constant disarray—interesting since no one seems to be in it much—and the only "unexpected" thing about my stove is that I find time to periodically use it.)

Teddie has been in the fashion industry for most of her life and quite successfully too. She owned and operated her namesake boutique in the heart of Santa Monica, one of Los Angeles' upscale areas and a trendsetter's paradise. In addition to designing exquisite pieces of jewelry, the clothing in her store also reflected her own personality: a fabulous, eclectic mix of classic shapes, whimsical accessories and super-cool, blinged-out fun. Her fashions showed a sensibility for what was on-trend and of-the-moment, yet nothing ever seemed to go out of style—and I am speaking from personal experience, as half of my closet came from her store, and most of my shoots and appearances were styled by her.

What was even more wonderful is that Teddie's store also reflected a consideration for her clientele's wallets. As she once said, "I could have easily opened up in Beverly Hills, but I don't want to charge six hundred dollars for a skirt. If I had a store in Beverly Hills, I'd have to do that just to cover overhead."

As with any business, some months were better than others, as were some years. But no one—including the most respected economic and financial

---

13 I have clearly given the Taco Bell excursion a great deal of thought.

experts in the world—could have foreseen the fiscal implosion that would take place in the United States during the late 2000s. Battle lines were drawn between lenders and small businesses; political finger-pointing and hyperbole was in overdrive in Washington DC and on Wall Street. Moreover, there was going to be a devastating financial storm through which everyone in America would suffer before the sun very slowly began to shine again—and at the forefront of that storm was the small business owner.

For the great majority of us who live, work and play on Main Street (rather than Wall Street), one thing was certain: things were never again going to be the same.

In Teddie's own words:

"It was a complete loss of identity. It was my name up there."

Teddie's story:

After twenty-two years of being in business and twelve years at my last location, I was forced to close my retail and manufacturing business. Because of the economic downturn beginning in 2007, I couldn't afford to carry the same great selection of inventory that I've always carried. I was not able to keep up with the failing economy, and with mounting [serious] health issues, I saw no other choice except to close.

Answers…but No Means

I did not go through a lot of "why me?" I felt I had the answers but not enough capital to keep the business afloat. I couldn't afford to spend money on what became a sinking ship. This did cause quite a bit of grief, as I've always prided myself on having great merchandise and being a shop that everyone loved to visit.

Getting Healthy and Figuring Out the Future

I began my business with thirty-five dollars in my wallet and a garage full of clothes that I had designed and manufactured. I was very proud of how far I'd come and what I had accomplished.

A lot of people around me either treated me as if I had not done enough [to save the business] or had advice that just didn't apply to me. People would say things like, "You need to advertise" when I had already spent thousands of dollars [on advertising], or "You need to be on the Internet." I like the personal touch, where you have real conversations with people. My store grew and thrived mostly by word of mouth.

A Work in Progress

I am moving forward with a whole new type of business, incorporating the knowledge I have absorbed along the way. I am working on my next incarnation, [and] I now have the time to get healthy and figure out what I want to be when I "grow up."

Love Your Dreams and Those Who Love You

Even if you have to "tweak" your business plan along the way, plenty of people are still able to make a go of their dreams—don't ever let the economy scare you. Also, whether you're fighting to save your business or if you're closing your business, don't neglect your family and friends in the process, because you can never get that time back.

HOW YOU CAN HELP

Someone who is bidding goodbye to her business is devastated, yet she is quite likely to be the recipient of judgment, criticism and unsolicited opinion. Do not pile on with that crowd—she needs solid, practical support, but she also needs someone to tell her that it's really okay to be sad.

Definite Do's

- **If she chooses to have a "Going Out of Business" (liquidation) sale, help her make the experience as positive as possible:** Brainstorm ideas with her as to when and how to have the sale and how to make it fun—serve inexpensive snacks, run a raffle (everyone who purchases over "x" amount will be entered into a raffle to win a prize from the store or a prize donated from another local merchant), etc.

- **Spread the word:** Tell everyone you know that your friend is closing her business and now is the time to get wonderful items, do their holiday shopping, treat themselves—whatever it takes to help drive traffic and boost her bottom line. Share on social media outlets and encourage your social media circles to share to *their* circles. Help make this occasion as upbeat and positive as you can.

- **Offer your help**: If you are able, offer to help, be it with the logistics of the sale (answering customer questions, checking stock, etc.), moving leftover inventory or store fixtures after the fact or even with the business and paperwork aspects of closing (on the important condition that you have skills in these areas).

- **Reassure her:** Whether she is closing and locking the door on her brick-and-mortar business for the last time or she is filing the last piece of paper with the state that officially dissolves her business, it will be a sad and difficult time for her and she will need reassurance. Remind her that regardless of how long she was in business, she was a success. She opened and ran a business, and that is an achievement to be respected and admired. Listen to her while she shares her hopes, fears and new goals, and reinforce her forward thinking.

Without a Doubt…Don't

- **Don't kill the dream:** *"Why start another business?"; "There's no demand for what you do"; "I told you this wouldn't work"; "Who needs the headache?"*

  For the record, I'm not sure that "I told you so" is ever an appropriate response to any kind of situation (and we will revisit this later in the book). Remember what I said earlier about the battering that self-esteem takes after a business is lost? Re-read it. She has just lost something that she built from the ground up, no matter the business in which she was involved. Her business was not a "headache" to her. It was her dream-come-true and then a dream-snatched-away, likely by circumstances that she could not control. Get behind her eyes and into her heart; you may then understand the magnitude of this loss.

• **Don't be an "expert":** *"Why don't you start something on the Internet"; "I have a great idea for something else that you can do* [... that has nothing to do with the line of business that she is in].*"*

I understand that the Internet has become the latest, greatest avenue on which to begin and grow a business, as witness phenomena like Amazon, Google, Facebook, Twitter, Huffington Post and YouTube. However, you may well remember the "Dot Com" boom of the late 1990s; it was soon followed by the "Dot Com" *bust,* with the cataclysmic collapse of untold numbers of businesses losing multi-millions of dollars. In other words, for every Amazon, Google, Facebook, Twitter, Huffington Post and YouTube, there are millions more businesses who tried and failed.

Does that mean that Internet is off-limits in terms of an alternate business model? Of course not—but let the idea come from her. Believe me, she is aware of the existence of the Internet. Ask her how *she* feels about having an Internet-driven business. Chances are that if she wanted her business to be on the Internet in any fashion, she would already be there. In other words, the Internet is not the solution to every single business situation or for every single person. As Teddie shared, "I like the personal touch," and for that reason, she intentionally eschewed the Internet in connection with her store. She knew that it was not for her and would not best serve her clientele.

Further, now is not the time for your "great idea" for another business, especially one that would take her away from what it is that she has been doing and the area(s) in which she is expert. The first thing that will go through her mind is, "If it's such a great idea, and if you're such an authority, how come *you* haven't done it?" Secondly, she is in her chosen field for a reason, and if she has a desire to change fields, it is a decision at which *she* needs to arrive on her own, and in *her* own time.

- **Don't ask for freebies:** *"I know it's marked down fifty percent but you'll let me have it for* [an even lower amount], *right?"; "Hey we're family, can I just have this?"; "If I help you, can I have some stuff for free?"*

  Her misfortune should not become your fire sale or bartering opportunity. She will price and sell her inventory based upon several factors, not the least of which is her obligation to settle debts and resolve any expenses involved in closing a business. However, she also likely has a deadline (self-imposed or otherwise) that she must meet to close her business and for that reason, she is probably already selling her inventory at a deep discount.

  If you are purchasing from her liquidation sale, do so at the price marked. Do not take advantage of your relationship, and do not further insult her or cause additional financial burden by asking for discounts on things that she is likely already selling at below-retail prices.

From Bad Thing to Brighter Days Ahead

No one will ever deny that the loss of a business is core-shaking. However, you also have the benefit of knowing that you have what it takes to begin and run a business—not everyone can say that. In other words, if you did it once and if it is your choice to do so, you can absolutely do it again.

On the other hand, if it is your decision to leave your field or decline opening another business, or if you are thinking of taking an entirely different career path, go ahead and do it! This is *your* life's design and you can design (or *re*design) it any way you wish. Today is not "forever," and the word "no" does not mean "never." Always remember, you do not have to settle for where you are…if where you are is not where you wish to be.

chapter 5:

The Challenge of Finances and the Finances of Challenge

Financial challenge manifests in all kinds of ways for all kinds of reasons. The reality is that despite even the best efforts, millions of people are literally one or two paychecks away from disaster.

The reasons for financial challenge are limitless. Divorce, death, job loss, legal woes, loss of a business, medical bills (a reality for most who live in the United States), children's higher education, and in more recent years, the economic devastation that millions have experienced through no fault of their own. The list of reasons for financial struggle is lengthy, and at one time or another (perhaps even more than once), most of us have paddled this worrisome canoe.

Doing the Right Thing Doesn't Always Matter

The sad fact is that you can (and should) do all of the "right" things when it comes to your financial house. You can pay all of your bills on time. You can sock away funds for a "rainy day." You can live within your means…and you can still wind up with your heart in your throat, spending restless nights wondering how you are going to manage and crying, "Why is this happening to *me?*"

It can also feel like as soon as you are making financial headway and you just *might* be able to relax, the universe inevitably delivers another reason for you to lose sleep.

A (Fake) Tooth for a Tooth

It was a particularly busy time in my office when a relatively minor toothache interrupted my schedule and landed me in a dental chair, one of my least favorite places on the planet. Thinking that I had a simple cavity, the dentist instead took X-rays, studied them closely, shook his head gravely and said, "If we're lucky, we're looking at 'only' a root canal." When I asked him what the presumably unlucky alternative might be, he replied, "We're looking at a dental implant."[14]

Several X-rays later, it was revealed that I indeed landed on the unlucky side of things and a dental implant would be necessary. More unpleasant surprises followed, most notably, the fact that dental insurance does not cover dental implants (or any of the implant processes), because—for reasons defying all logic—insurance companies consider dental implants to be "cosmetic" procedures.[15] In other words, the mid-four-digit bill for the one-tooth implant belonged to me.

Several months into the process and heading into the holiday season, I advised the surgeon that I was taking a break in the dental merriment to allow my wallet to recover. Literally twenty-four hours after putting the remainder of the dental work on a temporary hold, our refrigerator quit without any prior indication that it was quickly heading to Appliance Heaven. I had allowed myself to take a financial deep breath, and we instead found ourselves in an appliance store, shopping for a refrigerator that we certainly did not plan on purchasing at that (literal) season in time.

---

14 A dental implant involves oral surgery, a bone graft, the placement of a steel post that takes months to heal and the eventual placement of a prosthetic tooth.

15 The insurance companies' position on implants is that filling a hole in your face with another tooth to preserve the ability to chew, prevent the rest of your teeth from shifting and keep from looking like a bit player from the movie *Deliverance* is an optional cosmetic luxury.

Teeth and major household appliances aside, "Why is this happening to me?" is a very common lament during times of financial challenge. You are a decent, hardworking person and you do not deserve this kind of heartache. Nevertheless, when financial difficulty befalls, you must get single-minded and serious about what you are going to do in order to weather the storm.

GETTING ORGANIZED AND STAYING THAT WAY

Even though the first instinct is to hide from an unfortunate financial reality, if you are experiencing financial challenge, your next steps must also include some serious honesty. Serious honesty sucks, but it is necessary none-theless.

Begin by gathering your checkbook, your credit cards, your debit cards, your insurance policies and anything else that has anything to do with monthly output. This exercise will both show you *exactly* what you are spending every month and assist you with "trimming the fat" off of monthly spending. Most people do not have an accurate idea of how much money goes out each month and once you have made this determination, you are going to feel much better. Even though your financial situation will not instantly change, when you have a sound idea of in-versus-out and it is down on paper, the garbage that has been bouncing around in your head is now emptied and in front of you. You have begun your fat-trimming plan.

FINANCIAL FAT TRIMMING

Many are unaware that you can begin financial fat trimming simply by picking up a telephone:

1. Start with your cable television provider, Internet provider, tele-phone provider[16] and cell phone provider to see what rate reductions

---

16 I *do not recommend* disconnecting a landline as part of financial fat trimming. Cell phones may make landlines seem redundant—until you try to reach someone in an emergency, or cell service is not working due to disaster situations. You might consider discontinuing features such as call-waiting or call-forwarding, but don't eliminate the landline altogether.

are available. Many providers offer reduced rates and extra savings when you bundle services—for example, your cable, Internet and landline telephone. Even if these services are already bundled into one payment, you can still contact your provider and negotiate a lower rate—providers have gotten extremely competitive as they realize that your carrier choices are now vast.

You must also assess if you are paying for services that you do not use. For example, do you have the largest package that your cable provider offers? If so, are you really making use of every premium channel offered? How about the extra sports and movie channels? If you are making full use of these packages, that's fine—but if not, move to the next package down, or the one after that. The same holds for all of your telephone services—how many features do you have that you rarely or never use? Tally them up and cut them out.

2. Next, have a look at your utilities: electric, gas heating, water, trash collection, etc. Many utility companies offer "level pay" or reduced rates for people in financial hardship. See what they have to offer, and do not just assume that you won't qualify for relief. You may be pleasantly surprised.

3. Now examine the interest rates that you are paying on each one of your credit cards—easily done by visiting your accounts online. Call each company, advise them that you are contemplating transferring your balance to a company offering a lower rate and ask if they would be willing to lower your rate rather than lose your business. You may again be met with a happy surprise.

At this point, stop and determine how much financial fat you have been able to trim. Write that number down before you continue. If the number is very small, do not be discouraged. Think of it this way—even if you are saving ten dollars a month, that's $120 per year. If someone walked up to you and said, "Here's $120," would you turn it down because that number is too small? If so, please give that person my email address, because I will happily accept $120—or any amount of money that goes into the "plus" column on a budget sheet.

4. Review *all* of your insurance policies, including automobile, home-owner (or renter) and medical insurance.[17] You may be able to reduce your monthly premiums by raising deductibles slightly or eliminating coverage that you may not need. Contact the respective agents and see what savings might be available to you.

5. Lastly, examine everything on which you spend money regularly—and that means *everything*. How much are you spending when you visit the coffeehouse every morning? A small cup of black coffee five days a week can add up to approximately fifteen dollars per week, which is sixty dollars per month. How could you better use sixty dollars? Instead of the coffeehouse, go to your local discount store and get an inexpensive coffeemaker with an auto-on feature, set it to brew before you get out of bed in the morning, fill up a travel mug (which generally holds about three times the amount that you would get at a coffeehouse) and head out the door.

Complete this exercise with everything else that is eating away at your bottom line. What can you cut down, substitute or eliminate altogether? Write it down.

Experts are Expert for a Reason

If you are encountering serious financial difficulty that the above steps alone will not help mitigate, seek out *expert* assistance. For example, if you are unable to make timely credit card payments, contact the respective companies to work

---

17 If you have medical insurance through your employer, your contributions are likely fixed as part of a group policy. However, if you purchase medical insurance on your own because of self-employment, unemployment, retirement, etc., be aware that due to changes in health insurance laws in the United States, you may be eligible for medical insurance at a reduced rate and/or qualify for governmental assistance. Visit www.healthcare.gov or the website for your particular state for additional information.

out a repayment plan. If you are in trouble with rent or mortgage, immediately contact your mortgage company or property management company to find out what options are available. If you are struggling with medical debt (as are approximately *one-third* of all Americans),[18] contact the doctor or hospital billing department and work out a reasonable payment plan.

If all else fails, do not automatically dismiss bankruptcy[19] as an option. Obviously this is nobody's idea of a first option; however, depending on your particular circumstances, you may be able to declare bankruptcy while keeping certain assets (such as your home and your car). While not the most desirable of actions, the overwhelming consensus from those who have experienced bankruptcy is that it was for the best; they were able to begin rebuilding their financial lives and start anew with a clean fiscal slate.

Looking to a Bright Future

> *"Many people who commit themselves 100% to eliminating debt and saving money find that a certain joylessness creeps in. That's not a way to live, and that's not what I advocate. Austerity, yes; deprivation, no."*
>
> —Kevin O'Leary, Founder at O'Leary Financial Group
> and star of ABC's *Shark Tank*

I agree wholeheartedly.

Contrary to what many say or believe, I too am not one of those people who believe that financial challenge means that you do not ever get to have any fun or that you do not get to treat yourself periodically. Will you have to compromise the lifestyle that you previously enjoyed? Yes...for awhile. However, there is good news about financial challenge. While it may not

---

18 As reported by the *New York Times*, March 20, 2012: "Many Americans Struggling to Pay Medical Bills."
19 When contemplating bankruptcy or any kind of financial reorganization, it is imperative that you consult with legal experts that specialize in this very complex area of law. Most lawyers specializing in bankruptcy law will offer an initial consultation free of charge.

happen quickly, financial difficulty is something from which you can eventually recover, regardless of how serious your situation is, or the steps that you must take to rectify it.

HOW YOU CAN HELP

While you might not be able to ease another's financial burden in a practical sense, there are still a number of ways that you can be supportive without breaking anyone's bank—and even have fun in the process.

Definite Do's

- **Suggest low or no-cost ways to have fun:** These can include a picnic with homemade food (even something as simple as peanut butter-and-jelly sandwiches with potato chips and chocolate chip cookies); a nature hike; working out in your living room to exercise videos (which will get you laughing); a trip to an art gallery, museum or farmer's market. Also, check the "Events" section of your local newspaper to see what is going on in your neighborhood that is free of charge.

- **Provide your best cost-cutting ideas:** I am shameless about clipping coupons, checking for online coupons and deals,[20] doing research to find out which credit cards offer cash back, joining whatever free rewards club stores offer and using reward points to do everything from save money at the pump to getting discounts when dining out. I have also negotiated lower cable bills, homeowners and automobile insurance premiums and gym memberships. Help your friend in need

---

20 A fantastic resource to use when shopping online is www.ebates.com. Ebates is totally free to join, they have thousands of stores and services in their database and when you do your online shopping through Ebates, the store (or service) will reward you with a percentage of the purchase price. It doesn't sound like much until the quarterly check arrives—which can be anywhere from a few dollars to a few hundred dollars.

by providing these and other money-saving ideas to help her make ends meet. Just a few dollars saved here and there will add up quickly.

Without a Doubt…Don't

- **Don't be cliché:** *"Money isn't everything"; "Money doesn't buy happiness"; "Money is the root of all evil."*

  Let's get something straight. The person who says "money isn't everything" usually isn't up night after night worrying about how bills are going to be paid. They are generally the people who are not in financial straits. Further, the number of people who have used the "money is the root of all evil" misquote far outweigh those who know that the actual quote reads, "For the *love* of money is the root of all kinds of evil." In other words, it is the *love* of money that is considered evil, not money itself.

  The fact is that whoever says that money doesn't buy happiness has never been shopping with me. It is true that there are things that money doesn't buy. Money doesn't buy character, integrity, heart or compassion…and money most *definitely* does not buy class.[21] But happiness? Hmm…

  What money *does* buy is choice. Money buys financial peace of mind and security, both present and future. These are all facts that are not going to be easily erased with useless clichés.

- **Don't give financial advice:** *"You need to [buy, sell, invest] right now."; "I can help you out with this idea/software-du-jour/get-rich-quick plan"; "I know someone who has a great 'scheme'/knows everything there is to know about money/made a ridiculous amount of money in a week."*

  Though you may be well-meaning, unless you are a certified

---

21 For proof as to how much class is available for purchase, tune into any one of a sadly large number of alleged "reality" television shows.

financial adviser or well-established financial planner with a sound history of financial success (accompanied by references that can be contacted) and your advice is specifically solicited, your advice is not welcome or needed. Your advice may instead be taken as thinly-veiled criticism or condescension. Further, "get-rich-quick" schemes and other potentially shady ideas are never helpful. If she wants a specific financial plan or other actionable advice, she will seek it out—and if she wants that advice from you, she will let you know.

- **Don't pass judgment:** *"You should never have used your credit card(s)"; "If you hadn't bought that* [car, house, grindle reflincher or anything that *you* feel is unnecessary or frivolous], *you wouldn't be in this position; "You don't have a savings account? What's the matter with you?"*

    Have you ever heard that saying about closing the barn door after the horses have bolted? Consider the horses bolted…and closing the barn door after the fact isn't going to get those already-bolted horses back.

    Admonishments are not going to help whatever financial issues she is dealing with right now. If she has made mistakes in her financial planning (or lack thereof), or if she has otherwise been less than prudent when it comes to finances (and let's be honest, who among us *hasn't* made an error in judgment at least once in our lives), she is well aware of those mistakes and does not need you to point them out to her. She needs compassion and understanding—and if you have ideas that can help her in the immediate, share those ideas with a gentle heart. She will be forever grateful to you.

- **Don't invite her to go places that she cannot afford right now:** *"Come on, it's not* that *expensive"; "What's the problems; we used to go there all the time"; "It's just this once, you can do it if you really want to"; "Use a credit card, it won't make any difference."*

    You know, when Mike lost his ability to eat and swallow (due to his illness), we quit eating around him. We knew that just because he was physically unable to eat did not mean that he lost the desire to eat or that food was unappealing to him. To my mind, preparing food with yummy smells or eating in front of him when he had been sadly relegated to liquid sustenance administered through a feeding tube would have been just plain cruel.

The same line of logic applies here. Just because someone can no longer afford to eat at this restaurant or take advantage of that sale does not mean that she doesn't *want* to—and telling your cash-strapped buddy to toss common sense to the wind while encouraging her to whip out the plastic because you want or need a dining/shopping wingman is selfish.

Unless you are willing to change one of the above statements to, *"Let's go to this restaurant/sale extravaganza/concert/place that requires serious coin—and it is one-hundred percent my treat,"* do not make her feel worse than she is already feeling by putting her on the spot—or worse, tempting her to worsen her financial situation by encouraging an attitude of *"Well, I'm already drowning, what's one more meal/outfit/concert/thing I have no business doing?"*

From Bad Thing to Brighter Days Ahead

There is no absolutely no shame in experiencing financial challenge, especially considering that, with rare exception, just about everyone over the age of majority has endured this difficulty at some point in their lives. There *are* solutions and there *are* ways through. Do your research and avail yourself of some of the suggestions listed. Remember too, that everyone in the world deserves at least one financial "do-over" in their lives—and that includes you.

Chapter Six

BETRAYAL

BETRAYAL IS AN ENORMOUS WORD. YOU CANNOT EXPERIENCE BETRAYAL unless you first placed trust in a person. People who you do not know or do not trust cannot betray you. For betrayal to occur, there must first have been trust, along with the expectation that the trust you bestowed would be honored, treated with the utmost respect and ultimately reciprocated. Most certainly you reasonably expected loyalty in exchange for that trust, which is why betrayal is one of the worst kinds of bad things that you can ever experience.

Betrayal is the destruction of the relationship that you believed to have existed with another person, whatever that relationship perspective may have been. How? Without trust, there *is* no honest relationship, and betrayal is the great destroyer of trust. Betrayal causes you to question everything that you believed a relationship—and in some cases, your very life—to be. It leaves you feeling foolish, stupid, humiliated and angry beyond measure, naturally wondering what on *earth* must people be thinking and/or saying, and often-times questioning your own good judgment. After all, how could you *not* have known about the:

Affair
Secret or double life
Hidden financial issues/debts/obligations/payouts
Person you met online, with whom you fell in love and who turned out
to be a "catfish"[22]

…and numerous other betrayals of which countless women have been victims.
You are *not* lacking in intelligence, nor are you blind. How could something
like this happen to *you*?

The answer is simple.

It happened to you because you are decent and trusting and believe in the
inherent good in people—and that is a good way to be. However, in being
that kind of person, you are also running the risk of experiencing betrayal,
perhaps even more than once.

The women you are about to meet have all been victims of betrayals.
They courageously share their stories so you understand that when it comes
to betrayal, you are most certainly *not* alone—nor are you stupid, foolish,
ignorant or any of the other adjectives that you have likely been using to beat
up on yourself.

"My Life was a Lie": Discovery of Infidelity

Whether we got married in a house of worship in front of hundreds of people
or we married at the local courthouse in front of a judge, be it a full-out religious ceremony or a civil ceremony that takes no more than twenty minutes,
all ceremonies involve one common denominator:

Vows.

We vow to love, honor and respect one another; however, vows involve more
than just those select words. We vow to love when things are great and when
things suck. We vow to take care of the other person when they are sick, be it

---

22 As defined by www.urbandictionary.com, a "catfish" is (in pertinent part): "Someone who pretends to be
someone they are not, particularly to pursue deceptive online romances."

in body, heart, spirit or all three. We vow to hang in there together, whether things are "bucks-up" or the proverbial evil bill collector wearing the figurative black hat comes calling. We vow to have one another's back and not stick a knife in that back when turned. We vow to forsake all others—yes, *all* others—no matter how pretty or handsome one of those "all others" may be, or just how green that grass on the other side of the marital fence may appear.

So what happens when only one person at the altar takes these vows seriously?

Karen* is a lovely and serene presence in an otherwise chaotic world. A successful businesswoman in her own right, with children who are each successful in *their* own rights and with whom she enjoys loving and wonderful relationships, her personality is one of calm and effortless organization (which makes personalities like myself alternately extremely grateful and insanely jealous). Her heart for others is enormous, and she is as deeply committed to philanthropic causes as she is to her family, her friends and to her own frenetically growing business. Karen is equally committed in her relationships as well, devoted to a fault to the ones she loves—and you don't have to be a relative to be a recipient of that love.

Given all of the above, Karen would be the last person one would expect to be on the receiving end of infidelity. However, as her story teaches, you can be and do all of the right things, and experience this awful betrayal just the same.

Karen's story

My story involves my ex-husband's infidelity and how his betrayal affected my life and the lives of my two young daughters, and shook the foundation of our marriage.

For years, I was "mom and dad" to the girls, all while founding and working in a very successful business. My husband worked the second shift at a local distribution center and would not get home until after the girls and I had gone to bed. I got the girls up each morning, got them ready for school or daycare, and then went to work. The girls were very active and involved, which kept me busy. Additionally, the girls would spend time with me at my business and, to this day, they remember all the fun times that we had, even when there was a lot of work to be done.

One night as [my husband and I] lay in bed, he told me that he had something on his mind. He'd been having an affair for over a year with an older woman that he worked with. He was afraid I would see her driving our truck and wanted to tell me before I saw her. To say I was shocked was an understatement. I was emotionally devastated. I had been betrayed. He had broken our scared marriage vows. How could he? The thought that he had broken a promise he had made "until death us do part" was unbearable.

I felt frustrated and humiliated. I went into "mother-cub" protection mode, as I did not want the girls to know what was going on. I started staying up at night to see what time he was getting home. He would get off work and go over to the "other woman"'s house, have sex and then come home. He lied about his whereabouts and became verbally abusive with me.

The woman knew my schedule better than I did (this was before cell phones and social media) and followed me around. She punctured the radiator in my car while I was with my daughter at gymnastics. My husband told me that a bird did it with its beak. I later learned how far she was willing to go in her relationship [with my husband] as she tried to commit suicide and [thereafter] blamed my husband.

We had many arguments about her, as he was addicted to the relationship. His verbal abuse was awful, and there was physical abuse too. This behavior went on for months, until I finally told him that he needed to move out.

What Did *I* Do?

I asked myself "Why me?" over and over. What had I done in our marriage to drive this man, the father of my two girls, into the arms of another woman? I was running the household, taking care of our children day and night, working full time—what more could I do? Had our relationship started going downhill with all the pressure of family life? Was I not meeting his emotional needs?

Reconciliation...and Déjà Vu

It was vital to me to move on with life and learn to trust again. However, after being separated for a few months, he asked for forgiveness. I told him nothing could compensate for the infidelity and that he needed to demonstrate his commitment to our marriage. I suggested we go to counseling. It lasted only for a few sessions—he didn't like that the counselor was telling him he needed to put one hundred fifty-percent effort into the relationship to rebuild trust. We had to work on our communication issues without verbal abuse, and that added additional stress to rebuilding our marriage.

After the reconciliation, we were blessed with a son, and I thought that perhaps we had found our way. We bought a beautiful new home. I thought it would make my husband happy, that after working through all of our problems, he could have the home and the family that he always wanted.

Not long after moving into our new home, he started taking off again. We didn't know where he was going and when asked, he would snap at us and say that it was none of our business. He'd disappear for hours. The stress, the fighting, the verbal abuse had begun all over again. I wondered if I could be living this hell all over again. Had he been seeing someone? I had to do something, and that decision would be one of the toughest of my life.

Choosing Freedom at Last

There comes a time in your life when you realize that you can no longer live to please others. When you decide that you are "done," you just want to be free. I'd protected the girls so much when they were so young—wouldn't they rather be *from* a broken home than live in one?

I went see my attorney, discussed my options and moved out, taking the two youngest children with me. It was a very long [healing] road, and I was blessed to have had support from trusted friends and family. After four long years, I was granted a divorce, and I had my freedom.

During this difficult time, I turned to a man who I'd known for over twenty years within the business community. I'd see him at local chamber events and we'd talk about his kids and my activities. He too had gone through a very difficult divorce. He had always been a confidante; even if it was just a phone call of encouragement. He also saw that my self-esteem had been run through the mud—and with his words of inspiration, I soon realized that I had so much more to give to life and my children.

You Are Stronger Than You Think

Following my divorce, the man in whom I had confided for so many years got down on one knee and proposed. It was a surprise, as I never expected to get married again. He was a wonderful man who went out of his way to help me rebuild my life, my trust and taught me to live life to the fullest.

Infidelity is a betrayal like no other. It took me years to learn to trust again, but there is only one you and you have only one life to live. It's what you do with your life that matters and you are stronger than you think.

"Who ARE You?" Discovery of a Hidden Life

Most of us enjoy lives that are of our own creation. Be it on our own or with the person we love, we establish ourselves and the day-to-day that we call our lives. We have good days and bad days. We have bumps in the road and lovely seasons of celebration. We are secure in routine and we welcome moments of spontaneity. We also rightly believe that the lives we are building and leading are authentic—why would we believe otherwise?

Unfortunately for many women, "otherwise" shows up—and is blind-siding in its arrival.

Monica Lee, the author of *The Percussionist's Wife: A Memoir of Sex, Crime & Betrayal*,[23] was a loving wife who was married to her husband for sixteen years. Her life was decimated by the discovery of both the ultimate betrayal and criminal behavior. She describes the pain of that time, the mistakes that she admittedly made and most importantly, how she persevered and eventually triumphed over a horrendous set of circumstances.

---

23 To learn more about Monica and *The Percussionist's Wife*... (Monica Lee), please visit www.mindfulmonica. wordpress.com and www.minnesotatransplant.wordpress.com.

Monica's story

My husband and I had been married nearly eleven years when he was accused of raping an eighteen-year-old female high-school student. He initially told me that the incident for which he was accused was a fantasy created by this girl. I believed him.

After being questioned by the police, he admitted to me that he did indeed invite the student to our home while I was out of town. He allowed her to smoke pot on our porch and made out with her. He said that she was a willing partner and that she was lying about being raped. He begged me to believe and forgive him. For many reasons, not the least of which included our long history, his apology and my love for him, I decided to stand by him. He eventually spent time in jail.

I took me five more years of marriage to this man to figure out—and finally accept—the flaws in my husband that precipitated his infidelity, including his inability to be honest. We [eventually] divorced.

ANGRY AT THE WORLD

I percolated with blame and anger. I was particularly angry with the student who made the accusations against my husband, even after he told me that he had an illicit encounter with her. I irrationally blamed her, the school district, the police and the court system for pinpointing and punishing my husband. In retrospect, my anger was a symptom of my own sorrow and humiliation.

MISTAKES AND OPENED EYES

The legal process took eighteen months. During that time, I coped by focusing on my work. I was a marketing executive so I had a large staff and a lot of business travel to distract me. My husband (who was immediately terminated from his job at the high school) was not working, so I was responsible for all of the attorney's fees and fines. The responsibility of being the sole breadwinner made the attention I paid to my career seem reasonable, though it was also a convenient way to avoid addressing the relationship problems.

I thought we had a strong marriage [prior to] the girl's claims of rape, but when I look back on the years following the accusation and his time spent in jail, I realize that we didn't address anything in any depth. We behaved like we'd addressed our problems, but we were simply acting in our "happily-ever-after" roles. I didn't open my eyes to what was really happening until I embarked on an affair of my own. It was initially to address my sexual needs, but quickly opened my eyes to the lack of honesty in my marriage.

Cheating on my husband was an inappropriate and selfish way to address the loneliness that I was feeling, but I honestly don't know if I ever would've figured out how broken my marriage was without having confided in my lover. He provided the place of intimacy and trust that I didn't give my family and friends a chance to [provide] because I was so embarrassed.

Opening Up and Finding My Healing

I eventually realized that my husband was permanently flawed. The intimacy I craved in a marital relationship was not possible with him. I started opening up to others, and I felt renewed strength to take action.

The next few months were a whirlwind. I moved out, broke up with my lover, filed for divorce, started my memoir and began online dating. I met a new man whom I eventually married, and he encouraged me to finish writing the story about my first marriage. The process of writing my memoir and sharing the intimate details of my first marriage were incredibly healing.

Share Your Heart with Those Who Care

Share your heart with people with whom you feel safe. Talking about how you feel when you've been betrayed actually helps you sort it out. When I finally started talking about the betrayal, how humiliated I was and how I'd failed, that's when I realized I wasn't alone, and that people around me wanted me to be happy.

My life is so much better now. I found a man who loves me as I am and values respect and intimacy as I do. As I wrote in the epilogue of my memoir: "Sometimes the A-student in me looks back at my first marriage with regret and wishes the teacher would have accepted extra-credit work. I am certainly not proud to count myself among the divorced; [however] I am much happier."

From Beyond the Grave:
Betrayal Discovered After Death

Imagine just for a moment…

You have lost your husband. You have been through the arrangement making and the subsequent funeral. You are receiving visitors and sympathy cards, both by the dozens. People are regaling you with stories of how wonderful your late husband was and how greatly missed he will be. Meanwhile, you can barely make your feet. You feel as though you are on autopilot…and to an extent, you *are* on autopilot. After all, this level of grief is overwhelming and all-encompassing.

Time passes.

You continue to mourn both your husband and the life you have lost. Eventually you begin to go through things: paperwork, old bills, the piles of "stuff" that we all manage to accumulate over a lifetime…

Then you run across "it."

"It" might be a letter or a telephone bill in a desk drawer. "It" might be a receipt from a florist shop or credit card bills hidden in a desk drawer. Whatever form "it" takes, "it" manages to bring what little life you felt that you had left crashing down around you.

You have discovered a posthumous betrayal.

Betrayal is earth shattering under any circumstances; however, betrayal discovered posthumously is much worse for two primary reasons. It is betrayal that can never be directly confronted or explained by the perpetrator because the perpetrator is no longer here to either confront or to offer an explanation. Further—and perhaps even worse—it causes you to question everything that you had believed your life to be, the legacy of that life and everything that your life will be in the future.

Tiffani* and Anissa* both discovered betrayal after the deaths of their husbands. While horribly difficult to overcome, both women demonstrate that with the right emotional and practical support, you can begin to reconcile and eventually accept the experience of betrayal discovered after death—and find a place of peace.

Tiffani's story

Rich and I were high-school sweethearts. We married when I was nineteen years old and he was twenty years old. Everyone told us the usual things that people say when you get married young: "Why don't you wait till after college?" and "Young marriages don't last." But I knew better. Rich was the only person I ever dated and I knew I wanted to spend the rest of my life with him.

We were married for ten years when he was killed in a [work-related] accident. I was in so much shock that I can barely remember the first few days after the accident. I was left with two [young children] and I had no idea what I was going to do.

Several months later, I got up the guts to go through his things. He had a workshop in our garage and in back of one of the closets, I found a shoebox filled with cards and romantic notes from a woman he'd been seeing for almost three years. It looked like they had met online [by the contents of the notes]. At that moment, I felt like my whole life had been one big lie, and the guy I'd been in love with since I was sixteen was nothing but a cheater and a liar.

Shock and Questions

It felt like the first week after he died. I went back into shock. I didn't know what to do or where to turn. I didn't know who I could trust. I questioned everything he ever said or did. Was he really bowling every Thursday night or was he with her? Was he with her instead of working overtime like he said he was? Did his friends or family know? I didn't know what the truth was anymore.

It wasn't until a few weeks later when I really started to think about what he had been doing and what he did to our family. I kept asking myself, "What did I do to make him want to be with someone else?" I put all the blame on myself.

I Wanted to Scream

After the shock of finding out started to wear off, I got angry. I took my anger out on everyone around me. They just assumed that I was acting that way because of losing Rich. They had no idea what was really going on.

My first thought was to find out who she was so that I could meet her face-to-face. I went through Rich's laptop but I couldn't find any emails or information about her on his computer. The cards and notes didn't have envelopes so there was no way for me to find her. Except for not throwing out the cards and letters that I found, he covered his tracks.

While all this was going on, people kept asking how the kids and I were doing and kept telling me how much they missed Rich. I wanted to scream, "Rich was a bastard who cheated on us!" but I didn't think anyone would understand. I was so embarrassed and afraid that people were going to assume that he was having an affair because he was unhappy with me.

ACCEPTING WHAT I CANNOT CHANGE

I finally couldn't take it anymore and told one of my closest friends. She was so understanding and helped me realize it was not my fault and the responsibility of what Rich did was on him. She encouraged me to get help in dealing with that part of his death. I found a great counselor who helped me accept that I'll never really know his reasons for cheating and that if I'd faced off with the other woman, it wouldn't have made me feel better and could have made things worse.

The people who know about the affair ask me if I've forgiven Rich. I can't say that I've forgiven him and I don't know if I ever will. I also don't know if I will ever tell our kids the whole truth. But at least I know that it wasn't anything that I did. Rich made his choices, and I do not take responsibility for the choices he made.

THE RESPONSIBILITY BELONGS TO THE BETRAYER, NOT TO THE BETRAYED

The most important thing I can say is that whatever he did behind your back is what *he* did. You didn't do anything wrong. You owe it to yourself to realize that you're a good person, and no one can blame you for the wrong actions of your husband.

I really believe in getting counseling and telling a couple of close friends or people you can trust. I took my anger out on everyone around me and my family and friends didn't deserve to be treated the way I was treating them.

The time will come that you'll remember the good in your marriage and relationship. The affair will always be there because it's reality, but it will stop being the only thing on your mind.

Anissa's* story

Burt* and I were married for almost thirty years. He had his own business, and I worked part-time at a boutique. I didn't have to work but it was fun for me to work with people and be creative with fashion. We lived a very comfortable life by most standards. We had a nice home and entertained a lot. Our three children were grown and gone and we'd just started to do some traveling when Burt was diagnosed with cancer. He died about a year later.

After Burt died, I had the mail that went to his business address forwarded to our house. It was about a month later that I started getting mail from different credit card companies and a bank that were all looking for money. I had no idea these credit cards even existed, and the bank wanted a home equity loan paid off that I didn't know about. When I contacted these companies to let them know that Burt died, all they did was change the name on the accounts to "The Estate of," so they could send the bills to me. They were trying to hold me responsible for hundreds of thousands of dollars that I never knew about.

I also found out that Burt quit paying on a life insurance policy that we had going back to before he got sick—so there was no life insurance. There were also medical bills left over from when he was sick, and I was responsible for them too.

How Could I Not Know?

I felt like I'd been living a huge lie, thinking that we were so comfortable when we had no security at all. Burt intentionally let the insurance lapse, he ran up credit cards and now I wasn't sure I could stay in our house because of the home equity loan. I didn't understand how he could do something like this to me and to our family.

I went through the "If only I'd known" period. I know it's not logical to think that way. How could I have known about hidden credit cards and a house loan when the mail was going to the business? And why shouldn't I have trusted him to keep up the life insurance policy? Doesn't everyone trust their husband or wife? I felt ashamed and stupid.

GETTING SERIOUS ABOUT GETTING HELP

I didn't have time to be upset. Don't get me wrong, I was definitely upset but I knew if I was going to have any chance at keeping my house and anything else I owned, I had to get [legal] help right away. I could deal with being furious later on. I had to move very fast to try and find my way out of the mess that Burt left me.

HANDLING THE PRACTICAL WHILE DEALING WITH THE EMOTIONAL

I got an attorney who helped me negotiate with everyone that Burt owed money to. I had to pay the medical bills, but the doctors and hospitals lowered the amounts and didn't charge interest. Because the credit cards weren't in my name and my name wasn't on any of the [credit card] applications, I was not held responsible for those debts. We're still figuring out the home equity loan, but my attorney feels that it can be resolved through the sale of Burt's business.

There is still the emotional part that I'm trying to deal with. I used to think, "You're so lucky that you don't have to work and you still get to live like this." I felt humiliated and stupid when everything fell apart. I have to keep reminding myself that Burt was the one who was deceitful and selfish, because he knew what he was doing and that I'd be the one [left behind] to deal with it.

SHIFTING FOCUS TOWARD THE POSITIVE

There will always be a part of me that will be angry at Burt for doing what he did. He even had the chance to say something when he was sick and chose not to. But I'm trying to concentrate on the happy parts of our marriage, our children and my new grandchild. That's the only way that I can keep going with a positive attitude. I also don't want our kids' memories of their father to be all negative. I finally told them what I found [after their father died], and they were all pretty upset with him, but more worried about me.

I also found out that this happens to a lot of widows and widowers and I felt a little less ashamed; like I'm not alone. It's been a great learning lesson. If I ever do get married again, I'll make sure I know everything about the other person's finances and make sure that I have my own security. I will never put myself at risk and I will never just assume that everything is taken care of.

The most important thing that I did was get an attorney right away. I knew this was something that I couldn't fight alone and I couldn't just ignore. If you find yourself in this situation, get going right away and find the help you need. Also, let the banks and credit card companies know what's going on so they don't think you're ignoring them. If they see that you're trying to fix the situation, they will be more understanding.

Gone (Cat)Fishing:
Online Scammers and the People They Hurt

The advent of the Internet and social media has done and continues to do many wonderful things for us and the world in which we live. Among many other things, it has succeeded in shrinking our globe to the point that we can "meet" fantastic new people that live anywhere and everywhere.

Meeting new people and making new friends can also mean meeting new loves. Once stigmatized as only for those who were "desperate" (much in the same way that the Personals column in the "Want Ad" sections of newspapers once were), online dating has become accepted as commonplace. Approximately forty million people in the United States alone have tried online dating at least once, and I personally know quite a few people who met online and went on to marry. Without the Internet, the likelihood of these people actually meeting (let alone marrying) would have been all but non-existent.

I have advocated and taught "safe and smart" online dating for many years, and prior to meeting my husband Dave, I participated in online dating as well. Although Dave and I did not initially meet online, the fact that we once lived six thousand miles apart[24] meant that the Internet was an integral part of our initial friendship, a burgeoning romance and our subsequent courtship.

Yes, the Internet can be a phenomenal avenue on which to meet new people, make new friends and possibly even find the love of your life.

Until it isn't.

It's a sad fact that where there is good, there is generally also bad—very bad—lurking in the shadows. As much good as it can do, the Internet is unfortunately also fraught with scammers, criminals and predators—and if you are not vigilant, these vermin can creep their way into your life, your heart and even your checkbook before you realize that something is not quite right, let alone horribly wrong.

Marlene* is a beautiful, vivacious woman who is also highly educated and very successful in her chosen profession. Feeling particularly vulnerable after the tragic loss of her husband, she sought friendship via the Internet, as do millions like her. Hers is a story of caution to anyone who uses the Internet, and a story of hope to those who have been victimized by what has come to be known in pop culture vernacular as "catfishing."

Marlene's story

I lost my husband to a very brief illness. We were [out of town] for Thanksgiving when he became critically ill and went into a coma. I was living in hotels and the intensive care unit for a month before I had him transported home via air ambulance. He died ten days later.

Shortly after my husband's death, I sought pen pals through online dating sites. I had little experience with online dating sites and totally ignored the warnings about scams. I'm a smart, well-educated financial executive and I make good decisions—[I believed that] those warnings were not for me.

A few weeks after my husband died, I developed a very close [online] friendship with Mike*. We communicated on a website initially and then

---

24 Dave was born and raised in England and moved to the United States when he fell in love with this crazy American writer chick. And yes, he *does* have "the accent."

shared e-mails, texts and phone calls over the course of a couple of months. He was smart, educated and very convincing. When we talked on the phone, we seemed to click instantly, and he was the one that wanted to meet [in person]. I still had to walk the journey of widowhood but the phone calls, the emails, the texts, the love letters…I thought I had found the next man in my life.

Several months, many lies and $250,000 later, I discovered that the entire thing (including his name) was a scam. I was left to grieve three losses: the loss of my husband who was the love of my life, a broken heart because of someone I fell in love with and who scammed me, and the financial devastation that happened.

Billions of dollars are made through [online] scams each year. Scamming is big business, and scammers are very good at what they do. I hope to help educate others so that they never feel the pain of being scammed.

I Was a Target

Scammers target widows and their vulnerability. I was also targeted because in my [online] profile I said that was educated, I liked to travel and I was a businesswoman—all signs that I might have some money. Once Mike knew my name, he could easily research my husband's obituary and find out a lot about my life.

How Could This Happen to Me?

Losing the money was financially devastating for me. Losing the love that I had for Mike was worse. Losing my husband, the person who I thought Mike was and over $250,000—I was suicidal. How could I, a financial professional, be "taken?"

Finding the Help that I Needed

I reported the case to the police but they were very honest in telling me that there was little or nothing they could do. I also reported [the scam] to the FBI, and I'm in one-on-one counseling for grief and trauma.

USE YOUR POWER

I will not allow Mike to take away my power to be my authentic self. I take one day at a time to grieve and rebuild the life that was shattered both emotionally and financially. Also, my friends and colleagues who know the story are very supportive. They listen, accept and don't judge. They encourage me to forgive myself, and understand and accept that I was a victim and that I was manipulated by a professional criminal.

Don't share the word "love" or the words, "I love you" with someone you have never met in person. Insist on meeting and sharing feelings in person. Once I was "in love" online, there was no one that could convince me that I was being scammed. Be very careful who you give your heart to.

AN IMPORTANT NOTE FROM CAROLE

If your catfish experience is still ongoing and/or if the person is still in contact with you (or is attempting to remain in contact with you), take immediate steps to cut off all communication and protect yourself. Start by contacting your local authorities and if applicable, the FBI as well. If financial fraud is involved, call your bank(s) to see what steps can be taken. Change all of your telephone numbers and email addresses. Let your employer know about the situation, in case the person attempts to contact you at your place of employment. If necessary, investigate the steps involving obtaining a restraining order—and then get one!

Being the victim of a scammer is a horrendous violation in so many respects. It is like being robbed—and sadly, for many like Marlene, it is also literally being robbed. However, this is in no way a reflection on you as a person, nor is it a reflection on your character or your judgment. Should you learn from history and heed the warning signs and red flags? Of course you should. However, does it mean that you should never trust anyone ever again? Absolutely not. Why would you eliminate a lot of wonderful people based on the actions of one jackhole that managed to worm their way under your BS radar?

Most importantly, remember that you are the *victim*, not the perpetrator. You are no more "at fault" than a bank teller who was robbed at gunpoint. This means that in every sense of the phrase, it *really* isn't you! It well and truly is *them. They* are the criminal. *They* are the liar. *They* are the master of crime and duplicity. Lay the blame where it truly belongs—at the tail end of a smelly, horrible catfish—and be reassured that while you may not be able to see it just yet, good, decent and loving people truly do outnumber the evil.

HOW YOU CAN HELP

Betrayal Victims

Betrayal victims have a tremendous amount of anguish with which they must come to terms—even more so if the betrayal is discovered posthumously. In addition to questioning the lives that they were leading, betrayal survivors are also feeling ashamed, foolish and completely humiliated. Your role is now not only one of support post-betrayal, it is one of reassurance as well.

Definite Do's

- **Keep your eyes open and your ears alert:** Someone who is grieving a loss is obviously in mourning. Someone who is dealing with both mourning and betrayal can also become very angry, withdrawn and guarded. If you sense that someone you love who is going through a mourning process is holding something back or might need to talk about something other than the loss itself, be sure to invite that conversation. Tiffani admits that she was initially reluctant to share what her betrayal discovery had done to her. She says, "The reason I finally said something to my friend is because she figured out that I was hiding something and said, 'Is there anything else going on?' I felt relieved because then I was free to tell her and tell a few more people too."

- **Actively encourage her to get the help she needs as soon as possible:** If the betrayal involved anything of a financial nature that could jeopardize her future (losing a home, financial security, credit, etc.), she needs to seek appropriate help immediately. This is the one area of loss where—betrayal or not—she really cannot afford to wait. If the betrayal was the result of a scam, she needs to contact all of her financial institutions that were involved to find out what her recourse(s) might be.

If the betrayal was an emotional betrayal (most commonly infidelity), she can benefit greatly by talking to a trusted professional. There is a tremendous amount of anger involved, mixed in with confusion and sadness; she needs a starting point where she can begin working through and resolving all of these issues.

- **Invoke the "Hold Harmless" policy:** No matter the nature of the betrayal, be quick to let her know that she is not responsible *in any way* for the actions of her betrayer. As is said in law, she is "held harmless" from any and all responsibility. She did not drive someone into having an affair or hiding financial information or anything else that was done behind her back and without her knowledge. She has likely spent quite a bit of time beating up on herself; take her by the hand, look into her eyes and say very firmly and lovingly, "This is *not* your fault, and we are going to get you through this no matter what."

Without a Doubt...Don't

- **Don't even so much as imply that the betrayal was her fault:** *"How could you not have known he was messing around?"; "There must've been signs, you were just ignoring them"; "Why would you trust him to handle all the money?"*

  In seeing questions like these, my first thought is, how could anyone think that these statements are going to better the situation? How is it in any way comforting to make someone feel as though a betrayal is *their* fault?

  Understand that if someone has shared a betrayal with you, it was not done impulsively. She is already feeling like an idiot and has likely been hiding this information for awhile. She is devastated and has had to summon a measure of courage in even discussing the subject. Asking her how she didn't know about deceitful financial practices or infidelity only serves to make her feel like an even bigger idiot.

- **Don't be a mind reader:** *"He wanted to get caught"; "He obviously had trust issues"; "He probably didn't think you could handle finances"; "He just wasn't the monogamous type."*

  Unless you have a proven track record as a clairvoyant and you can also supply me with next week's winning lottery numbers, you do not get play the part of mind reader.

  You do *not* know who or what kind of person the betrayer was. Hell, even his own spouse didn't know—how could *you* know? Furthermore, you do not know what drives any person to cheat, lie, deceive or otherwise choose to betray those closest to him. None of us know. Scientists and clinicians hazard theories and conduct studies, but at the end of the day, people are who they are, and we really don't know how or why a moral compass simply quits pointing toward the direction of Right, Moral and Decent.

  You don't know why the betrayal occurred anymore than his victim does. Do not hazard hurtful theory to the contrary.

- **Don't share what you believe you would do in the same position:** *"I'd find that woman and let her have it"; "I'd burn all his stuff"; "I wouldn't have any problem handling this because I'd never waste tears on a liar."*

  Have you ever heard the expression "armchair quarterback"? It's a reference to those who are very much like I am when watching football—sitting in the comfort of their home or in a sports bar, shouting various strategies to the coaches and quarterback and screaming profanities at the television when things don't go the right way.

It is a lovely luxury to be in the "armchair"—to call plays and shriek disapproval at the television. I know this because I do it every week during football season. However, I have never once been the coach who is either "good guy" or "goat," depending on a final score. I've never been a quarterback who is expected to execute flawlessly in a matter of seconds, while three-hundred-pound men try to stand on his neck.

The armchair is indeed an exquisitely easy place to be.

There is another arena where armchair quarterbacks exist, except this time, those who sit in these metaphorical armchairs have the ability to wreak havoc. They are the family members and/or friends who feel that somehow, a victim of betrayal is also the rightful catch-all for ill-placed advice.

It is quite easy to sit in that armchair, look in on another person's life and criticize, disparage or share what you believe you would do, given the same set of circumstances. My question to those people is quite simple:

How do you know?

How on *earth* do you have any idea what you would do if you had just buried your beloved and were trying to find your way through a hellish haze of grief, while continuing to run and support a household (that might include children)…only to discover that your late beloved is not the person you believed them to be?

How do you *really* know what you would do if you discovered that your entire financial foundation was actually built on quicksand?

Finally, could you honestly predict how you would react if your husband/significant other told you there was "someone else," or if you discovered they were living an entirely separate and hidden life away from you?

Instead of putting on some kind of bravado that you will hopefully never need, or providing what-if scenarios and speculative fairy tales, a much better response would be something along the lines of,

"I have no idea what I would do in your situation. This must be so terrible for you, and I'm so glad you trusted me enough to share."

In other words, instead of sharing some fictional Superwoman scenario (which I pray will never befall you), get out of the armchair and get into the game by being a loving and compassionate source of support.

Scamming Victims

Victims of online scammers experience violation on numerous levels. In addition to being violated—and as with betrayal victims—they feel embarrassed, foolish and completely humiliated. Their trust has been seriously breached, and their ability to trust once again is so undermined that they have difficulty trusting even their own judgment. Your presence can help assuage all of these feelings and help her regain trust both in humankind and in herself.

Definite Do's

- **Be a confidence booster:** A victim of a scam is likely questioning her judgment and her ability to make wise choices. Remind her that she is not to blame; rather, she is a victim of a liar and a sociopath. Marlene shares, "My friends now rally around me and I vet things through them." Be one of those friends who rally and closes ranks around someone who needs all the reinforcement she can get.

- **Offer practical help:** In addition to the obvious emotional fallout, she may also be dealing with the scam situation from a practical aspect. The scammer(s) may still be in contact with her in any number of ways and for any number of reasons. Any continued contact with a scammer (particularly if the contact involves money) is potentially dangerous—if not to her pocketbook and/or her physical well-being, then to her psyche.

  If she has not already done so, urge her to contact her local authorities, as well as her local branch of the FBI. Help her gather, collect and collate any evidence of the scam that she has, keeping in mind that in an emotional state, she may overlook something that can be a crucial component in effecting justice. Things like voice mails, emails, wire transfer receipts, bank statements, etc., can help authorities with a potential prosecution, and these are things that can be easily overlooked, forgotten about or lost altogether.

Without a Doubt…Don't

- **Don't make her feel foolish or humiliate her further:** *"How could you fall for this?"; "I can't believe you didn't see the warning signs"; "Why would you trust someone on the Internet?"*

    Victims of Internet scams spend a great deal of time beating up on themselves. They don't need you to pile on or point out the obvious. It's rather like when people assume free license to park good manners at the curb and point out to a pregnant woman nearing term that she is big enough to warrant entry as a float in the Rose Parade—why would anyone *do* that?[25]

    The same concept applies here. Your girl is already feeling like an idiot and kicking herself around the block. She really does not need any further admonishing—she has suffered enough, and depending upon the circumstances, she may well suffer consequences for the foreseeable future.

- **Don't rush her into the resumption of dating:** *"You have to get back out there"; "When you fall off a horse, you have to get right back on"; "I know the perfect person for you, let me fix you up."*

    I have actually fallen off a horse and you know what? I did *not* "get right back on." I lay on the couch for two weeks, nursed bruises and cracked ribs, and took a lot of really fabulous medication. Why?

---

25 These same people clearly assume that pregnant women do not have mirrors.

Because falling off of a horse *hurts*.

A victim of a scam (catfish or otherwise) has suffered a genuine loss. She has lost a person who she believed to have existed, to the point of entrusting them with her heart (and as Marlene has shared, more than just her heart). As with any loss, there is pain, grief and a mourning period that must be respected. If we are indeed likening this experience to falling off a horse, there is healing to be accomplished and there is no hurrying up any part of the healing process.

The day will come when she will be ready to dip her toe into the dating waters once again, but as with any other step forward on a Healing Journey, that time frame is determined by, and belongs solely to, her. When she is ready, believe me, she will let you know. Until that time, do not push her into anything.

- **Don't question her judgment as to her future:** *"You're still using the Internet to meet people? Are you crazy?"; "I'd be afraid to go out ever again"; "How can you even trust yourself now?"*

  Have you ever tried to un-ring a doorbell or put toothpaste back into the tube? Probably not, and for good reason. It cannot be done.

  Likewise, a scamming victim cannot undo her mistake. The bell has been rung. The toothpaste is out of the tube. The mistake has been made. It is done. However, as awful as this mistake is, one mistake does not necessarily mean that similar mistakes are in her future. On the contrary, she has learned a very difficult lesson the hard way. She needs reassurance and reinforcement, not someone to question her ability to dress herself.

From Bad Thing to Brighter Days Ahead

Whether your betrayal discovery is present-day or posthumous, betrayal as a whole is an impossibly maddening situation. All betrayal situations involve huge loss—a serious loss of trust and a loss of confidence. You are mourning a plurality of losses and so much more.

You have every right to want answers to your questions, the first of which is most likely "Why?" However, if the betrayal is posthumous, you know that you are not going to be able to confront the betrayer on this horribly hurtful issue. If you attempt to confront the situation as a present-day betrayal victim, you will likely receive more lies and deceit; victims of scammers will receive all that and perhaps even worse. You could also be endangering your physical well-being; after all, if an obvious sociopath has the capability to perpetrate scams without a second thought or any kind of conscience, who knows what other crimes they are capable of committing?

It is therefore up to you to learn how to deal with the completely justifiable anger that you are experiencing and eventually get to a place of peace in your heart:

1. **Whether present-day or posthumous, if your betrayal situation involved infidelity, do *not* meet with, or otherwise engage in confrontation with, the "other person" under *any* circumstances**: Despite what you may have seen on television or in the movies, there is no advantage to be gained by starting a bitter war with someone who doesn't deserve your time or your very limited energy. The person with whom your spouse was being unfaithful does not get to play any kind of role in your life. Relegate them to where they belong; to a pathetic and unimportant part of history. These people deserve no more attention than that, and you have far more important things to do with your life, both now and in the future.

   If anyone has tried, or is trying, to confront, harass or intimidate you, or otherwise make your life difficult, seek help immediately. If you feel threatened or as though your life, safety or welfare is in imminent danger, *do not hesitate* to contact your local law enforcement agency.

2. **Begin journaling:** Get your feelings onto paper. You can be as sad or as angry or as bitter as you want in whatever colorful language you wish. And believe it or not, you will feel better for getting it all out.

3. **Reach out and connect with others who have had similar experiences**: You do not have to go into any specifics; the fact that you share a common betrayal experience is enough to garner the support that you will receive from a community that understands.

4. **Consider seeking counseling or therapy**: If your betrayal situation involves any kind of financial issue, you will also want to consult legal and financial counsel as soon as you can.

Finally, make every effort not to define your life by the betrayal that took place. Define yourself instead with these adjectives:

Caring.
Loving.
Loyal.
Devoted.
Compassionate.
Beautiful...inside and out.

Because even after all that you have experienced...
...that is *your* truth.

Chapter Seven

Unkept Promises and Shattered Dreams: A Broken Engagement

The romantic proposal that left you breathless. Declarations of love meant to last a lifetime. Showing off a beautiful ring to friends and family. Obsessively poring over what feels like hundreds of bridal magazines. Trying on dresses by the multitude and selecting bridesmaids. Engagement parties, lunches, showers, bachelorette parties, registering for gifts, selecting flowers… all of this and so much more comprises one of the most exciting moments in a woman's life: an engagement, followed by impending wedding plans and a happily-ever-after marriage.

And then…it is over before it ever happened.

Perhaps he got a case of what is commonly referred to as "cold feet." Maybe he woke up one day and decided he preferred bachelorhood to the prospect of being one-half of Mr. and Mrs. The Two of You. You might have discovered a huge secret or bachelor-party-gone-horribly-wrong error in judgment that was your personal deal breaker (for which no one would blame you). Whatever the reason, your engagement is broken. The wedding is now cancelled, and you are left heartbroken and likely feeling angry, foolish and maybe even humiliated. *How* will you face your family? *What* will you say to your friends?

In addition to the emotional side of a broken engagement, you may have also incurred financial obligations (scheduling ceremony and reception venues, booking various vendors, putting deposits down, etc.). Is the money lost? Are you being held liable? Where and how do you even begin to recover?

Meet Lisa, a successful actress-turned-entrepreneur who was engaged to the man of her dreams—until the dream turned into a nightmare. Lisa's journey of love, betrayal and determination to triumph teaches us that happily-ever-after not only exists, it can be entirely different than what you originally imagined.

Lisa's story

When I was twenty-three years old, I was in love and engaged to marry the man I was living with. He never wanted to spend a moment apart from me. When he got a job offer in China a few weeks before the wedding (supposedly a two-week assignment), I told him to go. He was to have returned before my bridal shower but he never came back—I never saw him again. He tortured me for months, calling me, telling me he loved me and he just had cold feet. I waited by the phone and cried for weeks.

I finally found out from our best man that my fiancé had run off and married a Chinese girl. I cancelled the wedding but did not think to tell my fiancé's parents, assuming that he would've had the decency to tell them he'd left me. Instead, his parents arrived for the wedding, and we had to spend a humiliating week together. His parents were horrified, and I was beyond devastated.

Just when I thought that it could not get worse, I discovered that he'd taken all of the money from our joint account and run up all of my credit cards to which I had added him. He not only broke my heart and my spirit, he broke my bank account as well. I later discovered that I was not his first victim and that he was a true con artist.

Shock and Survival

I moved into a self-hate phase, where I thought there was something wrong with me. I thought that I wasn't "good enough" to keep him. I believed that no one would ever really love me. I was in shock and did not really believe it was over. I kept thinking he was going to come back and that we would work through whatever he was going through. I never thought he was gone forever.

After I realized that he had actually married someone else and that he had stolen my money and maxed out my credit cards, I realized that I had to protect myself. I jumped into survival mode, cancelling credit cards, changing bank account numbers, changing my phone number and all of my account passwords.

Auditioning My Way Forward

I had no confidence left in my judgment or instincts. When I found out that I had my savings wiped out and had $17,000 in credit card debt hanging over me, I knew I had to pull it together.

I'd left a career I loved (as an actress) to work at a talent agency because my fiancé did not want me to tour. When I realized that I no longer had to give up what I loved doing, I auditioned for the national tour of *Les Misérables* and got it. I remained on tour with *Les Misérables* for years, paying off his debts, saving money and rebuilding both my finances and my self-esteem.

Back on My Feet Again

Les Misérables saved me. I got back on my feet financially. I made friends, I had a career that I loved and I saved enough money to buy an apartment in New York.

After touring for many years and healing both my heart and my finances, I started my own company called Road Concierge,[26] which specializes in travel for Broadway and music tours. Within five years, I'd built the company to such a profitable point that I was able to sell it, having a choice of four different offers from four different companies. I got a dog, who is the true love

---

26 To learn more about Lisa and Road Concierge, visit www.roadconcierge.com.

of my life, and I was able to buy my dream house in Pennsylvania. I get to live in both Manhattan and in the country.

FAILURE IS NOT FALLING DOWN...

Getting over the hurt and pain of what happened was not easy. It is honestly a pain that will never go away, but time does help. I made sure that I spent time with my real friends. Since I had a ton of friends who had already bought plane tickets, and I'd already paid for most of the wedding, on the actual wedding day, I threw an "unwedding." I turned the saddest day of my life into a day where I was surrounded with love and support. No one can ever break you, and nothing is so bad that you will never know joy again.

Winston Churchill said, "When you are going through hell, keep going." Another mantra that I repeat every day of my life is "Failure is not falling down—it is *staying* down." I genuinely don't need a man to be happy. I am able to support myself financially and care for myself physically. I have a large network of friends and a great family. I have a real career. I have the cutest dog in the world who I cherish so much, and I've had several romantic relationships in the years that have passed.

There are awful things that happen in life, but you will never know the moments of joy and the highs that are coming if you don't believe that it is possible. At twenty-three years of age, my heart, my faith and my finances were all broken. At thirty-seven years of age, I look better than I did at twenty-three years, my finances are in order, I have a happy life—and the knowledge that I was able to do it all on my own.

Don't settle for breadcrumbs—you deserve the entire bagel. Don't look for happiness outside of yourself when you can find it within.

HOW YOU CAN HELP

A broken engagement oftentimes involves shock, disappointment, embarrassment and despair. The person left behind to pick up the pieces has likely never needed support in the way she does right now. You can be one of her "she-roes" and help ease the way for a peaceful recovery.

Definite Do's

- **Rally around:** Regardless of how the engagement ended or which party ended it, your girl is devastated. Stand ready to listen, wipe away tears and offer a strong shoulder—she needs her girlfriends right now.

- **Offer practical help:** Depending on where she was in the process, she may need help returning gifts; making calls or sending cards advising of the cancellation of the wedding; and calling venues to cancel and (hopefully) get her money returned either in part or in full. She may need to move from the home that she and her ex-fiancé shared. Help her make lists of everything that needs to be done and everyone who needs to be contacted. Assist with packaging any gifts that need to be returned.[27] You might offer to be the one to make the phone calls to the vendors. If either apartment or house-hunting is involved in the process, you can get involved with that as well (see Chapter Two, "Loss of a Home," for additional suggestions).

- **Remember her even after the dust has settled:** A broken engagement is one of those things that is easy for everyone else to quickly move forward from—except for the one who has gone from bride-to-be to bride-who-isn't. After about a month, send a funny or sweet card, get together for lunch or dinner, schedule a girls' night out (or in)…in other words, let her know that you are still there for her.

---

27   Many gift-givers will offer to let the bride-to-be keep the shower and/or wedding gift. Whether she chooses to accept that offer is up to her; however, it is proper to at least attempt to return any gifts given in advance of a wedding that did not take place.

Without a Doubt…Don't

- **Don't state the obvious:** *"It's better that you found out now rather than later"; "A broken engagement isn't as bad as a divorce"; "You are so much better off."*

  A broken engagement may well be the preferable option over divorce, and it may be better that the relationship ended prior to the marriage, but now is definitely not the time to point it out. She knows all of these things intellectually, but she is not feeling "better off" right now. Since she was never thinking in terms of divorce (as is the case with most brides-to-be), comparing her heartbreak to something she was never anticipating is useless.

- **Don't push her into dating or coupling off too soon:** *"You need to get back out there"; "Now is the time to try online dating"; "I know the perfect guy…"*

  I have never believed in setting any time parameters for any kind of recovery circumstances for anyone other than myself, especially when it comes to dating. When and how to resume the dating process is entirely up to the person affected.

  After any kind of relationship loss—be it through broken engagement, divorce or death—the newly-on-her-own woman needs time to absorb and digest her loss. She also needs to take time to figure out who she is now, since she is no longer one-half of a couple—and as we well know, we are not the same person post-loss as we are pre-loss. Until she expresses an interest in dating again, do not push—the presence of another person is not a "replacement" for who and what has been lost. When she decides to resume dating again, it needs to be her decision made for the *right* reasons.

- **Don't say, *"I told you so"* or any phrase remotely resembling it:** *"I knew you were making a mistake"; "I knew he was no good for you"; "What did I tell you?"*

Remember what we discussed in Chapter Four ("Bidding Good-Bye to a Business")? We all enjoy being right, but just how important *is* it to you that you are right? Is it more important to be right than to be a source of support and comfort? What purpose is served in doing the I-Told-You-So Dance? It will *not* make her feel better and if it makes you feel better, shame on *you*.

* **Don't give any advice whatsoever about what she should do with the ring:** *"Throw the ring away, that'll teach him"; "Keep the ring, it's too pretty to get rid of"; "We need to have a 'ring party,'"* [a gathering where a group of women apparently get together to bury the ring/throw it into a body of water/auction it off to the highest bidding friend].

The matter of the engagement ring is one of the most personal and emotional factors in a broken engagement. Her ring is a symbol of a future promised, and now, that future is lost. *She* needs to be the person to figure out the logistics of what to do with the ring, and cutesy-sounding vengeance suggestions are not at all helpful.

Not only is the decision concerning the engagement ring an intensely personal decision, in many states, it is also directly governed by law. There are dozens of cases on point[28] stating that an engagement ring is not a "gift," but rather, a "promise." If that promise is not fulfilled by an actual marriage, the engagement ring is to be returned to its original owner—in this situation, the person who offered the ring in engagement. By suggesting any of the above (or similar) activities, you may be unknowingly pushing your girl into winding up a defendant in a civil lawsuit.

If the engagement ring is a family heirloom, there is no question that the ring must be returned to the giver's family. Outside of those

---

28 A "case on point" means that similar lawsuits have been brought and tried, verdicts have been rendered and the case is published and used as precedent and reference for subsequent cases.

circumstances, let *her* be the one to bring up the matter of the ring and what she plans to do with it.

From Bad Thing to Brighter Days Ahead

Regardless of who broke your engagement or why, the end of an engagement is devastating, since it likely ended your relationship as well.

However, while you may be feeling devastated beyond measure, there is *no reason* to feel embarrassed, ashamed or humiliated. No matter who broke the engagement, the fact is that your family, your loved ones and your true friends are going to stand steadfastly by your side and support you through a very difficult period of your life.

Your key to brighter days ahead is to *take your time.* Just as Lisa did, you need time to recover, get your feet back under you and get to know *you* again, none of which can be accomplished in a hurry. Do not rush to start dating again, jump headlong into another relationship or hurry up and do anything, other than tend to the matters that need to be resolved right away (cancellation of wedding vendors, gift returns, etc.).

After the emotional and practical chores that are involved in the ending of an engagement are completed, you have a right to take your time and redesign the direction that your life is going to take. Take that time for *you.* You deserve it.

Chapter Eight

I Did…Now I Don't:
Surviving Divorce

I HAVE SO OFTEN SAID THAT NO BRIDE IS STANDING UP FRONT IN THE BIG white dress thinking about the possibility of widowhood. At that moment, all you are thinking about is *that* moment. You are also likely thinking about the napkins matching the tablecloths at the reception, how the groom had better not smash cake into your face and that you cannot *wait* to get out of the jillion-dollar wedding shoes that are pinching your feet and into a pair of flip-flops.

The same thought processes hold true regarding divorce. No one is standing up front in the big white dress thinking, "This whole thing is going to devolve into arguments, animosity, unimaginable pain, fights over who-gets-what and how-much-is-owed-to-whom, custody battles and ultimately end in hardened hearts."

All weddings represent promises of a forever marriage. All marriages begin with glowing hopes for a bright future filled with endless potential. Everyone has the same dreams in their heads and hearts of dancing happily-ever-after, both at the reception and into the sunset.

So it naturally goes without saying that divorce—no matter who initiates it—is one of the most painful processes that one can ever endure.

Your Bags Are Packed (You Chose to Leave)

There is a long-existing and very tired myth implying that the person initiating divorce is not at all suffering, that her life is instead about to become one big fun-filled re-entry into the wild life that many imagine post-divorce life to be. Such is not generally the case.

The decision to file for divorce is generally fraught with anxiety. Further, and regardless of the reason(s), the woman who has found it necessary to file for divorce is also likely looking at assuming primary custody of children. This is in addition to the possible measurable loss of income to her household.

It is rarely a decision that is made quickly or lightly.

Kamrin's dreams of a happily-ever-after life with her husband ended in her escape from an alcohol-fueled abusive marriage. She both challenges the myth of the hard-partying divorceé and provides insight for those in the position of filing "first paper."

Kamrin's story

I fell in love with Terry when I was twenty-three years old. He was gorgeous and had a very outgoing personality. He was always the life of the party. Everyone loved him and thought he was the nicest guy. After dating for a little over two years, we moved in together and got married three years after that.

What I refused to pay attention to during the time that we were together was that Terry was an alcoholic who was verbally, emotionally and physically abusive later on. Whenever Terry would drink too much or treat me badly, I constantly told myself that "It will get better when..." I thought it would get better when he got a better job and started earning more money. I thought it would get better after I finished school, got my degree and got a better job. I thought he would stop after we got married and had a baby. I saw all the signs and kept telling myself it was going to get better—except with alcoholism it never gets better, it only gets worse.

After years of Terry's alcoholism and abuse, I decided enough was enough. I'd been abused in almost every way possible, our son was beginning to suffer from the constant fighting and yelling and I was scared of what Terry was capable of. I already made the mistake of thinking that his alcoholism would go away. I wasn't going to wait for the abuse to get worse or be directed at our son.

When I told Terry that I was filing for divorce, he started crying and begging for us to go to counseling. I'd already gone to counseling by myself a year earlier because he refused to go, and after six months, even the counselor told me to leave the marriage for my sake and for my son's sake. When I told Terry that it was too little too late, he started making threats about what he would do if I left him. I'd listened to his threats for almost eleven years at that point, and I couldn't listen to it anymore.

I filed for divorce, took my son and moved out. On the same day we moved, Terry got drunk and got the first of his three DUIs.[29] I've never regretted the choice to leave.

I'M A GOOD PERSON

I didn't understand what I did to deserve being treated the way that Terry was treating me. I worked very hard and I'm a good person. He constantly told me that everything going wrong in his life was my fault and I was the one who made him drink. When he got fired from jobs, it was my fault. When our son got sick, it was my fault. He lost all interest in me sexually. He always made me feel terrible about myself. It was my counselor who taught me that alcoholics accuse others of what they see in themselves.

STAYING STRONG IN THE FACE OF CRITICISM

I had to tell my family and friends that I was leaving Terry. Except for my two closest friends and my mother, no one had any idea that Terry was an abusive alcoholic. He covered it up in public and I was too embarrassed to

---

29   "DUI": Driving under the influence of alcohol, drugs or any other substance causing impairment.

tell anyone. Everyone thought he was this perfect guy and we were such a cute couple, so the divorce was a huge shock to a lot of people.

I did get some criticism for leaving. Some people said that I should stay and get counseling with him or stay with him because of our son. It's easy for other people to say those things when they aren't the ones in fear for their life. It was hard to be told that I was messing up my son's life or I was being unfair to Terry but I had to remind myself that I deserved fairness too and my son deserved to grow up in a safe home.

I Had to Work Through the Pain

Right away, my girlfriends assumed that I wanted to go out and party. I had more freedom to go out, and I enjoyed myself after years of living in fear of what was going to happen at home. But people didn't understand that I was hurting too. I really liked being married and having a family. I didn't want to end my marriage. I never saw divorce in my future, and I had to work through the pain of it. Everyone thinks that just because you filed the papers, you don't hurt, but it's not true.

Life became a lot more peaceful when I didn't have to deal with a drunk husband almost every night. My son became much more relaxed and laughed a lot more. I lost a lot of weight due to the stress, and I began to get healthy again. I eventually started dating again and remarried six years after my divorce.

Listen to Your Heart

I waited much longer to leave Terry than I should have because I listened to too many people telling me to stay. I don't believe you should file for divorce because you've had an argument, but you also know if things aren't right and if they aren't ever going to be right.

Life is too short to be with the wrong person. It doesn't make you a bad person to leave a marriage that isn't working. It just means you aren't with the right person for you. You have a right to be happy, and if you have kids, they have a right to be happy too.

Left in the Lurch (You Were Left Behind)

So much about a woman's life is about the ability to control our lives. Regardless of marital status, we have control in ways that women of eras gone by did not enjoy. We have the capability of deciding the trajectory of our lives, which naturally extends to career, relationships and marriage. Eventually, we also likely make many of the major decisions regarding child bearing and child rearing—a fact that is borne of statistical probability. We are also likely contributing heavily to or making most of the financial decisions that affect the household.

And then it happens.

The control is wrested away.

The person with whom you expected to spend the rest of your life one day informs you that your life—the one that you had carefully planned, designed and executed—is about to change forever. The person to whom you committed your heart and your future emotionally and practically, the person with whom you dreamed, hoped, laughed, cried, had (or planned to have) children, announces that they are no longer interested in sharing those precious things with you…

…leaving you alone in the blink of a tear-swollen eye.

Meet Michelle, a mompreneur,[30] who was once a happily-married mother of a then-infant son. Without warning, Michelle's world was turned upside-down when her husband announced that their marriage was over.

Michelle's story

A number of years ago I went through the worst time in my life—a divorce. My then-husband came home one night, went upstairs, packed his bags and walked out the door, saying, "I am leaving and starting over." He walked away from both me and our ten-month-old son.

---

30 To learn more about Michelle, visit www.michellemorton.wordpress.com.

Why Didn't He Love Me?

At first, I was in shock. I didn't believe it was really happening because it happened so fast. Why didn't he love me? Why didn't he want to be a family anymore? Wasn't I good enough? Wasn't I pretty enough? What did I do wrong?

Looking to the Future

My biggest concern was my son. How was I going to take care of him? I moved through my feelings of shock quickly because soon after he left, I discovered that he was dating a sixteen-year-old high-school student.

I never wanted to reconcile, because I would never love him again. My feelings were of disgust. The word "embarrassed" is an understatement. I had to face everyone I knew, knowing what he was doing. I had to work through a lot of gossip, as he was from a prominent family and there was a lot of talk.

After I stopped feeling sorry for myself, I told myself, "No more!" It was time for me to think about my future and the future of my son.

Taking Another Chance on Love

It took time to heal, but I eventually realized that his issues were about him and not about me. It took time to learn to trust, but I did. I was afraid of being hurt again, but I knew that if I didn't take a chance at loving again, I may never have the life that I wanted and my son would not have a family.

My Life Is Full

Today, my life is full. I am happily (re)married, I have three amazing sons and I am excited about my future. No one knows what the future holds. If you are afraid of life, it will pass you by.

Trust yourself. You have to work toward creating the life that you want and deserve.

You will never forget the pain, but don't let it control you. Don't let it cause you to be bitter. Don't ever give up on you!

HOW YOU CAN HELP

Statistics continue to tout that fifty percent of marriages end in divorce. Loosely translated, this means that if you do not already know someone who has been directly affected by divorce, you will at some point. Here's how to help:

Definite Do's

• **Suggest a "girl-time" activity:** It really doesn't matter which side of the divorce papers you are on—a woman's self-esteem and confidence levels can plummet after the process. She may feel unattractive, unworthy and experience everything from hopelessness to outright despair. This is a wonderful opportunity to suggest activities that will boost her spirit and help her feel a bit better about herself.

   Depending on both financial abilities and her idea of fun, you can suggest things like a spa activity, a mani-pedi or a low or no-cost makeover. Finish off by hitting a local happy hour—you will both be feeling and looking great. Will any of these things fix all of the feelings that she is experiencing right now? Of course not. However, she will get out of the house, she will be with someone who obviously cares and she will be smiling.

• **Listen:** Just that one word—"Listen"—is so powerful. She needs to talk. She needs to be angry. She needs to be disappointed. She may even need to be relieved, happy and excited. Whatever place she is in (and you do visit several of those different "places" on the journey post-divorce), be ready to listen without judgment and without reproach.

• **Assist with adjustments:** If she is the one who's moving out of her home, volunteer to help. Gather boxes, help her pack and/or help her unpack at her destination. Bring in coffee and cupcakes if you are moving in the morning or wine and a cheese-and-cracker tray if you are unpacking later in the day.

If she has children, the adjustments that she is making also involve adjusting to life as an only parent—also a challenge. If her children are younger, volunteer to babysit or take the kids out to give her a few hours to herself. If her children are teens or adults (and if it is appropriate), suggest a time to get together with them to see how *they* are adjusting.

- **Steer her toward support:** There are many wonderful support groups for the divorced, both in-person and online. Encourage her to investigate these groups—particularly important if factors such as infidelity or domestic violence were part of her marriage.

Without a Doubt...Don't

- **Don't initiate "ex-bashing":** *"I don't know how you could have married such a loser"; "What a waste of time he was"; "I can't stand him."*

  If she wants to discuss her ex-husband and his faults and failings, by all means, listen with the kind ear that she needs and respond in a supportive manner—but do not be the one to bring it up. A marriage takes two, and your perception and her reality may be two different things. If you do not like him and/or if you've never liked him, that's fine, but she does not need to spend time questioning herself based upon your opinion.

- **Don't dig for details:** *"Did he hit you/have an affair/drink/do drugs/ etc.?"; "Did you stop having sex?"; "How much money are you getting?"*

  If her ex engaged in any one or all of these heinous things, she will let you know. If her sex life or her financial matters are up for discussion, she will let you know. Please be the support that she needs, rather than behave in a manner befitting nosy neighbor Mrs. Kravitz from *Bewitched*.

- **Don't appear to assess blame in any way:** *"If you paid more attention to him, maybe he wouldn't have strayed"; "Do you think you put work before your marriage?"; "If you never had kids you'd probably still be married."*

  What is going to be accomplished by asking these questions of a newly divorced woman? Guilt? Shame? Remorse? Second guessing an entire life?

  The rule remains the same: if the results are not going to be to the positive, the statement should not be made—and questions like these cannot in any way have a positive result.

  One more thing: Animals "stray". People do not. People ostensibly choose and have control over their actions. People are supposed to know right from wrong. People do not "stray." People *choose* to behave in the ways that they behave.

FROM BAD THING TO BRIGHTER DAYS AHEAD

Years ago, a fantastic business colleague once shared that she had been married prior to her current marriage, stating that "Some of us need to be married twice—the first time lets us know who we *shouldn't* be married to." She has been happily remarried for over twenty years.

No one will argue the fact that no matter who initiated the proceedings, divorce is one of the most distressing events that anyone can experience. It is one of the biggies on the proverbial "trauma list." However, divorce in no way means that there is not a wonderful life ahead of you. Yes, you will have to endure pain, you may question yourself as never before and you will be surrounded by opinions—many of which will not necessarily be helpful. However, as Kamrin and Michelle have both shared, the best truly can be yet to come.

As with any other loss, take your time in recovering. Pay attention to you and your needs, remembering that when you are taking care of you, the result is a more productive employee, a more engaged mother and a much happier woman.

Most of all, open your heart to the possibilities that your future holds for you. There is no age limit or statute of limitations on love—and when the time is right for you, and if you choose it, there can be a fabulous future with love in it, waiting just for you.

Chapter Nine

HOPE INTERRUPTED: INFERTILITY, MISCARRIAGE, STILLBIRTH AND HYSTERECTOMY

As women, we have all been raised to believe that pregnancy and childbirth should be normal.

Natural.

Integral parts of a woman's life.

After what seems like a lifetime obsessed with the prevention of pregnancy, we believe that we will easily become pregnant when we choose to cease said prevention. We steel ourselves for morning sickness, swollen appendages, baby showers and nursery decoration. We eagerly anticipate the day when we meet the tiny person we will love more than anything and anyone in our lives, and who will transform us forever. We eventually give birth and after a (physical, emotional, hormonal, mental and financial) recovery period of our determination, we may decide to do it all over again.

The process certainly was never presented as complicated when explained by both our mothers and our biology teachers.

But sometimes...things do not go as planned.

Sometimes...the seemingly simple things are not just complicated...

The seemingly simple can be devastating.

Infertility

From the time that we were old enough to begin playing house, a majority of us began picturing ourselves in the role of Mommy. We played dolls (many of which had better clothes and accoutrements than some of us did growing up), we played "house" and most of us even stuck a pillow under our top.

Admit it—you did too. Just to imagine.

As we matured, most of us spent a great deal of time concerning ourselves with the prevention of pregnancy, reasonably assuming that when we wished it, becoming pregnant would be no problem—and for many millions of women, getting pregnant is indeed no problem.

Except for the women for whom it *is* a problem.

Clearly, there is nothing wrong with being childless by choice. However, many women are not able to make that choice, instead having that "decision" thrust upon them for any number of reasons: medical conditions, certain medications or medical protocols (such as chemotherapy or radiation), the medical necessity of hysterectomy or perhaps worst of all, a "mystery" situation that the medical profession cannot readily identify or explain. Yes, we are fortunate to have made amazing technological advances that can assist women with infertility issues, but those amazing technological advances also come with amazing price tags that many cannot afford and that are not covered by most medical insurance. Moreover, many infertility treatments also involve side effects that are challenging to say the least.

So how do you cope with the reality of infertility when all you've ever wanted is what should come so naturally?

Pamela Mahoney Tsigdinos is the award-winning author of *Silent Sorority...*[31] Her book explores the stigma associated with infertility and the effects of living involuntarily childless. She shares her personal journey through infertility and how she thrives today.

---

31 To learn more about Pamela and *Silent Sorority...* (BookSurge Publishing), please visit www.silentsorority.com.

Pamela's story

My life contained the usual milestones: college, dating, new jobs and marriage. With each new stage of life, friendships grew deeper. One by one, my friends announced pregnancies and our life experiences diverged. The majority of our social circle moved down one path: parenthood. Others came to the conclusion that [having] children was not for them. Our path wasn't quite so clear.

After a year of carefully-timed sex with no positive test [results], it dawned on me that fertility operated on a much broader and grayer spectrum. Life became complicated in a way that I'd never imagined.

My husband and I quietly devoted a decade to increasingly invasive diagnostic tests, surgeries and procedures. Weeks turned into months and years. Each new doctor visit and stage of trying to conceive came with the expectation that we would succeed. Trying to decode this biological mystery took on a life of its own. Infertility all but became a second job as we endlessly researched and tried both Western and Eastern medicine.

Beyond the physical and financial tolls, the emotional strain was traumatizing. Infertility became an alienating, shaming force in our lives. The most intimate act now felt like a chore.

THE HEARTBREAK WAS TOO MUCH TO BEAR

In the earliest days of trying to figure out what was preventing me from getting pregnant, a cavalcade of emotions raged in my head: frustration, embarrassment, anxiety. There was envy mixed with resentment when seeing people—especially those who didn't seem that interested in being parents—getting pregnant or complaining about their children's demands.

The doctors kept reassuring me that they would find the solution. With nothing to directly blame for our lack of success, I started second-guessing myself. Was I somehow sabotaging [myself]? All of the magazines said to "just relax"...how *could* I relax?

My prickliness was not just about infertility—it also came as result of encountering judgment about being a "non-mom." As long as I was in active-problem-solving mode, I was mostly able to keep my anger under control. I reassured myself that my day would come.

After 4,380 days of trying to get pregnant, somewhere just past forty years old was about the time that hope flew out the window. It was replaced by despair, darker than I ever imagined possible. Sobs routinely welled up and racked my body. A lava-like rage bubbled up, only to retreat to numbness.

The heartbreak became too much to bear—especially when most of the world didn't recognize our losses or offer the support reserved for "legitimate" grief.

Making a Life in the Long Shadow

Wondering how we would possibly cope with another failed cycle, we grew weary of living in indefinite limbo. After exhaustive conversations, my husband and I loosened our grip on our fragile dream. We began allowing ourselves to imagine a life not driven by twenty-eight-day cycles and heartbreaking vigils.

Infertility involves two individuals who love each other and yet cannot joyfully, spontaneously conceive—but there's more. In the wake of conception failure, I discovered that as hard as the loss of pregnancy normalcy was, making a life in the long shadow of infertility has its own challenges. With the judgment surrounding this difficult human experience, it's not surprising that many choose not to speak about it—however, the silence can be deafening.

Infertile couples and the three-billion-dollar infertility industry are driven toward one outcome: successful pregnancy and delivery. This is where attention and assistance is focused. I learned the hard way that there is a rough landing for those who decide to end treatment. We are left to find our way back to some kind of normal within a society that celebrates motherhood. We're surrounded by parents preoccupied with childrearing—at work, on newsstands, on television and on the Internet. Those of us who "opt out" don't want to be pitied, but we also don't want to seem like we didn't want it bad enough.

I Needed to Forgive and Accept

The transition took a long time to achieve. A part of me was convinced that if I allowed the transition, it would somehow mean that all of my efforts associated with trying to have a child would be negated—that a chunk of my life would evaporate.

Most of all, I worried that by accepting a life as a family of two would mean that I didn't work hard enough to provide a nurturing landing for my embryos; that I didn't want or love my children and that I had failed them; that my children didn't matter as much as someone else's children. I have been dogged by guilt on so many levels.

I thought it my obligation to carry the pain like a badge of honor, to never let go of the heartache or it would mean that my attempts didn't matter. Worse still, I thought that I'd become like most everyone else around me who acted as though infertility is nothing more than a bruise that goes away. It doesn't. It stays with you always. It leaves scars, but not in places that people can see.

In distilling all of the emotions, I realized that like Antonio Salieri, the embittered composer in the film *Amadeus,* I needed to not only forgive others for their ignorance, I also had to accept my own physical shortcomings. Today, I no more hate my uterus than I do my lungs. In sharing what I've learned about disenfranchised grief, [32] I began to actively mourn the losses we'd endured and found peace. By giving voice to my experience, I tapped into a well of strength and resilience and cultivated a community of women whose lives don't involve parenting.

Today, birth announcements or photos on supermarket checkout stands of newly pregnant, aging celebrities no longer evoke envy or anger. I've learned to appreciate my body, my life and my relationships in a new light. I tread lightly in our newfound joy and our life lived without the limitations they face, so as not to appear indifferent to their struggles and the demands on their time.

I AM AT PEACE

I encourage those experiencing infertility to actively mourn the losses, both tangible and intangible. It's only in submitting to pain that healing begins. Be gentle with yourself and with your friends and family too. They mean well, even if they don't always know how to express it. One of the most beneficial ways to work through grief is to help someone else with *their* grief. Among my proudest achievements is giving women and men a safe and supportive

---

32 Grief that is not acknowledged by society.

environment to acknowledge and come to terms with their losses.

After years of struggle, I am at peace. I'm a happy woman who is grateful to be on the other side of infertility hell. I adore my husband more than ever. I cherish my friends. I feel a certain agelessness, a magic that comes with embracing the unknown. There is more than one happy ending to the infertility story.

My husband and I continue to push forward, to shape and define a life outside the beaten path. We challenge each other to uncover new possibilities and seek new adventures and discoveries that will enrich our understanding of the world and our place in it—which is what we would have encouraged our children to do.

HOW CAN YOU CAN HELP

A woman who is undergoing treatment for infertility or is coming to grips with living with infertility is dealing with a host of simultaneous emotions and, outside of her immediate family, she likely does not have a great deal of support. There are several ways that you can lend positivity and hope to her life—a life that includes a future dramatically different than the future that she had originally planned.

Definite Do's

- **Be understanding if she is not ready to talk just yet:** While it is true that many women do want to talk, the fact is that infertility has dominated her life, perhaps for many years. She may simply want to take a break from the entire dialogue.

  Pamela shares, "While most people focus on the physical aspects of infertility, it's the emotional wounds that take the longest time to heal. A gentle response might be, 'Take as much time as you need. We'll be here for you when you're ready,' or 'You're probably tired of explaining this stuff to people. Is there a good resource where I can learn more?'"

- **Offer support as to whatever decision(s) she has made:** If she has decided to either seek out or continue fertility treatment, support her decision. Ask questions as to what is involved and if she'll need practical help—for example, many women are prescribed bed rest immediately after treatments and need help with meals, household chores, etc.

  If she has decided against pursuing infertility treatment or she is going to suspend/discontinue treatments altogether, she will need both support and comfort. This is a loss for her—the loss of the hope of having children, and the loss of ability to change that reality. In addition to tears, there may also likely be anger, bitterness and even an assessment of blame directed at herself. Encourage her to take her time in mourning the decision that she has so bravely made.

Without a Doubt...Don't

- **Don't imply that adoption or surrogacy is a cure-all solution:** *"There are plenty of children already in the world for you to adopt"; "You should check other countries for available children"; "You can always get a surrogate."*

  We're not talking about phoning up for a pizza. The reality is that fewer women are choosing to give up babies for adoption, as it has become far more socially acceptable to be a single parent than in times past. Further, adopting a child from a foreign country is not quite as easy as television shows and celebrity magazines would have you believe and of late, has become increasingly difficult.

  Adoption is an arduous and not-always-successful process that needs to be entered into with the greatest of consideration. As Pamela further shares, "While adoption is noble, it is not a 'cure' for infertility. An adopted child is not a generic replacement for a longed-for biological child."

  We have also become conditioned to the fairly recent phenomenon that is surrogacy; however, surrogacy is also not something that anyone can "always get." As with all fertility methods, surrogacy is an emotional and expensive undertaking that is not readily available to everyone and to suggest otherwise is inaccurate. If surrogacy is an appropriate option for her, she will be the one to mention it.

- **Don't recommend home, folk, herbal or other alternative remedies as a means to pregnancy:** *"What really works is* [fill in the blank with a methodology outside of conventional medicine]*"; "I couldn't get pregnant for the longest time until I* [started getting massages/acupuncture/meditating/dancing naked with birch twigs]."

  Does your first name begin with the word "Doctor"? If not, you do not get to give medical advice.

  I understand wanting to help in any way possible. When Mike was battling ALS, we too received "try this/that/the other" suggestions by the boatload and we understood that it was the good in people's hearts that motivated their suggestions. However, without hesitation (and with a few sarcastic remarks and eye-rolling episodes), Mike shunned every single suggestion that was not made by one of his doctors.

  Any woman and/or couple dealing with infertility has done more research on the subject than anyone surrounding them. They have consulted with numerous specialists, and they have likely also tried the "outside-the-box" remedies. Whether something may have worked for you or for someone you know is immaterial—when it comes to infertility, the only person with whom a woman struggling is concerned is herself.

- **Don't imply that her infertility is somehow her fault:** *"Quit stressing about it"; "Have you ever thought that you can't get pregnant because of your weight?"; "If you quit obsessing about getting pregnant, it will probably happen"; "Did you ever use drugs/take birth control/ have unprotected sex/get an STD?"*

A woman dealing with infertility issues is likely also feeling a great deal of guilt. She is already replaying a full-length movie of her life on a mental loop to try to determine what she may have done "wrong." Any statement that implies that something in her past caused her infertility is completely inappropriate.

If she is experiencing stress, she is in good company, as I have never known *any* woman (including yours truly) who does not experience stress on a daily basis—yet most appear to be able to reproduce in spite of that fact. The same thing goes for body weight. Yes, being seriously overweight or underweight may interfere with reproduction, but women at both ends of the weight spectrum still can and do get pregnant. If her body weight is of serious concern, she will have that discussion with her doctor.

Finally, her medical history as a whole—drug use, birth control use and certainly her sexual history—is her personal business, the business of her spouse/partner and her doctor. If any of these things have contributed to her fertility issues, her doctor will have discussed the matter with her, and unless she chooses to do otherwise and discuss it with you in turn, it is a private matter.

- **Don't suggest a "substitute" for parenthood:** *"You're free to travel whenever you want"; "Now you can concentrate on your career; you can't do that when you're a parent"; "Look at all the money you're saving."*

  While there may be truth in these observations, here are the realities:

1. Traveling and vacations are momentary, no matter the exotic locale to which you travel or how long the trip. Anyone who wants to become a parent and is unable to do so will not be readily comforted by thoughts of palm trees and tropical drinks.

2. It is true that oftentimes, careers are put on the back burner or compromised in the interest of parenthood—it was certainly the

case with my career. However, ask me what I would do if I had to do it over again and I assure you that I would do the same things for the same reasons. Absolutely no one remembers the trial motions that I drafted in 1994 or the sales awards that I won in 2003—but I remember every moment of motherhood, and my daughter remembers a mother who was there for her without fail.

As with traveling, a high-flying career is not exactly the same as parenthood. Anyone who wants to become a parent is more than happy to make any career sacrifices that need to be made.

3. There is no argument—parenthood is expensive. However, prospective parents are well aware of the financial undertaking involved and would still far prefer a child over another savings account.

There *is* no substitute for parenthood, and anyone seeking to become a parent is not going to be comforted by the prospect of fancy vacations taken at whim and will, the acceleration of careers or any other supposed "replacement." There is no such thing as a "replacement" for parenthood and to suggest otherwise borders on the ridiculous. Instead, allow her time to her figure out how she wants to design her life and if asked, offer suggestions and helpful insight.

Miscarriage/Stillbirth

There was a time that miscarriage was treated as though it was little more than a biological function gone awry. Women were routinely dismissed with an "It happens all the time, it's no big deal" attitude and treated as though it was not an overwhelming loss. There was only one problem with that attitude.

It *is* an overwhelming loss.

While most medical experts agree that miscarriage is not an unusual phenomenon, it is nonetheless a devastating event for the expectant mother, generally filled with guilt, anger and overwhelming sadness, necessitating compassion and sensitivity in regard to this very real loss.

Daisy White, the founder and owner of Daisy White's Booktique[33] in England, experienced the devastation of three miscarriages. Katy Larsen, the owner and founder of Somewhere Over the Rainbow, a store featuring pregnancy/infant loss memorial items, experienced both multiple miscarriages and the stillbirth of her daughter, Hannah. Both women share how they eventually emerged from their extremely difficult heartbreak.

Daisy's story:

I suffered three miscarriages before the birth of my two boys. The traumatic experience, difficult pregnancy and emergency Caesarian section births with both boys led me to suffer PND[34] and quit my job.

DISBELIEF AND FLASHING BACK

I couldn't believe it was happening. As I went to each scan to check for a heartbeat, I held my breath, hoping it would be okay. Later I had flashbacks, even long after my children were born.

FINDING A FOCUS

I have always written, but interest from a literary agent led me to start writing seriously, which made me focus on something other than my [miscarriage] experiences. My children were a great source of happiness but I couldn't seem to hold onto that feeling. When Ollie was three years old, I set up the Booktique and focused myself on both writing and building a business.

I DEFINED MY SUCCESS

I still have occasional flashbacks and panic attacks but I can now control them. My confidence is back and I don't feel [like] a failure anymore! I now have my own business that I can fit around the kids. I am so lucky.

---

33 For more information about Daisy please visit www.daisywhitesbooktique.co.uk.
34 Known in the United Kingdom as post-natal depression and in the United States as post-partum depression.

Dealing with the Worst…Your Way

When the worst happens, deal with it as only you can. You know yourself better than anyone. Look after you, be patient and give yourself time to heal. Cry or scream, go out and book a spa day…in a tiny way, it will help you begin to move on.

Katy's story

I lost my stillborn daughter, Hannah, under horrific circumstances in the emergency room of a hospital…in a supply closet. Losing Hannah was my inspiration for the charitable business I run and for my activism to bring attention to the devastating consequences of infant loss.

What Could I Have Done?

The [healing] process was grueling. Why was my baby taken away from me? What could I have done differently? It was a challenge like none other. I had difficulty just getting pregnant, I'd already experienced miscarriages and now I'd had a stillborn.

Turning Anger into Action

Anger became an emotional force that led me down an incredible path. I turned that anger into action. I first started a ministry called Delivering Hope for Hannah and provided care information and handmade memory boxes to the hospitals in my state that are without labor and delivery departments. I also began gifting handcrafted items to other mothers in pain, which eventually became Somewhere Over the Rainbow. All proceeds from remembrance items are used to gift such items to families on similar grief journeys.

My business is how I keep Hannah's memory alive. I can parent my children who are physically with me, and Somewhere Over the Rainbow is my way to parent Hannah.

Finding a Purpose All Around Me

Even without Hannah, life is indescribably complete—because Hannah *is* here. Finding a purpose for her life has given mine even greater purpose. I had a daughter after I lost Hannah, and I'm blessed to have them both.

Hannah has touched people in places I have never [visited]. Her name and her story travel with every handcrafted item that I send. She is all around me and fills our lives with an incredible richness and genuine appreciation.

HOW YOU CAN HELP

You have the ability to be a great source of comfort and support to your friend or loved one who is dealing or has dealt with either one or both of these very sad situations. Keep in mind that she may very well have experienced the worst sort of negative comments and that you may be the only source of positivity that she has right now.

Definite Do's

- **Make sure that she is physically taking care of herself:** In addition to the emotional, there are obviously the physical ramifications of miscarriage and stillbirth. Due to this kind of loss, she may dealing with things on only an emotional level and not paying vital attention to her physical recovery. Do your best to ensure that she is keeping her post-trauma doctor appointments in order to ensure that her body recovers completely.

- **Be willing to listen:** I use the word "listen" a lot in the "Definite Do's" because it is such an important word. Remember, she may not have a lot of people willing to listen to her feelings of anger, sadness or guilt. Be the reassuring presence in her life. Be open to hearing whatever she has to say, and be quick to reassure her that you will be there every step of the way for her as she begins the Healing Journey.

- **Get her around others who have experienced the same loss:** One of the first lessons that I learned in serving the widowed community is that one of the fastest avenues of comfort is getting the widowed around other widowed. The same lesson applies here. She needs community with others who have experienced a similar loss. She needs to understand that she is not alone, that her feelings are completely justifiable and that there is both hope and recovery. Encourage her to research the Internet for support, consult her doctor and ask for references from hospitals, all of which can steer her in a positive direction.

- **If you sense that she is in a place of despondency, *do not hesitate to intervene immediately*:** One of the horrible offshoots of miscarriage and stillbirth is that although she does not have a baby, she is still left to deal both physically and emotionally with post-partum *everything*. This may put her into a place of crushing despair, where she may feel tempted to cause herself harm. If you so much as suspect that she is in a place of crisis, do not hesitate to get help immediately. Organizations such as the October 15th Organization[35] and the International Stillbirth Alliance[36] support those who are suffering by providing all kinds of forums, education and resources.

Finally, if you feel that hers is an emergency situation, call 911 or your local emergency services (and if applicable, the National Suicide Prevention Hotline),[37] contact her doctor and if possible, accompany her to the hospital.

---

35 For more information, please visit www.october15th.com.
36 For more information, please visit www.stillbirthalliance.org.
37 National Suicide Prevention Hotline: In the United States: 1-800-273-8255. Outside of the United States, visit www.suicidehotlines.com/international.html for a list of countries that are served, along with hotline telephone numbers

Without a Doubt...Don't

- **Don't ask morbid questions or dehumanize the situation:** *"Was it deformed?"; "It wasn't really a baby"; "Miscarriage is better than giving birth to a freak."*

  Lest you think that no one in the world is stupid enough to say anything as awful as the foregoing statements, I rush to remind that these are actual quotes that women who have experienced miscarriage or stillbirth have endured.

  Whether or not you believe that a miscarried pregnancy wasn't "really a baby" is immaterial. First, this is not about your particular beliefs right now. Secondly, I can attest that from the moment the pee stick from the pregnancy test turns blue or shows the "plus" sign and/or the doctor says, "Congratulations," in your mind, there is a baby inside. It may not yet be true from a technically biological standpoint, but from an emotional standpoint, it *is* true—and the woman who is suffering this kind of loss is the one whose truth must be respected.

  Asking questions about a fetus' physical condition is beyond inappropriate—and referring to any child as a "freak" (be they in or out of utero) honestly does not warrant the dignity of response. If the mother-to-be wishes to share this kind of incredibly intimate information, she will volunteer it. Otherwise, she does not need people painting grotesque visuals for her. She is suffering enough.

- **Don't pile on the guilt:** *"Maybe you're too old to have a baby"; "What were you eating/drinking/taking?"; "You should have been exercising more/exercising less/working/not working/continuing to have sex/ not continuing to have sex"* etc.

  Once again, does your first name begin with the word "Doctor"? If the answer is "no," you do not get to offer speculation, and you *definitely* do not get to offer this kind of useless insight. Just as with women struggling with infertility, every woman who has experienced miscarriage or stillbirth is already feeling guilty. Every single woman who has experienced miscarriage or stillbirth is already questioning her age, weight, height, workout regimen or lack thereof, sexual history, medical history and everything that she has ever ingested, going all the way back to the Bartles and James wine coolers that she drank to celebrate finishing college finals. Why in the name of common sense would anyone pile onto Guilt Mountain by causing her to question herself any more than she is already?

- **Don't sweep her loss under the carpet:** *"The sooner the loss, the easier it is to get over"; "You can always get pregnant again"; "Just avoid places where kids are."*

  Statements such as these are ways of saying, "What's the big deal? It's so easy—you can get pregnant again just by wishing it, and until then, don't walk through children's departments in stores, and don't go anywhere near an elementary school. Problem solved."

  Really?

  What if she can't "always get pregnant again"? Perhaps getting (or staying) pregnant *isn't* easy for her. Moreover, just because there were not years upon years invested in a child does not mean that she hasn't lost something that was extraordinarily precious.

  Finally, if anyone thinks that avoiding places where children congregate somehow makes things "all better," I would hope that level of intelligence is not being permitted to operate motor vehicles. Unfortunately, we see this particular "suggestion" later on in the book in an even more unbelievable application.

  You have been warned.

- **Don't use spiritual or philosophical clichés to question her parental ability:** *"God doesn't want you to be a parent; "Everything happens for a reason"; "I guess it just wasn't meant to be"; "God knows best."*

  I am always amazed at the number of people who seem to know

precisely what God wants. Guess what? No one has any idea what God wants for another person. You know who knows what God wants? God. Any discussion about what He wants should be left between Him and anyone who wants to speak directly with Him. Miscarriage or stillbirth is not some kind of divine punishment or retribution, nor is it the universe telling someone that they are not meant to be a parent.

Although a number of people are comforted by the thought of everything happening for a predetermined reason that is beyond our comprehension, the reality is that the same thought doesn't carry the same level of comfort when told to you by someone else. When you say "Everything happens for a reason," the person to whom you are saying it is thinking one of two things: either "What possible reason could there be for me not to be able to have children?" or, that you simply do not want to listen to her any further and instead choose to write off this terrible situation with an overused cliché.

Hysterectomy

Why include hysterectomy in a book about bad things? Because hysterectomy has been universally dreaded and derided as a bad thing. There has been much controversy surrounding hysterectomy, from its necessity as a surgical procedure, to the myth that along with her reproductive equipment, a woman also undergoes the surgical removal of her libido and her very womanhood. Many women indeed believe that they will be somehow "less" if they need to undergo this procedure. Others believe that menopause[38] will be either the stereotypical nightmare or punch line that has been portrayed throughout both time and media.

None of the above is accurate.

---

38 A total hysterectomy will result in "surgical menopause." If undergoing a partial hysterectomy, you may not necessarily experience surgical menopause, as a remaining ovary may continue producing hormones.

A True Story 2.0

Sue and Diane are my gorgeous cousins (sisters) who have been gorgeous throughout their entire lives. Nowadays looking more like siblings of their children rather than their mothers, they are still gorgeous—and just as beautiful on the inside as they are on the outside. We were inseparable throughout childhood and remain close to this day.

As we collectively entered adolescence years ago, certain "things" began to change—and definitely not to my favor. Sue and Diane both escaped the agonies of cringe-worthy acne, oily hair, a mouth full of metal, the lovely nicknames accompanying that mouth full of metal and many of the other tribulations and awkwardness that had no problem finding me (an overbite necessitating braces, rubber bands *and* headgear; oily hair and severe acne everywhere except my knees). Additionally, because of their stunning looks (and accompanying stunning height), Sue and Diane also attracted the attention of many a male admirer wherever they went.

Try being short, flat-chested, stringy haired, metal-casted, freckle-faced and constantly broken out next to all *that*.

I *so* badly wanted to be Sue and Diane. I *so* envied them their effortless looks and personalities to match. I coveted their omnipresent confidence and wit, their smoothly glowing skin and their perpetual California tans.

(I instead sported perpetual California burns.)

As if all of that was not challenge enough, my cousins also "got their growth" (as it was ever-so-delicately referred to in the 1970s) about a year and a half before the same wonder of nature visited me. I felt even more left out. How sophisticated it all seemed to be, discussing bras and cramps and feminine products of one kind or another...and there I was, five inches shorter, broken out beyond belief, period-less and with a chest that resembled a wooden plank.

I felt like I was left behind by Mother Nature to play Candyland and hopscotch.

I constantly whined to my parents about my washboard-like chest, my pimply complexion and being without a reason to bitch about cramps. They gamely tried not to laugh at my laments, while saying things that we all heard from our parents—things like, "It will happen for you too"; "Everyone is different" and "Don't be in a hurry." They meant well and I knew that—but then again, they were not suffering from the whole chest-like-an-ironing board/menses-challenged/Candyland-hopscotch syndrome either.

The one thing that I wish my parents *had* said is "Be careful what you wish for." You see, the universe actually heard my laments—and the universe has a really peculiar sense of humor.

I soon found myself in a 34C bra, which was okay I suppose, except for the fact that nature thereafter forgot to apply the brakes. Winding up in a significantly larger size prior to exiting my teen years, I now look at my chest (a few decades and one child later) and laugh.

You know what happens when you are naturally top heavy and then you have a child? *Gravity*, that's what happens. Picture two party balloons. Got it? Now envision those party balloons about three days after the party is over. That's me now. I long ago embraced that I am top heavy. I just wish that the "twins" were still located in the general geographic area of my chest.

Little did I know that a burgeoning bustline would be the least of my problems.

Two months shy of my thirteenth birthday, I got my period for the first time. This "miracle of womanhood" for which I had so longed instead found me doubled over and in agony, scarcely able to move and not feeling especially sophisticated. Was this *really* the future for which I had been yearning? I didn't remember Sue or Diane (or anyone else I knew) experiencing debilitating pain. All they ever did was complain about discomfort for a couple of days each month, worry that boys would glimpse female paraphernalia languishing in their seriously-cool, suede-fringed purses[39] and rue the days that their monthlies coincided with pool parties and beach gatherings.

What was wrong with *me?*

What none of us could have known was that decades of pain and struggle would follow. Simply put, as was done with the Ford Pinto in 1978, my female equipment should have just been recalled.

---

[39] It was the '70s, after all.

Once on the menstrual treadmill, I thereafter endured twenty years of varying horrendous female issues. I was blessed with wonderful doctors and specialists, all of whom I constantly frustrated with the assortment of challenges that I presented. Bleeding that would not stop. Incapacitating pain. A myriad number of different medications that did not help.

Surgical intervention began when I was fifteen years old, initially to try and quell the borderline-hemorrhaging that occurred each month. I underwent my first open surgery (involving an incision) when I was nineteen years old. The surgery was of an emergency nature, necessitated by a ruptured ovary that needed to be re-sectioned. One year later, the Fallopian tube "kinked,"[40] and also had to be re-sectioned. Shortly afterward, doctors began the surgical removal of cysts in varying sizes and lower abdominal locales.

By the time I was twenty-four, the doctors had no choice but to remove the completely-remodeled left ovary and tube. At that point, I was nowhere near getting married or having children and I was now watching the chances for the latter trickle down the drain. I was clearly a walking mess in terms of the female reproductive system—what were my chances of ever having a child going to be?

You know what? Miracles *do* happen.

With all of the problems that I'd experienced, the one problem that I did *not* have was getting pregnant. Four years after the (really-long-word-alert) salpingo-oopherectomy, I married and quickly (and quite intentionally) became pregnant. While the pregnancy itself unsurprisingly presented its own set of difficulties, I eventually gave birth to a beautiful miracle named Kendall Leah, who was delivered via Cesarean section and came out hollering and hungry. She truly is my "miracle baby," a fact of which she takes great pleasure in constantly reminding me.

Though doctors were hopeful that childbirth would alleviate at least some of the aforementioned problems, I unfortunately picked right back up where I left off after Kendall was born, with the same problems, pain and subsequent

---

40 Picture a garden hose squeezed in half. Imagine that to be your Fallopian tube. Now try walking upright. Enough said.

surgeries. By the time I reached my thirty-first birthday, I had endured nine major surgeries, and found myself yet *again* in horrendous pain.

Unable to work, unable to function as a parent both enjoys and needs to, wonked on pain medication for months and fed up with the physical and emotional toll that being unhealthy for so much of my life had taken, enough was finally *enough*. Relying upon the trusted advice of my specialists, and realizing that there were no alternatives, I prepared to undergo a total hysterectomy.

I then bid a sad goodbye to my dreams of ever having another child, reluctantly signed the forms and reported to the hospital for my tenth major abdominal surgery.

WHY ME?

I admit to a very long "Why me?" process that began in my teens and continued for many years. Everyone seemed to have only the usual once-a-month complaints and were able to take solace in chocolate and Midol,[41] while I was being hauled out of various workplaces in ambulances because the pain and bleeding were frighteningly severe. Further, my condition yielded little in the way of understanding from many of my workplace superiors—whoever heard of bursting ovaries and kinking tubes? What was the big deal about a period? All women have them. Why couldn't I be like everyone else and just pop an aspirin and go back to my desk?

I also indulged in "Why me?" in the days prior to the hysterectomy. Even though I knew how fortunate I was to have had a child at all, I'd always envisioned having two children. Because of the medical necessity of the hysterectomy, that choice was taken away.

I felt like one big walking short circuit.

A BLESSING IN DISGUISE

After the hysterectomy, I felt better both physically and mentally than

---

41 You know, if the makers of Midol really wanted to make bank, they would figure out how to *combine* chocolate *with* Midol.

I had in my entire post-adolescent life. No more monthly dread. No more terrible, one-sided pain and wondering what was wrong *now*. No more pain medication that put me on Planet Twinkie. No more wondering if the pain was leading to something even more serious than major surgery, like cancer. The physical well-being and peace of mind was fantastic. I also truly embraced how blessed I was to have had my one child, because the odds had been so stacked against me. Remember, by the time I tried to get pregnant, I had already lost fifty percent of my reproductive apparatus.

After surgery, the doctors informed me that because of the condition of the uterus and remaining ovary, I would likely never have become pregnant again—and if by some chance I *had* become pregnant, I would not have been able to carry a child to term. To my mind, the hysterectomy saved both my body and my psyche from undergoing much more pain and heartache.

All Is (Mostly) Well

Unfortunately, the surgeries did not end with the hysterectomy. Because of the number of surgeries I have undergone throughout my life, I now deal with scar tissue that needs to be surgically removed. While chances are high that repetitive surgery will be part of my life for the rest of my life, my overall health is so much better, and my quality of life is phenomenal.

Your Body = Your Decisions

I will never say that the decision to undergo a hysterectomy should be entered into lightly or quickly. I firmly believe that hysterectomy is a last resort, not a first option. Your own situation must be analyzed carefully, risk factors must be discussed and you absolutely *must* feel comfortable with your physicians and their opinions. If you do not like what one physician is saying, or you do not feel that you are being treated with the sensitivity and compassion that this situation warrants, consult with someone else. This is especially vital if a hysterectomy is being recommended and the recommendation is contrary to your plans to have children.

I will also never say "Don't be afraid" because it is a ridiculous thing to say. *Any* surgery is scary. After thirteen abdominal surgeries, I am still scared when it is time to go to the hospital, and I doubt that will ever change. Surgery is not like tennis—you do not get better at it with practice.

While recognizing that every woman is individual and reactions to medical procedures are never identical, I do wish to dispel some of the popular myths that surround hysterectomy.

MYTH: "I'M NOT A WOMAN ANYMORE."

Your female body parts—*any* of them—are not what define you. I am no less a woman because I do not menstruate and can no longer reproduce anymore than our brave sisterhood who undergo mastectomies are "less" after the fact.

What makes you a woman is *you*—your head, your heart, your compassion, your goals, your dreams, the way you approach life and the way you live life. I say it constantly: you are not defined by who or what you have lost—and that includes body parts.

MYTH: "I WON'T WANT TO HAVE SEX ANYMORE."

The most important desire-producing organ that we have is the brain. The absence of hormone-producing egg-makers and a uterus does not govern my desire level. I came through my hysterectomy believing that I was *finally* going to be whole, healthy and happy...and not only is that exactly what happened, once I discovered that sex could be pain-free, my libido shot through the roof.

A hysterectomy does not compromise your desire level unless *you* believe it will. A hysterectomy does not eliminate your ability to achieve orgasm unless *you* believe it will. If you are concerned that a hysterectomy might interfere with your sexual capacities, please do not hesitate to discuss this with your doctor.

MYTH: "MENOPAUSE WILL MAKE ME CRAZY/INSANE/GROW A BEARD/ NOT CARE ABOUT SEX ANYMORE."

The whirlwind of stories surrounding menopause are numerous, scary— and largely untrue. Yes, there are physiological effects. Yes, things will change. However, you will not go crazy, you will not grow a beard, menopause is not horrible and, as stated above, your sex drive does not automatically pack up.

Not everyone who goes through menopause (surgical or otherwise) suffers menopausal symptoms. *If* you should suffer symptoms and *if* those symptoms become uncomfortable, they are both treatable and manageable. I did experience physical menopausal symptoms, and when they first occurred, I immediately communicated with my doctor and tried a different number of ways to manage them until I found what worked for me.

I realize there is much debate in our current culture concerning medication to treat menopausal symptoms and because of the ready access of information, it is easy to become overwhelmed. Communicate with your doctor and explore all of your options together. If your doctor gives the go-ahead, try several different regimens to see which works best with your body. Review your diet and see if anything might be either contributing to menopausal symptoms or helping to mitigate those symptoms.

Most importantly *relax*. Be it surgical or natural, menopause is absolutely manageable.

HOW YOU CAN HELP

A hysterectomy is major surgery, requiring a significant amount of recovery time—and that is just the physical aspect. Because doctors are messing with reproductive equipment, there is likely going to be a period of hormonal adjustment. Of course, there are indeed emotional ramifications of hysterectomy as well. Keeping all of these things in mind:

Definite Do's

- **Help her get organized prior to surgery**: You can help by running through a simple checklist with her beforehand. Does she have anyone staying in the house during recovery for the first forty-eight to seventy-two hours? This is a matter of safety, as she will have been under a general anesthetic and trying to manage after abdominal surgery. If she is in a two-story home, bear in mind that stairs are neither easy nor fun to navigate post-surgery—how will she deal with meals, bathing, dressing, etc.? Does she need to pay any bills ahead of surgery? These are not things that she should begin thinking about the day that she arrives home from the hospital. You can help her get organized prior to surgery, which helps immeasurably with recovery post-surgery.

- **Offer to visit, but be understanding if she cannot receive visitors:** Prior to my most recent surgery, I had every intention of welcoming visitors and even bought pretty pajamas and robes so that I would be presentable.[42] Unfortunately, I suffered post-surgery complications and was simply not up to having visitors. I had to turn everyone away.

  Even though you have the best intentions, and even though patients really want to receive visitors, the fact is that they cannot predict how they will fare after surgery. If she has to say "no visitors" for the time being, be understanding, stay in touch with her and let her know that as soon as she is ready, you cannot wait to visit.

- **Bring a small get-well gift that is not flowers:** Don't get me wrong, I *love* receiving flowers…but not when I have to worry about hauling them home from a hospital or caring for them when I can barely move.

  Instead, bring something that will help to make her feel better physically and emotionally. Examples include a book or a small bundle of magazines tied with a ribbon; body wash and loofah; an eye-gel mask that can be chilled in the refrigerator; moisturizing lotion (general anesthesia can have a drying effect on skin) and complementing body mist or an aromatherapy candle. These items can be inexpensively purchased at a drugstore and will bring a smile to her face.

---

42 Far nicer than my standard at-home uniform of oversized sweat pants, fluffy socks and skull-emblazoned t-shirt.

Without a Doubt...Don't

- **Don't question her judgment and/or the necessity of the surgery:** *"Do you really have to do this?"; "I'd think again. It's not like you can change your mind"; "What if you want to have children [or more children]?"*

  A hysterectomy is not like a cheeseburger—you cannot just order one because you feel like having one. A hysterectomy is *not* an elective procedure. It is a medically necessary, emotionally-wrought procedure, over which your girl has already agonized. Causing her to second guess a decision that has likely been weeks or months in the making does not help. She has consulted with doctors, she has weighed pros and cons, she has carefully deliberated. Your role is supposed to be supportive, not a source of doubt or uncertainty. Stand strong with her.

- **Don't share horror stories:** *"Aren't you afraid of getting an infection in the hospital?"; "You'll never be the same again"; "I know someone who had a hysterectomy and they almost bled to death/never wanted to have sex again/couldn't have orgasms/had the most horrible scar."*

  What is it about people facing surgery (or for that matter, pregnant women facing the inevitability of labor) that moves those around them to share horror stories? Exactly *how* does sharing the story of a nightmare surgical experience help someone facing the same procedure who is trying to prepare themselves mentally and emotionally?

  Answer: It does not help. At all.

  This is really pretty simple. As stated in Chapter One ("How Can I Help?"), before you are tempted to share anything along these lines, please ask yourself:

1. *"If I were her, would I want to hear what I'm about to say?"*
2. *"Will what I'm about to say bring comfort and reassurance?"*

3. *"Will what I'm about to say be to any advantage?"*

The answer should be clear—horror stories of *any* kind are useless and potentially damaging. If you have any such stories, please keep them to yourself. Concentrate instead on being positive, uplifting and supportive—do not put visuals akin to a horror movie into her head.

From Bad Thing to Brighter Days Ahead...Times Three

Infertility

The decision to explore the options that will be offered to you regarding infertility is intensely personal, and that decision cannot be made by anyone other than you. However, as Pamela beautifully pointed out, there is nothing wrong—at *all*—with deciding to forgo those options and live a life of your specific design.

If you do wish to have a child and pregnancy is eliminated as a possibility for you, you should explore every option that you consider realistically available to you. However, I do not at all wish to minimize or trivialize the very real emotional and psychological impacts that infertility can have on a woman. For that reason, you may also wish to consider talking to a mental health expert who specializes in infertility issues to help you deal with the very understandable feelings with which you may be coping.

Please know that despite what anyone else may say to you, infertility is a biological function, and sometimes biological functions—well, they just *don't*. However, this in no way diminishes you as a woman, and it certainly does *not* mean that you are not meant to be a mother, if that is what is in your heart. Continue your research, surround yourself with people who can help you and know that your worth as a woman is not now, nor will it ever be based on reproductive ability.

Miscarriage/Stillbirth

Although there may be those around you who (intentionally or otherwise) attempt to trivialize these devastating experiences, know that there are *many* more people who stand ready to support you during and after these terrible losses.

As with any other loss and bereavement experience, your best allies on your Healing Journey are education, support and community. In other words, do not try to do this alone. Avail yourself of the resources provided in this chapter. Surround yourself with a community of understanding and support. Reach out to others who will figuratively or literally wrap their arms around you and say, "I get it, because I've been there too."

Also important to remember is that that your body has been through a physical trauma and that you must take care of yourself in order to be a ready, strong and active participant in your own Healing Journey. Keep your doctor's appointments and follow orders closely. Eat when your body asks you for food (mini-meals that are easily digested are the best) and get plenty of rest. Do not resume any exercise regimens without first getting your doctor's clearance to do so.

Remember, it does not matter how important your loss is to anyone else. Miscarriage and stillbirth are losses of great magnitude and deserve to be recognized as such—and it is really okay to do just that.

Hysterectomy

If a hysterectomy has been recommended to you, there is generally a legitimate medical reason behind the recommendation. No one likes surgery, least of all me. However, the preservation of your health is far more important than risking your health by eschewing the idea of surgery or foregoing surgery altogether.

If you are uncomfortable with a surgical recommendation, get as many other opinions as are necessary, until you are comfortable with the consensus of medical opinion. If you are not comfortable with your treating physician and/or surgeon, ask for a recommendation to another with whom you will feel comfortable.

Most importantly, please remember that as a woman, you are not defined by the sum of your "parts". You are instead defined by the size of your heart… and you are truly and honestly going to be okay.

Chapter Ten

LIFE'S LIGHTNING STRIKE: SERIOUS INJURY

EVERY SINGLE DAY, WE GO ABOUT OUR LIVES IN A FASHION THAT WE TAKE FOR granted. We get into cars, onto trains and planes and travel from Point A to Point B. We go to work. We run errands. We participate in sports and hobbies. We travel on vacation. We shepherd children to and from countless and varied activities. We live our lives expecting little in the way of catastrophe—and we should. How much life would we miss if we took up residence in the Land of Something Horrible Might Happen?

However, there is no denying that whether we are simply getting into a car or climbing the side of a mountain, living life in the ways that we both see fit and enjoy also carries risk, and that risk involves the possibility of getting hurt—sometimes badly.

Serious injury is like being blindsided in football without the benefit of protective gear or offensive linemen to block whatever harm is headed our way. Serious injury is something that no one expects and for which few are prepared. We never expect to be the ones who are inflicted with or affected by life-threatening injuries—and there is logic in that expectation. I continually teach and fervently believe that life is not meant to be lived in the constant fear that something awful may happen to us or to our loved ones. Yet, the sad fact is that, as with so many other bad things, serious injury *can* happen to us or the people we love—and it happens where, when and to whom we least expect it.

The two women you are about to meet are perfect examples of how life-threatening injuries suddenly invaded and forever changed lives, ultimately taking them in new directions that they could never have imagined.

Sustaining a Serious Injury

Christine King [43] was training for the Miss Fitness USA contest. As the name of the contest implies, the training and preparation involved is incredibly demanding and takes an extraordinary level of commitment. Christine had that level of commitment and the results showed. She was fit, she was ready to compete for the title and she was ready to win.

All of that commitment—and her entire life—was devastated in a split-second accident. However, that tragedy would also alter the trajectory of her life and lead her down a path that she could never have expected.

Christine's story

I was in rigorous training for the Miss Fitness USA Contest when I was in a serious Jet Ski accident. As I was pulled from the water, I repeatedly said "I cannot feel my legs." I had been left with a broken back, and doctors were unable to say whether I would ever walk again. The accident had caused a lumbar vertebrae explosion and after surgery, the doctors said that I didn't die because I was so fit—and those positive comments convinced me that I *would* walk again.

I decided that if I *was* able to get out of that bed, I would dedicate my life to helping others get fit as well. During my rehabilitation, I studied and became nationally certified by the American Council on Exercise. I also became a Post-Rehabilitative and Medical Exercise Specialist.

---

43 To learn more about Christine King, please visit www.lifeonlybetter.com.

This Happened for a Reason

When the accident occurred, I was in the strongest part of my life, both physically and mentally. After I regained consciousness, I knew that I was paralyzed from the waist down. I knew that I might be in a wheelchair for the rest of my life—but I also immediately knew that this happened for a reason.

I Had a Larger Purpose

When the doctors told me that I didn't die because I was fit, I had a purpose and a focus. I knew that my full-time job was to rehabilitate and take advantage of every day. Each day, I went to the gym, returned home to study for my personal trainer exam, took a nap and went back to the gym for another hour or two. I was fast asleep by 8:00 p.m. and I started all over again the following day.

I knew that I would never return to my position as vice president of a video production company. I had a larger purpose. I was highly focused, motivated and knew what my mission in life would be.

I Am Truly Blessed

I "hung my shingle" at the health club at which I had rehabilitated and within months, I was booked solid with personal training appointments. However, I realized that my mission needed to be larger. I had visited Florida frequently, both before and after my injury, and thought it would be a perfect environment to reach my niche. I was fortunate enough to have contacts who connected me with private [golf and country] clubs in South Florida.

I was blessed with the gift of life, the ability to walk again and the privilege to help others. While walking with a slight limp and dealing with internal injuries is no picnic, I must reinforce that I am truly blessed.

Your Number One Job Is to Focus on Recovery

I've built a business that continues to grow through my original mission and also through the new opportunities that are presented to me each day After being in this industry for over sixteen years, you realize that there is always someone whose situation is worse than your own. There is always someone hurting more than you, and the more opportunity I have to reach out into the world, the more I fulfill my life's work.

Your mind and heart will guide you to take each day and do everything you can for that day to improve your wellness and strength. Your number one job in life is to focus on recovery. No matter how severe the situation, you *will* get better. There are people in your life (some of whom you may not even have met yet) who are there to help you get better and to support you during that process. You've been there for many people in your life, and now it's your turn to accept the assistance of others.

Serious Injury of a Loved One

Lee Woodruff[44] is someone who I am convinced has discovered the secret of the forty-one-hour day. Blessed with four children and a globetrotting husband (Bob Woodruff, correspondent for ABC News), Lee is a *New York Times*-bestselling author and contributor to *CBS This Morning* on CBS News. She constantly travels the country, yet always has time for everything and everyone. She is an active participant in her children's lives. She bakes and blogs, parents and presides over a multimillion-dollar charitable foundation benefitting returning military troops; she always looks amazing and she never fails to return an email from wherever she is on the planet.

(For the record, I have one-half of the number of children that she has; I can't remember the last time that I baked anything but I'm positive that there was bribery or a holiday involved and my email return rate is usually within the same *month*.)

After the death of longtime *ABC World News Tonight* anchor Peter Jennings, Bob was moved into the anchor position. Less than thirty days later, Bob was embedded with a unit in Iraq when the tank in which he was riding was hit by an IED (improvised explosive device), critically wounding Bob and his cameraman. Clinging to life, Bob underwent numerous life-saving

---

44 To learn more about Lee and the Bob Woodruff Foundation, visit www.leewoodruff.com and www. bobwoodrufffoundation.org.

surgeries and would thereafter spend thirty-six days in a coma, followed by intense therapies to aid in both his physical and neurological recovery.

Bob's physical condition was not the only thing that a roadside bomb shattered. The world that he and Lee had so carefully crafted and fiercely loved also imploded. While theirs is a story that has a triumphant ending, the road to that triumph was long, difficult, fraught with uncertainty and unbearably painful. Would Bob ever awaken from the coma? If he did wake up, would he recognize Lee, his children, his family? In what sort of physical and mental state would this catastrophic injury leave this vibrant husband, father and journalist? Would there be any semblance of that life that they loved so very much?

Would *any* part of their life ever again be the same?

Lee's story

The president of ABC News does not make social calls to employees' wives at 7:00 a.m. on Sunday mornings—not even a co-anchor's wife.

"We've been trying to reach you," David Westin said. "Bob has been wounded in Iraq."

I sat up, trying to process the information. "Wounded? What do you mean wounded?"

"We don't have a lot of information right now, but we are getting it as fast as we can. We are getting him the best care possible."

I interrupted him. "David…is my husband alive?"

"Yes, Lee…but we believe he may have taken shrapnel to the brain."

He was alive; I'd start with that.

REWINDING THE "TAPE"

I remember thinking that I could "rewind the tape," and that if I imagined the scene enough in my head—if I could recreate the movie of the bad thing that happened in my mind—I'd be able to redo it, because surely this wasn't really happening.

I had been through a few dings and dents before (losing a baby, two miscarriages). With some good therapy and some great friends, I had come to the realization that bad things happen to people and that it's completely random; bad things are not "punishment" for something. Look at just about everyone's lives and you'll see they have had some [bad] thing. But I do remember feeling "Why me...again?"

"Plan B"—One Day at a Time

I had to slow my brain down and take it day-to-day. I had a big "Plan B": sell the house, go back to work full time and get health insurance through work. It was all about protecting the kids and making sure their lives weren't negatively impacted by what had happened.

I would find my mind flying ahead and getting worried about things that I couldn't control. Making lists helped tremendously. Talking to an accountant, and doing new wills and DNRs[45] were achievable goals which helped mitigate some of the anxiety that I felt about the future.

Frankly, there were days where *I* got sick of me. You have to give in to the low days; the 3;00 a.m. panic when you wake up wondering how you are going to do it all. I told myself that everything looks better in the morning, and it's so true. But each time I accomplished something on my own or crossed something off my list of things I needed to do to feel safe, I told myself I could do this. There was a lot of me talking to me in my head. When things felt like it was all too much, I went outside—to walk, hike or look at the sky and realize there was a whole big world out there.

An Ever-Changing Landscape

Moving forward is a constant process. It's different for everyone, but traumatic situations or losses force you to reckon how precious life and time is... and many people (myself included) shift their priorities. Before [Bob's accident] I was a freelance writer taking assignments from corporate and media clients. Afterward, I focused on writing only what *I* wanted to write and working on book projects that I wanted to spend time on. I became better at saying "no" to work and "yes" to time with friends and family.

---

45 In medicine, "DNR" means "Do Not Resuscitate." It is a legal order in place to respect the wishes of a patient who does not want CPR or advanced life support administered in order to "allow natural death."

Life is an ever-changing landscape. If I leave myself open to where this fork in the road will take me, I will have a different answer every year—and that's exciting to think about.

FORGIVE YOURSELF—YOU WILL SURVIVE

Although your experience will never be forgotten, it will recede. One day you'll wake up and it won't be the first thing you think about. Time helps move things forward and provides healing. You will backslide—progress is slow and one good day may be followed by two bad ones—that's the roller coaster of recovery. Forgive yourself. Human beings were built to survive.

HOW YOU CAN HELP

If an injury is serious, you must realize that both the injury and the recovery process are also not going to be pretty, nor is it going to be easy to see. In other words, you will need to mentally prepare yourself—it is not an easy dynamic in which to participate. However, your key focus must be on your girl (or whoever in her life has been seriously injured), rather than on any discomfort that you may be feeling, given the situation at hand.

Definite Do's

- **Use words of encouragement often:** Lee says, "I was helped by hearing things like 'There are no words I can say that will make you feel better, but I want you to know I am here for you and I care for you and I will be here for the long haul' or 'This sucks and I'm so sorry this happened to you.' Empathize, don't sympathize—no one wants to be the object of pity."

  Christine shares, "[My visitors] shared great words of hope and love. Surprisingly, [some of these people] weren't very close friends, but mere acquaintances who had heard of my story from the health club or the newspaper. It touched my heart unlike anything I've ever felt."

It's really quite simple. Be the love-boost that is so badly needed right now.

- **Offer practical assistance:** What can *you* do to help either the patient or the household in a practical sense? For example, are there children who need looking after? Plants that need watering? Pets that need attention? Meals that need preparing? Anything you can do to help the patient or caregiver keep their focus where it belongs will help them feel calmer. While get-well gifts are great, telling someone, "Don't worry, it's been handled," (whatever "it" may be) is even better.

- **Encourage her to seek support:** I honestly do not know of one instance involving life-changing injury or catastrophic illness where counseling has not been involved. However, many people put on that "brave front" that I despise and view seeking help as a sign of weakness. The reality is that serious injury flips the paradigm that was once a normal life. No one can go through something like this without a "road map." This is where counseling proves invaluable.

  Encourage the person with whom you are closest (be it patient or caregiver) to talk to someone in a position to help—a doctor, cleric, social worker, mental health professional—anyone who can help them cope with what has happened and how they can begin to design their future, both immediate and long term.

Without a Doubt…Don't

- **Don't question or pass judgment:** *"Why were you doing something so risky/dangerous?"; "You should have known better than to…"* [fill in the blank]; *"How could you be so foolish?"*

  At one time or another, everyone wishes that they were Mr. Peabody and Sherman with a Way-Back Machine that would enable them to go back to the day *before* their particular bad thing occurred.

Lee earlier described her own attempts to "rewind the tape" of the events that landed her husband in grave condition with life-threatening injuries. Unfortunately, there is no Way-Back Machine and there is no "Life-Delete" button. The situation at hand is, in fact, the situation at hand.

Passing or questioning judgment saying anything that might be interpreted as "How could you have been so careless/stupid/reckless/foolhardy?" does nothing except perhaps cause *more* anxiety or guilt, or make someone feel like less than an adult. It is a safe assumption that the patient and their loved ones did not go out of their way to create a tragic set of circumstances. Please do not imply otherwise.

- **Don't engage in avoidance.** *"I just can't stand to see them that way"; "What if I see them and pass out?"; "I hate hospitals."*

  I would love to meet the person who says "I *love* hospitals!" or the person who lives for nothing more than to see someone in pain. It is time for all of us to agree that we *all* hate hospitals, we *all* hate seeing people suffering and collectively resolve to never say anything like this again.

  Recalling her own hospitalization, Christine again shares, "When tragedy hits, you learn who your friends are. The people I expected to be at the hospital were nowhere to be found. While lying in the hospital alone, I had to reconcile these issues. I believe that due to the extreme nature of my injury, they simply were unable to handle visiting me. It hurt my feelings a lot."

  As with any other situation where you are in a position to offer help and support, this too is not about you or your discomfort level. It is about people in need of compassion and understanding. If visiting is permitted, please kick your fears to the curb and pay a visit. Be the one providing compassion, not the one who is too self-absorbed to be available to someone in need.

- **Don't assume that you know how someone feels or what they should or should not be doing during a recovery process:** *"I know exactly how you feel, because when I broke my leg* [followed by your own story]*"; "You think you have it bad…"; "I've been through the exact same thing and you have to* [fill in the blank with medical opinions]*."*

Are you sensing a pattern?

This is a wonderful time to pull another reminder from Chapter One ("How Can I Help?"). Even if your experience is identical to the one before you right now, this is not your moment. This moment is about someone else and their very serious challenge—do not engage in spotlight-shifting.

Remember one other very important point: Any attempt to compare what someone has been or is going through to an experience in your past is completely inappropriate. You cannot know how someone else feels because you are not them. When it comes to matters of health, every person is different. It therefore follows that their physical, emotional and psychological reactions will also be different. I can almost envision Lee rolling her eyes as she shares, "Never presume you know how someone feels or that your [situation] is just like theirs, e.g., 'Oh, I know how you feel. I lost my cat last Thanksgiving.'" Similar would be the statement above made by someone who had previously broken their leg. While certainly no fun, a broken leg is not comparable to someone who has suffered a broken back as Christine did or almost lost their husband to a roadside bomb, as was the case with Lee.

If you do have direct experience with the same or similar serious injury, or you've been a caregiver to someone whose life was hanging in the balance due to a life-threatening injury, use that experience for good by being a knowledgeable source of support—not as an opportunity to regale an audience with your tales.

If your opinions are actively solicited for things like physical therapy recommendations, recovery protocol, caregiver respite, etc., or if someone asks you for referrals or input, by all means, offer away. Such questions are a clear signal that your insight and opinions are welcome and necessary. Otherwise, leave "I know how you feel" at home.

- **Resist the urge to indulge in clichés:** *"God never gives you more than you can handle"; "Everything happens for a reason"* [*that* one again?]*; "What doesn't kill you makes you stronger."*

  You have seen these clichés sprinkled periodically throughout the book and with good reason—they are overused too often to count. The bigger problem is that these clichés help no one. Aside from the fact that you may be talking to someone who was perhaps almost killed (or is caring for a loved one who was almost killed), and making reference to newfound strength after near-death is inappropriate, these worn-out dime-store clichés and philosophies come off as insensitive and "canned."

  Now, be they patient or caregiver, if the person of concern looks at you with great conviction and says, "I know that God put me in this place for a reason" or "I am/they are going to come back from this stronger than ever," or sentiments to that effect…by all means, take them seriously and offer discussion—because in this case, it is a belief system. Otherwise, the use of clichés tends to come off about as sincere as something that is pulled out of a fortune cookie.

FROM BAD THING TO BRIGHTER DAYS AHEAD

If you have been victimized by a serious or life-threatening injury, the most important thing that you must do is the one thing that we girls tend to be really poor at—you *must* put yourself at the top of your to-do list. As Christine teaches, your recovery *must* become your full-time job and full-time focus. Everything else is secondary.

Listen carefully to your doctors, therapists and ancillary recovery team and follow the protocols that have been designed for you. Ask a million questions and don't feel stupid for doing so. If you do not like a particular course of therapy, medication, etc., speak up. If you do not care for any one of your professional caregivers, find one with whom you will feel comfortable.

You must also understand that most who have suffered this level of insult to the body generally need psychological support as well. You may very well be suffering the effects of post-traumatic stress disorder, situational depression or similar issues and these issues are equal in their ability to permanently injure. Unfortunately, for reasons that I have yet to understand, society tends to equate asking for emotional support with weakness. Just because psychological wounds are not visible to the eye does not mean they are not wounds all the same. Please do not ignore this very important area of your recovery.

To those who are caregivers: As caregiver to my late husband, I learned a very important lesson the hard way—caregivers are no good to anyone if they aren't taking care of themselves. I'll also admit to being one of those people who saw asking for help and/or accepting offers of help as weakness and failure. The result? When Mike was mid-illness, I wound up in bed with a case of shingles,[46] all because I had compromised my immune system by not properly caring for myself.

As with serious or terminal illness, a life-threatening injury affects both the patient *and* their loved ones. While your primary focus is obviously going to be on the patient, someone must also be focusing on *you*. Contact your doctor or a social worker at your local hospital for respite resources and if possible, to get assistance in the home. Let those around you know that you gladly welcome pre-cooked, heat-and-eat meals, offers of overnighters for the kids, grocery runs and even "patient-sitting duty" for a couple of hours so that you can get out for a bit—or perhaps just get a long shower and some uninterrupted sleep.

While the journey of recovery is long, you will also encounter victories along the way—and it is vital to celebrate those victories. Christine had no idea if she would ever walk again. Lee's husband sustained injuries so critical that they had no idea what life would look like. Through sheer determination and an

---

46 And once you awaken the shingles virus in the body, even though the degree of severity varies from episode to episode, it will likely recur throughout the rest of your life. It is also not fun.

undeterred mind to recovery, Christine is walking and runs a thriving business. The Woodruff family endured tremendous challenge during Bob's lengthy recovery; however that journey eventually saw Bob's return to ABC News. Lee went on to become a bestselling author and television correspondent, and their children are all doing wonderfully well in their respective pursuits.

Aside from incredible courage, the primary thing that these two women have in common is that while they readily admit to facing almost-overwhelming challenge, mixed in with plenty of those inevitable "bad days," neither one gave up. Each resolved that the set of circumstances that so seriously threatened everything they held dear was *not* going to win. While each saw their lives altered in ways that they never expected, both have embraced and moved forward into their futures with hope, determination and conviction.

You can too.

Chapter Eleven

THE BLACK CLOUD OF UNCERTAINTY: SERIOUS/LIFE-THREATENING ILLNESS

IT IS ONE OF THOSE THINGS THAT WE ALL BLITHELY ASSUME "HAPPENS TO someone else"...

Until it happens to you or someone you love.

Receiving a diagnosis of a serious illness is one of the scariest fears realized. Be it your own illness or that of someone you love, a stone-cold fear permeates the patient, their household and their loved ones, and that black cloud of uncertainty settles in and becomes a constant companion.

When serious illness invades your life in any measure, the illness figures largely in how you are going to live your lives from that point forward. Depending on your relationship perspective, an illness can determine everything from where you actually live to when you can go out for a cheeseburger.

Your Own Diagnosis

Having experienced the ramifications of serious illness as a caregiver to both my late husband and my father, I can emphatically attest that the presence of serious illness in your life changes absolutely everything. However, little will impact your life more than when that serious or life-threatening diagnosis happens to *you*. A myriad number of questions loom large: "What will treatment involve?"; "Will I be in pain?"; "How am I going to be able to take care of myself/my family/my job?"

"Am I going to die?"

Sonya[47] is a cancer survivor and spokesperson for cancer awareness. Anita Mahaffey[48] is also a cancer survivor and owns a very successful business. Soania[49] is a surgeon, business owner and philanthropist. These women have each received and faced devastating personal diagnoses; however they all persevered and collectively refused to let their diagnoses define who they are or keep them from achieving goals and fulfilling dreams.

Most importantly, we learn that while we cannot control many of the life circumstances handed to us, our *reaction* to those circumstances is certainly both within our control and vital to our respective outcomes.

Sonya's story

My story began when I was diagnosed with ductal carcinoma (breast cancer). As part of the diagnosis, I needed to have eighteen lymph nodes removed to see if the cancer had spread. I had blood work done in preparation for my first surgery and while I was waiting in the pre-op room, my surgeon and her nurse entered and asked to speak to me privately. The blood work revealed that I was two weeks pregnant with my daughter, Faith.

I'd been told during my initial surgical consultation that I would have to harvest eggs if I ever wanted to have children. I realized I was going to do possible harm to myself by staying pregnant. My surgeon also warned me that since I'd been exposed to testing involving high doses of radiation, the fetus was at very high risk for deformities and intellectual disabilities. I [subse-

---

47 To learn more about Sonya and her story, please visit the American Cancer Society on YouTube at http://youtu.be/05fyEPAM5go.
48 To learn more about Anita and her company, please visit www.cool-jams.com.
49 To learn more about Soania, please visit www.designingacure.com and www.myhippylicious.com.

quently] went through three surgeries (including a double mastectomy) and my first four rounds of chemotherapy while pregnant.

I Felt Chosen for the Journey

I felt chosen to undertake this journey and I wasn't sure why. My only choice, given my circumstances, was to remain calm and faithful...I felt that God would do the rest.

Weighing the Information

Once diagnosed, I wanted to know what my treatment options were. I asked for the necessary information in regards to treatment and surgery and how we could move forward with aggressive treatment, but keep the pregnancy safe. I was one of the first patients that the physicians had followed who was contending with both cancer and pregnancy. It was a relief knowing I had a team who were working to help me fight [the cancer] and ensure my pregnancy was safe.

A month and a half after being diagnosed, I had a double mastectomy. Reconstructive surgery usually happens at the same time as a mastectomy, but my breast surgeon didn't want to have me under anesthesia for an additional seven hours while pregnant. When my tumor markers shot up at thirty-seven weeks, I was hurriedly induced. I had a CAT scan the day after giving birth to Faith and found out that I was "free and clear" (no new tumor activity). One week after giving birth, I resumed my chemo schedule.

In 2012, I had three uterine hemorrhages. It was Faith's birthday and I wanted to celebrate by taking her on her first flight. I met two friends in San Diego, California and the next morning, I began hemorrhaging. My friends rushed me to the emergency room, as I had lost four pints of blood. I went into cardiac arrest and my daughter watched me almost die. I had to have four transfusions and an emergency D&C in order to stop the bleeding. Since that time, I've had several more surgeries, including a secondary reconstructive surgery, a uterine ablation and a partial hysterectomy.

FOCUSING ON GIFTS

Ten surgeries later, I am continuing to walk by faith. I have a wonderful support system of family that has supported me throughout my journey. I focus on the gift of each day and that we should all live more richly. I pay attention to sunrises and sunsets, I recognize people for good works, I always have an encouraging word to share and I try to make time for things that are important. Being engaged and present with my daughter is very important to me. Whether we are doing mani-pedis or coloring, I want her to know she has my undivided attention.

I feel healthy and I plan to make the most of it. I'm planning to take Faith back home to Guam, and I also plan on becoming a certified Zumba instructor. I have a lot to do, and I plan to be around for it all.

DON'T BE AFRAID OF FAILING

I live now paying much closer attention. I'm hypersensitive to the needs of others, I'm joyful for no reason and I eat chocolate every day without guilt. Faith saved my life and feeds my soul.

I live everyday "out loud." I hope to make an impact with the life that I have left and to inspire others to do the same. As human beings, we all have moments of reflection where we consider how we are living and how we could improve our lives to make a better impact. I would ask that anyone contemplating those thoughts to *move!* People shouldn't wait for a life-altering situation to give them a new lease on life. Don't be afraid of failing—there is a gift in every experience.

Anita's story

My first episode with head cancer was in my early twenties. After dealing with recurring head cancer three times, I lost my left eye and eyelids when I was thirty-nine years old. This was my third surgery and the tumor was about two millimeters away from entering my brain. If the surgeon did not take drastic measures, I would have died. There was no alternative but to remove a wide margin around the tumor which included my left eye, optic nerve and eyelids.

TRYING TO FIND SOLUTIONS

When I was first told that I needed to have surgery to save my life, I went into a deep funk. I spent every day trying to find another solution. I went to faith healers, crystal healers, explored cancer treatments online—and finally accepted the inevitable.

After the surgery, my jaw was locked and I needed physical therapy to open my mouth. I needed a prosthetic. I was scared because I didn't know if the "beast" would come back. They had already taken my eye and eyelids and I looked like a freak. I wore a patch for about six months and people never failed to comment on it. It was a constant reminder of my "defect."

LEARNING TO LOVE MYSELF AGAIN

After beating cancer three times, I decided that my only insurance policy would be to live life in the best way possible. It's not in my nature to sulk in a corner and hide behind my prosthetic face. I really needed to learn to love myself again. I decided to make serious changes, knowing that I wanted to be happy and never wanted to suffer through another bout of cancer.

EAT CHOCOLATE EVERY DAY!

After so many surgeries, I certainly was not a fan of invasive cosmetic procedures. I did what I could to improve myself physically, but the real work was the internal. By changing my way of thinking, I noticed huge changes. Being mindful and staying healthy has become a way of life. Following are some of the changes that I've made:

- Inaction causes worry, and worry causes me to waste precious energy. I choose to use my energy for positive purposes.
- I start my day by thinking how I can make life good for those around me. I try to commit to at least ten random acts of kindness. When those around me are positive and happy, it comes back in a big way.
- I've committed to exercising every day for the rest of my life. When I'm tired or worn out, I listen to my body and go on a mellow walk

or practice yoga. When I'm more energetic, I go on a long hike, run or practice Pilates.

- I stick with natural foods, fresh vegetables and fruits, whole grain breads and cereals, nuts, lean proteins and low-fat dairy. I drink water, tea, coffee and an occasional glass of wine or champagne. Life is a continuous celebration which should never be squandered.
- I love chocolate, so I indulge in a little each day. I have my chocolate, my latte and I think about all of the things for which I'm grateful.
- I do what I love and I love what I do. My passions include my family, my business (a pajama company which manufactures pajamas for temperature regulation), public speaking, mentoring businesswomen, reading, volunteer work and exercise.

These simple yet effective life changes have allowed me to stay energetic, happy and healthy despite the difficulties I've faced.

I LIVE THE BEST LIFE POSSIBLE

I have been cancer free for almost fifteen years. At the ten-year mark, I joked that my doctor "fired" me from his office. When my doctor told me that I had almost zero chance of the cancer returning, it was one of the happiest days of my life.

I have a fabulous and supportive husband, three great children and a successful business. I've learned so much going through the dark times. When it's dark outside, the stars shine the brightest. I wouldn't be the same person I am today had I not gone through my ordeal. My life hasn't been easy, but it's been like a roller coaster: lots of exciting ups and downs and in the end, the ride was a good one.

Soania's story

My symptoms began with a slight tremor in my right thumb. I'd heard patients describe tremors before but to experience it was medically intriguing to me. Around the same time, I was scheduled to undergo surgery to remove a benign brain tumor. The surgery was successful and as I recovered, I was too preoccupied to pay any attention to the tremor that was very sporadic and quickly dismissed by my neurosurgeon at my follow-up appointment.

A couple of months after surgery, my husband (who was also at the start of his career as a urologist) and I were excited to find out we were expecting our first child. But as my pregnancy progressed, so too did the tremor—so much so that I consulted a neurologist/colleague at the clinic where my husband and I had started our practices.

After much neurological testing, my colleague looked at me and slowly and carefully stated that he thought I had Young Onset Parkinson's Disease. I immediately dismissed his diagnosis as a lapse in clinical judgment. However, a few months after my initial diagnosis, a second assessment from one of the foremost experts in the field confirmed this diagnosis.

For almost a decade, I immersed myself in growing my practice and my family, welcoming three daughters. The tremor worsened in my hand, began in my right foot and ultimately progressed to the left side of my body. I did the absolute minimum to manage my diagnosis, not wanting to face what challenges life had presented.

The disease was taking over my body. I mourned the day I had to give up assisting in the operating room, and suturing in our urgent care. I hated that I had to "time" my medications so that my hands would not be shaking when I gave immunizations or conducted exams. It infuriated me that the tremor would give me an air of nervousness when I was so sure in my knowledge and skills. But the disease permeated all aspects of my life, from caring for my young children, to taking care of my home, to my relationships. Something as simple as an invitation to a social event entailed careful timing of my medications and as a result, I began to isolate myself.

DENIAL AND AVOIDANCE

For a long time, I focused on the difficulties that I faced on a daily basis and all that I felt I was giving up, because it wasn't my choice to slow down. My husband and I were enjoying parenthood, we had blossoming careers and we were building a new house. Life should've been ideal considering what we were blessed with, but there was always a shadow hanging over me.

I was angry that at a time when life was so exciting, I had to deal with this diagnosis. Although no one could tell from my happy demeanor, I didn't like the fact that I rarely laughed. I was so intent on distracting myself with "busyness" that I was exhausting myself. I became consumed with thoughts of the disability I was facing. What about my plans to travel with my husband when we retired? Was I going to be physically functional for my daughters as they journeyed through their lives? I spent almost a decade in denial and avoidance and it was a time of anger, fear and hopelessness.

OUT OF ADVERSITY COMES STRENGTH

My Parkinson's continued to worsen and my ability to cope deteriorated. But out of adversity comes strength, and this experience led to a pivotal time in my life. My future included Parkinson's but I gradually realized that my life experience would be very different, depending on how I faced this challenge. It was a necessary change. It became clear to me that I'd chosen to be fearful and pessimistic, and I recognized that this approach wasn't working. I came to realize that although the diagnosis was not within my control, the way I faced this challenge was mine to determine, moving me from a position of helplessness to one of power.

USING LIFE EXPERIENCE TO HELP OTHERS

With the necessary paradigm shift, the years of inner turmoil and self-doubt came to an end. I recognize that I wasn't really living when I was in that state of mind. This was a powerful life lesson, and one that is applicable to all areas of my life. I embraced my diagnosis and chose not to let Parkinson's define my life; for as long as I can, I will thrive despite its limitations. This realization allowed me to move beyond my disease, to focus on those variables in my life over which I have control, to give back to my community and to use my expertise and life experience to help others.

EMPOWER YOURSELF...LIVE YOUR PRESENT

Parkinson's disease presents challenges on a daily basis. It's a progressive neurological disease, so, with time, I expect my condition will deteriorate. But

I choose to remain optimistic, to keep my focus on research that will bring about better treatments and ultimately a cure. I try to control the variables that I *do* have influence over, optimizing my general health and emotional well-being so that I can live well. I know that there is much that can be done to live well with Parkinson's or any other chronic illness—empower yourself and become an active participant in the management of your condition.

You have to abandon your fear of the future in order to begin living your present. You may not have a choice in what challenges life may bring, but you do have a choice in how you face those challenges. That power of choice can move you from a position of hopelessness to one of empowerment.

Serious Illness of a Spouse

Having been the spouse sitting across from a doctor while he delivered horrible news to my husband, I directly relate to that brain-blender into which you are thrown, as you quietly listen to words that you cannot even comprehend. Your headspace goes into immediate caregiver mode, while your heart tries to grip a new reality. How are you going to care for an ill spouse and care for your children at the same time? What about medical treatments and side effects? Is insurance going to cover everything? How are you going to work? What's going to happen to your household?

What's going to happen to *you*?

Louise* is a highly-respected professional in her industry, one that often calls for twelve to fourteen hour days, a tremendous amount of traveling and working even while on personal time. She has actually traveled the spousal illness road once before and using her experiences from the first time, she shares what it is like to again be the spouse to a man battling a life-threatening illness who depends on her for both practical and emotional support.

Louise's story

After quickly losing a significant other to a very serious illness, it took six years to wake up in the morning and feel somewhat normal. I finally got back to a semblance of a life, piecing it back together day by day, and I began experimenting with relationships and dating again. I'm very fortunate that I met somebody and we fell in love. A year into [the relationship] he was diagnosed with lymphoma.

BAD LUCK AND SELF-BLAME

I felt like, "Oh my God, am I bad luck?" Self-blaming was a large part of this process. I was in disbelief, and just trying to understand how lightning can strike twice.

DEFINING A NEW ROLE WITH A NEW ATTITUDE

The first time around, I was sort of okay with denial. I didn't encourage [my involvement in] any handling of personal finances, his will and so forth. I [thereafter learned that] denial is not fair to anyone, and refusal to look reality in the eye is not helpful.

I realized that my role is to support and help in any way possible. This includes having a great attitude. That's one of the things I'm learning in my "aging and sage-ing"—that attitude is so important in work, relationships, family, home [life] and especially when your partner is going through a serious health challenge. Just be there to support, encourage and be a cheerleader.

I TOOK POSITIVE ACTION AGAINST STRESS

The stress was immeasurable. My hair began to fall out and my previously lush locks were now straggly strands. However, when I'm scared and undergoing a lot of stress, taking positive action helps me. Research and reading helped. I found a great article about an island where "people forget to die." I carried it around with me everywhere and would show it to people, telling them that they had to read it.[50]

LISTENING AND LOVING

Your role is to be a true partner, to give love and support as much as

---

50 "The Island Where People Forget to Die", *The New York Times*, October 12, 2012.

needed. Listening is an act of love. That's the best thing you can do…just listen and not say a word.

Serious Illness of a Parent

We are a population that is living longer than ever before. It naturally follows that the chances of having to one day care for an ill parent have greatly increased. Additionally, caregivers of ill parents are often in the position of simultaneously caring for their families, which presents even greater challenges in terms of time, energy and even financial outlay.

From an emotional standpoint, that ill person isn't just a "case"—they are also the one who nursed us when *we* were ill. What happens when roles reverse—and what happens when you are on the threshold of adulthood and you are thrown into a role that only you are able to fulfill?

Tory's story

I was like any other high-school graduate until the day my mother was diagnosed with breast cancer. I immediately became Mom's caregiver, driving her to treatments, grocery shopping when she wasn't feeling up to it and taking her to get her hair done. I rubbed her back when she was vomiting after chemo, and hung out with her on the days that she didn't want to get out of bed.

There was a remission in her illness, at which point I moved to Maui. Because I had stayed home during my freshman year of college to care for Mom, this was a big move; it was the first time I lived on my own. Almost two years to the day after I moved to Maui, I received a call from Dad, saying that Mom's cancer had metastasized and that she had approximately three months to live. The news was devastating. I put my condo up for sale, arranged to have my dog watched until I could fly her to California and moved home the following day.

I began managing all the duties that Mom had been responsible for: cooking, cleaning, laundry, grocery shopping and accounts for our family business, as well as helping manage doctor appointments and medication regimens. After trying two types of chemo, we were told there were no other options and that making her comfortable should be our priority. We then found a naturopath and enjoyed it so much that I started taking massage therapy classes at night so I would have a tool to help Mom manage her pain. I now have a massage practice.

My mother lived three and a half years past her recurrence date. Her quality of life was our number one priority: we continued to travel, laugh and maintain traditions. There was certainly a power struggle, but as with any relationship, we worked on our differences and came to a common ground.

I watched my mother take her final breath. It was an intimate, peaceful moment, shared only with my father, brother, Mom's sister and our dog, Bailey.

WE DID NOT DESERVE THIS

"Why me" was literally my first response. I had done everything "by the book" and I had the "perfect family." How the hell could this happen to *me*? I was a good kid. I had maintained a 4.0 grade point average and had a scholarship to college. Mom was an awesome mom. She didn't deserve this—and I certainly didn't deserve a world without Mom in it.

It didn't take me long to realize that the word "deserve" should be eliminated from the dictionary.

WHAT DO I DO *NOW*?

I had two very distinct "What do I do now" moments. The first was when I was living in Maui and my dad called to tell me Mom's cancer returned. The last thing he said to me during that phone call was "What are we going to do?" Following my arrival home, I became the team captain and "lead question-asker." The following three and a half years were filled with "What do I do now" moments.

The other "What do I do now" moment was when Mom passed away. I was angry and heartbroken but above all, I had no idea what to do. I had been so organized and one step ahead while she was sick. But this time, I felt like I'd failed miserably. Literally every moment of the last three and a half years had been scheduled, and I never considered that she would *actually* pass away. I hadn't made an after-she-dies grief plan.

TURNING GRIEF INTO ACTION

I was a month and a half shy of my twenty-fifth birthday when my mom passed away. I thought that by twenty-five I'd have a college degree, a career, a husband, a house, etc. After a self-pity party (and a few cocktails), I decided I was going to do something about it.

After Mom's passing, my brother, my father and I purchased one-way tickets to Bangkok, Thailand via Maui with the intention of healing. We scattered Mom's ashes on her favorite beach in Maui and then spent months backpacking Thailand. It was a life-changing experience.

The caregiving experience is something most people are going to face in their lives (there are sixty-five million informal caregivers in the United States). I thought that perhaps there was a way I could help others. While traveling in Thailand, I began outlining *The Medical Day Planner,*[51] a guide to help caregivers and patients stay organized throughout the care process.

TOMORROW BRINGS AN OPPORTUNITY FOR CHANGE

Caregiving is an exhausting, selfless act of love. We become caregivers because we *care.* That doesn't mean that you stop caring for yourself in the meantime. Delegate tasks, ask for help, find time to do what it is that you love and have a life outside of caregiving. There will come a point when your caregiving duties come to an end and more than ever, it is then that you realize you still have a life outside of caregiving.

The process is ongoing, and it's important to remember that the process is always changing. There is always tomorrow…and tomorrow is an opportunity to wake up with a different outlook, attitude or feeling. The opportunity for change is always present.

---

51 To learn more about Tory and *The Medical Day Planner* (Victory Belt Publishing), please visit www.toryzellick.com.

Serious Illness of a Child

It was in the overnight hours a few years ago that Kendall fell ill—literally. She was so sick that she had lost consciousness and as she fainted, she hit her head on the bathtub. After a frantic call to 911 and a hurried ambulance ride, one of the paramedics took me off to one side in the emergency room and informed me that when they had taken her pulse, her rate was forty.

I felt my insides turn to stone.

Kendall later remarked that she felt silly having her mother in the emergency room with her. After all, she was in her early twenties and took that to mean that as an adult, she should no longer be reliant on a parent during crises.

I listened to her, gently kissed her on her cheek and responded, "You may have outgrown childhood…but I will *never* outgrow motherhood."

Without a doubt, it was one of the smartest things that I have ever said—and spoken on behalf of mothers everywhere.

Let's face it. Despite what our children would prefer to think, no one knows them like we do. We know *everything* about our children: their personalities, their quirks and their idiosyncrasies. Everything there is to know…we know.[52]

We also know when something just isn't right—and when something is not right, it strikes cold fear into our hearts. We put on a smile for our children and reassure them that everything is going to be okay—while our insides turn to Jello. We make bargains with our higher power to spare our child and give their pains and trials to us as we try to convince ourselves that everything *is* going to be okay.

But sometimes everything *isn't* okay.

Shannon is a bubbly and extraordinarily intelligent young woman with big goals, big dreams and an even bigger heart. If you utter the words "I need…", Shannon is already on the case. She's a woman of action, a true go-getter.

Shannon has also endured a difficult set of challenges, first with the death of her husband and soon followed by the diagnosis of her son with a serious illness. Her story is one of both heartbreak and hope for parents everywhere.

---

52 Usually well before *they* do.

Shannon's story

My story begins like many: I met a boy and fell in love. Unfortunately, the ending was not "…and they lived happily ever after." I married Tim on November 1, 2003. We had our son, Lucas, on August 3, 2007. On May 6, 2008, Tim was killed on his way to work when a semi failed to yield to oncoming traffic. At the time that Tim died, I was twenty-six years old, he was twenty-nine years old and Lucas was nine months old. I had to reconfigure my life so that I could financially take care of my son, our house and our lives.

By June 2010, I had my daughter Ashlynn and although still single, I was moving forward in my life. Lucas (then three years old) had stopped walking. His daycare facility thought that he'd been playing a game, as he was sitting down a lot and dragging himself along the ground. I was quickly aware that he was unable to hold his weight on his legs.

In a panic, I took him to our local hospital. After a few blood tests and without much explanation, they put us into an ambulance and rushed us off to a larger hospital about an hour from home. The following two weeks were spent in the hospital with Lucas undergoing testing. Sitting in a hospital room and fearing for the life of my child, all I wanted was my [late] husband.

After what seemed an eternity, we received a diagnosis: Lucas was diagnosed with Becker's Muscular Dystrophy. In some ways, that diagnosis brought relief, as we could finally a put name to what was ailing Lucas and we could form a plan of action. It was also crushing, as this disease is not well-studied and does not currently have a cure.

Please Let It Be Me Instead

When Lucas was diagnosed, I pleaded with God to help me understand why I was being handed so much at such a young age. I was very angry for a long time after Lucas was diagnosed. I was angry with Tim for being gone. I was scared that Lucas was going to die before me and how unfair that was. I begged for it to be me and not him.

Let Him Be a Kid

After having already gone through immense tragedies prior to Lucas' hospitalization, I was an emotional wreck for quite some time following his diagnosis. I didn't socialize, and I kept to home and my school work. I couldn't handle going to meetings about Lucas' illness as I was simply terrified.

I still have a hard time not sobbing when he tells me that his legs hurt. However, his doctors told me to let him be a kid and that's what I focus on the most—letting him be a kid.

I Am Where I Am Supposed to Be

I learned to put one foot in front of the other and allow myself to feel how I need to feel. I spent a lot of time telling myself what I should be feeling, and I let people tell me what I should be doing. I learned to be free with my emotions. I am where I'm supposed to be.

With Lucas's diagnosis, I have tried to take a deep breath and let life lead the way. I've had to learn to let him be a kid because for the most part, he's a normal boy. Yes, we have rough days, and there are plenty of times where I have cussed Tim out for not being here to share this difficult path. But now, I try to have a more active role in fundraising for the Muscular Dystrophy Association[53] in hopes that they can find a cure for Lucas.

Finding Smiles in the Little Things

When you are a parent of a child with special needs, remember to take time to breathe. It's okay to take breaks because a happy mommy is a good mommy. If you are feeling stressed, find a sitter and go to a movie or dinner with a friend. It's really okay, and you need to give yourself permission to do so.

You also need to be aware of your limitations. Don't feel ashamed if you need to ask for help. Make sure you are well educated on the disorder or disease that your child has so that you're aware of what you need to be doing—but don't forget that you know your child best. Some of the best advice I got was

---

53 For more information on the Muscular Dystrophy Association and other resources and support for patients and families affected by over forty neuromuscular diseases, please visit www.mda.org.

to let Lucas be a kid. It's important to keep them safe, but more important that they enjoy life.

It's natural to worry, but don't let worry become central to your life. Focus on the little things that make you all happy. Some of our best days are when we sit down as a family and make popcorn, watch movies, play board games and put puzzles together. Those are the moments that count.

HOW YOU CAN HELP

Hearing that someone you care about has been diagnosed with a serious illness is terrible—but it is not nearly as terrible for you as it is for those affected. News of an illness remains one of the most common situations where I hear "I just don't/ didn't know what to say" from those who surround a patient and their family.

This is not the time for you to recoil in fear because you cannot find words. Rather, this is your time to shine as a beacon of strength. Even if you aren't feeling strong on the inside (and that's absolutely normal), as you have learned, you need to save those feelings for when you are on your own. It is now time for you to be the person that those in need can depend on.

Definite Do's

- **Inquire about the condition with a willingness to hear an honest response:** *"How are you **really** feeling today?"*; *"What's going on today?"*; *"What's the latest?"*

  Take a quick review of Chapter One ("How Can I Help") and the story of Joel and Rob. Remember, they never hesitated to ask Mike how he was feeling, and in doing so they acknowledged what he was going through.

- **Show sincere interest in the situation:** *"What's the doctor saying?"*; *"How is treatment going?"*; *"What are the next steps?"*

  Here again, you are creating an atmosphere where the patient or caregiver can share not only the particulars of what is going on, but also share their feelings; both good and bad (and there will be a mix of both).

- **Call or email before you pay a visit:** *"I'd love to come by and see you—is* [date and time of day] *good for you?"; "What can I bring for you?"*

  Always contact the household before paying a visit. Your schedule is not necessarily their schedule, and you never know what is going on within the household or with the illness at any given time.

- **If medically permissible and appropriate to your relationship, continue physical affection with the patient:** I fondly recall the nighttimes, when Kendall was asleep and I'd gotten Mike into his hospital bed for the night. We would tune into late-night reruns of *Friends* and *MASH* and I would sit as close to the bed as the chair would allow. I would take his hand (by now completely atrophied by the illness) and manually interlock his fingers with mine. I hugged, kissed and continued as much tactile connection as possible. Mike was a very affectionate person and even though he could no longer physically reciprocate, he loved that we sustained as much of a physical connection as the illness permitted.

  Similarly, I strongly encouraged Mike's visitors to both greet him and depart with a hug, kiss, handshake (the visitor would physically pick up Mike's hand and grasp it) or however they would have greeted him absent illness. It was a subtle way of reminding him that despite the illness, he was *still* Mike…and though he may have appeared and sounded different, he was still the same teddy bear of a guy.

  You too can continue whatever level of affection that you enjoyed with the patient, as long as it is not medically dangerous to do so. Greet the patient with a hug, kiss, handshake or in whatever fashion you would have prior to the illness. Even if they are unable to reciprocate, affection still contributes to helping the patient feel more normal and less like an "illness" or a "disease."

- **Keep normal life as a part of the patient or caregiver's life:** *"You won't believe what's going on at the office right now"; "Did you see* [a television show, the latest Internet sensation] *last night?"; "How are the kids doing in school?"*

  While illness definitely needs to be acknowledged and discussed, the patient does not want to focus exclusively on the illness that has upended their life. Despite illness, life does continue, and patients battling serious illness still want to enjoy as normal a life as they are capable. This includes conversations about work, kids, relationships, the latest reality television fiascos, the current prices at the gas pump or whatever else contributes to feeling as normal as possible under the circumstances.

  Also feel free to share what is going on in your life without feeling like you are burdening the patient with your problems or that your life is somehow insignificant in comparison. Conversations such as these can act almost as a respite from what has invaded a once-peaceful household.

- **If the patient or caregiver are able, offer to take them out for coffee, a meal or some other pleasant diversion:** Nothing feels better than a temporary break from illness, disease, doctors, insurance companies and anything else that is associated with illness and disease. It can be just a couple of hours out, but what a difference a couple of hours can make. It can give a patient a feeling of normalcy, and it can refresh and revive a weary caregiver.

  On the occasions that we were able to go out, I loved the fact that someone else was bringing food and cleaning up afterward. It did not matter if we were at a sit-down restaurant or a fast-food joint—just periodically being out for a little while did wonders for me, which in turn helped me to be a better caregiver to Mike and parent to Kendall.

Without a Doubt...Don't

- **Don't trivialize either the illness or a patient's feelings about it:** *"Don't be afraid"; "You'll be fine"; "Doctors are wrong all the time."*

  Statements such as these essentially shut down the patient's need to talk about their illness and their feelings concerning what the future holds. They don't know if they're going to recover. They don't know what they may have to go through in order to get well—or they may know *exactly* what treatment entails and it is frightening. Whatever the case, they need to be able to discuss the general uncertainty of the situation. They do not need to be concerned with the true undercurrent of statements like these—that you are too uncomfortable with their illness for them to speak frankly.

- **Don't negatively compare their situation to your own experience or to the experience of someone else you know or knew:** *"I went through the same thing and got so sick, I wished I were dead"; "I knew someone who had the same thing and they* [died or suffered some kind of terrible consequences].*"*

  Have you ever noticed that no one ever tells a story that goes, "I knew someone with the same illness and absolutely nothing terrible happened as a result." It always seems to be the horror stories that get shared.

  When I was twenty-six years old, I underwent a tonsillectomy, which is not as simple as undergoing the same surgery when you are five years old. Between the time that surgery was scheduled and the surgery itself, I was regaled with numerous stories of others' unimaginable pain, massive hemorrhaging and worse. I couldn't help wondering how *any* of those stories were supposed to help me. Now, a tonsillectomy is not a serious illness or a major surgery—can you imagine how it must feel to be an audience to horror stories when you are actually dealing with a set of horrific circumstances?

  There is no advantage to be served in talking about any kind of potentially negative or scary outcome. The point is to lift the patient and provide them with hope and optimism, not add to the storm of fear that is already brewing.

- **Don't criticize or otherwise question treatment protocols:** *"Doctors don't know anything, you need to see…*[someone who is not medically trained]*"*; *"You shouldn't do that treatment, you should do* [anything that is potentially unhealthy or illegal, against a treating physician's orders or that is medically unproven or unsound].*"*

  Unless you are a doctor who specializes in whatever illness from which the patient is suffering, your job is to offer support and a kind ear, not to question a treatment regimen or a patient's judgment. If you have heard something interesting on the medical front that may pertain to the patient's illness, you might inquire as to whether they or their doctor has heard this interesting news; however, direct suggestion of alternative or unconventional treatments (as well as any that may be illegal or dangerous to the patient's health) are completely inappropriate.

- **Don't insist on visiting if the patient or family requests no visitors:** *"I'm coming over and I'm not taking no for an answer"*; *"I'm on my way over right now."*

  Your need to visit will always be outweighed by what is going on with the patient, as well as with those charged with the patient's care. If you are asked not to visit on a particular day or at a certain time, you must realize that there is a good reason why a patient and/ or whoever is caring for them is making that request. You are obligated to respect either the delicate balance of the household that is coping with serious illness, or if it is a hospital or other facility, the rules of that facility.

  When visitors are present, everyone (including the patient) feels they have to entertain. You cannot assume that simply because someone is ill, that they (or their family members) wish to entertain visitors. A household that is dealing with serious illness is not like a twenty-four-hour convenience store that is open whenever you feel like dropping in—and out of concern for their patients' welfare, hospitals are very rigid when it comes to visitors.

If you wish to visit a patient and you are told that the particular day or time that you have selected is not convenient, be understanding in asking when a better time to visit would be—and then honor the request.

- **Don't *ever* drop in on a patient unannounced, whether they are in their home or in a hospital or other facility:** *"I was in the neighborhood and thought I'd stop by"; "SURPRISE!"; "This was the only time I had available to visit."*

  This is not only rude and inconsiderate to the patient and all members of the household, you do not know that you won't be interrupting a treatment or preventing the patient and/or their caregivers from getting necessary rest.

  I recall one Sunday when a visitor dropped in unannounced. Not only didn't we have caregiving help on Sundays, Mike and I had also been up all night long the night before with his respiratory difficulties. We were both exhausted and in no mood to do anything but close our eyes—yet despite several subtle hints, the guest did not feel compelled to leave...for almost five grueling hours.

  This sort of "surprise" is inconsiderate to any patient as well as to the people or facility that are charged with their care. P.S.: Caregivers need rest too.

- **Don't proselytize or otherwise "force" spirituality where it may not be welcome (Part I):** *"What doesn't kill you makes you stronger"; "God has a plan"; "Now is the time for you to think about...* [joining or converting to a religion with which the patient is currently unaffiliated]. *"*

  Even the most spiritual people do not necessarily want to hear about "God's plan" or anything along these lines. The same holds for attempting to convert someone to another faith during what is likely one of the most frightening times in their life—and if they do not happen to be spiritual, you have not only crossed a serious line, you are likely going to be asked not to return.

If a patient and their family need spiritual counsel or guidance, they will say so and they will solicit it accordingly. No matter how well intentioned, unless you know the patient and their family very well and you know them to be of a spiritual nature, opening this line of conversation is improper at best and, at worst, incredibly offensive and upsetting to patient and family alike.

- **Don't stay away because you "can't handle it":** *"I can't stand to see you/him/her 'that way'"; "Sick people creep me out"; "What if I catch what they have?"*

  First, if there is any danger of you catching whatever a patient is fighting, you will be disallowed from visiting at all. The week prior to Mike's death, I had a terrible case of the flu and while very sympathetic to my need to be with him, his doctors and the medical staff understandably would not let me anywhere near him.

  As to being "creeped out," I invite you to revisit Chapter Ten ("Life's Lightning Strike: Serious Injury"). Just as with serious injury, this is not about you or your discomfort. No one is saying, "Don't be sad" or "Don't be upset." You just do not get to use your feelings as an excuse to avoid a difficult situation. You will also be conspicuous by your absence. People *do* notice.

FROM BAD THING TO BRIGHTER DAYS AHEAD

There is no denying that serious illness is one of the scariest bad things that you will ever encounter. Regardless of how or to whom this particular bad thing is happening, your best allies are always going to be education, support, proactivity and perseverance. Whether you are the patient or the caregiver, do not try to cope with serious illness on your own. There is wonderful support available to you, and all you need to do is reach out for it.

Most importantly, remember that where there is life, there is hope...and where there is hope, there is life.

Chapter Twelve

When "Get Well Soon" Takes a Sad Turn: The Matter of Terminal Illness

LITTLE IS MORE FRIGHTENING IN LIFE THAN REALIZING THAT A SERIOUS illness is not going to be cured and the patient transitions from chronic to acute...to terminal.

A fun subject? Hardly—and yet it is one of the most important subjects that we can discuss. Why? While it's almost unbearably painful, being part of another person's sunset is one of the most unselfish kindnesses that we can ever show to another—because it is a kindness that can never be repaid.

Jodi O'Donnell-Ames knows what it is like to live with ALS, as she lost her beloved husband, Kevin, to the illness. She shares her story of receiving the diagnosis, their journey as a family and how she overcame her grief by helping others do the same.

Jodi's story

I married Kevin in 1992, we were blessed with our daughter Alina and we were on top of the world. Kevin was thereafter diagnosed with ALS and my world came crashing down. I became Kevin's nurse, his arms and his voice.

I realized how fortunate I was to have had six years to say goodbye to him. I counted my blessings.

In 2007, I started Hope Loves Company,[54] the only nonprofit in the United States that supports the children of ALS patients. Miracles do happen, and my life and happiness returned.

Proactivity in the Face of Uncertainty

I wasn't angry, just very sad for all of us. How did my young, healthy, handsome husband get this terminal illness? I immediately wanted to learn everything about ALS in order to be proactive in the fight. I was depressed and needed to take action. If I didn't use that energy for advocating, I'm not sure I would have lasted.

Caregiving Led to Advocacy

From the time that I was young, I was a natural caregiver, and the nurturing skills kicked in and supported our journey with ALS. I was a nurse twenty-four hours a day, seven days a week for six years. Kevin was on a ventilator, he was paralyzed, he had a feeding tube and could not speak. When he died, there was an empty hole.

After his death, I had all the time in the world and no one to share it with. I remember many sleepless nights, and I sent out an email at 2:00 a.m., asking someone to *please* give me a job, a purpose. I got a response and started my work as the Director of Communications at the ALS Hope Foundation. That job was the catalyst for much more to come.

A New Purpose Healed My Pain

Six years after losing Kevin, my skills and experiences were woven into a purpose. I understood my role in the process of healing and giving. I'd remarried and was raising three children, all of whom lost a parent to ALS. I observed how my loss could help others so I became an EMT in order to give

---

54 To learn more about Jodi and Hope Loves Company, please visit www.hopelovescompany.com.

back to my community. I trained to be a certified massage therapist because massage helped Kevin greatly. I then started Hope Loves Company. The more I did, the more my purpose evolved and healed my pain.

I am happy now. I'm remarried, I have three amazing kids and I wake each day excited about reaching out to ALS families. I *love* who I am and what I'm doing. Most of all, Kevin is always with me, as I continue our ALS work in his memory.

RESPECT AND LOVE YOURSELF

Everyone needs time to heal from enormous loss so be gentle with yourself. There is no "normal." Respect and love yourself enough to accept the ingredients for healing: love, support and patience.

Surround yourself with positive people. If you are having a difficult time becoming the person you want to be, find that person or a group of them and immerse yourself. Wellness is contagious! Keep positive quotes around your home, embrace your journey and acknowledge that you're doing the best you can.

HOW YOU CAN HELP

When terminal illness strikes someone you know (or one of their family members), you have the opportunity to show grace, compassion and strength as someone faces the end of their life. You can provide comfort to both the patient and those who surround them. Sadly, this is also a time that many people tend to either shy away or disappear into the woodwork altogether, as if their sudden absence will go unnoticed. You can choose to be there when others may choose otherwise…there are few greater gifts that you will ever be able to provide.

Definite Do's

- **Check in on other members of the household:** Are people eating regularly? Are there children who are in need of rides to school, help with homework or just a hug and a willing ear? Make offers of help when and how you are able. One of the best offers that we received came from another family at our synagogue who offered to have Kendall to their house for a weekend respite. Their lovely gesture gave Kendall a badly-needed break from the reality of the household and just let her be a kid—something that goes by the wayside when there is a terminal illness in the family.

- **Send greeting cards:** Not e-cards…actual, need-to-put-a-stamp-on-it greeting cards. Because a terminal illness is involved, you don't want to send anything that reads "Get Well Soon" because the sorry reality is otherwise. However, a card to let the patient or caregiver know that you are thinking about them is perfect—and do not be afraid to send (appropriately) humorous cards too. During such a difficult time, a laugh—any way you can get it—is welcome and appreciated.

- **It's okay to be honest about your feelings:** One of my favorite stories involves the bartender of our favorite restaurant who had become a close friend over the years. We dined at the restaurant on our wedding anniversary, which by unfortunate coincidence was Mike's first day in a wheelchair…and even sadder, the last time that he was able to go to that restaurant.

  As was our tradition, we went into the bar to enjoy a drink after dinner with the bartender. The two men engaged in their usual round of insults, telling each other how ugly they were and so forth.[55] While this typical nonsense was going on, the bartender very subtly passed me a note. I excused myself to the restroom and opened the note.

  It read only, "I want to cry."

  I loved that note so much. It let me know that in the midst of

---

55 I can just imagine ordering martinis with my best friend and then telling her that she was so ugly, she must have bribed someone to marry her. I will never understand male bonding.

behaving as normally as possible under the circumstances, our friend was also letting me know how devastated he was to see Mike obviously progressing in the illness.

It is perfectly okay to be honest about your feelings. It *is* awful. It *is* scary. You *will* want to cry. It's also very comforting when those who surround you acknowledge these things.

Without a Doubt…Don't

- **Don't make light of the situation or instill false hope:** *"There's going to be a miracle"; "You're not going to die"; "You're going to beat this"; "When you get well, we're going to…*[participate in an activity, travel or something that is likely not going to happen].*"*

One of the reasons that doctors take so long prior to issuing a terminal diagnosis is because "terminal" is the absolute *last* diagnosis that they want to give. Doctors do not take pleasure in rendering a dismal diagnosis and a gloomy future. It then follows that if a patient has been diagnosed as terminal, they are indeed likely terminal. It is true that doctors cannot pinpoint time frames with one hundred percent accuracy and they would be the first to say so. However, if a doctor says that someone is terminal, respect must be paid to that diagnosis and the reality that comes along with it.

When you deny a patient's reality, you are also denying them the very real need to talk about what is happening to them. A pleasant attitude is one thing, but pretending that the situation does not carry the gravity that it carries is wrong. When you acknowledge the situation at hand, you have also given the patient permission to talk, cry, laugh, rant or, in short, feel however they feel at that moment (and those moods swing widely and frequently). Creating that environment for the patient is paramount to providing comfort at such a difficult time.

- **On the other hand, don't "bury the living" either:** *"What's the point in* [treatments, therapies, etc]*; you're not going to get better"; "You should let nature take its course"; "Have you planned your funeral yet?"*

  If the patient has been prescribed any kind of treatment whatso-ever, it is your job to support that decision, whether you agree or not. The treatment may be palliative in nature and may help them feel more comfortable during an otherwise painful process. It may slow the progression of the illness. It may be experimental, and seeing no harm in trying something new on the medical horizon, the patient is willingly participating in a clinical trial, or has given permission to have an experimental medication administered. Whatever the case, the decision is not yours to make, and, to put it mildly, these suggestions and opinions are unwelcome.

  The same goes for funeral planning. Unless you are an immediate family member (and I mean *damn* immediate), the discussion of funeral plans is not your subject to broach. If the patient brings up any specific wishes or things that they would like you to handle or be part of, by all means, do not shut them down. Listen care-fully, ask questions if necessary and take them seriously. Otherwise, bringing up this most sensitive of subjects is inappropriate.

- **Don't proselytize (Part II):** *"Have you gotten right with God?"; "You need to start praying right now"; "I'm going to bring some people over from my* [house of worship or religious affiliation] *to talk to you."*

  In the interest of time and publishing real estate, I could simply refer you back to Part I of don't proselytize; however, this area seri-ously does warrant a quick revisit.

  As with any other areas where you might be called into a bad-thing support role, this is *not* about you right now and that includes your religious beliefs. If you wish to pray for the comfort, peace and welfare of the patient and their family, I am all for it—I do it too.

If seeking comfort for your own heart is accomplished with prayer or meditation, I wholeheartedly encourage it. However, unless a patient or their loved ones ask you specifically to pray with them or otherwise participate in spiritual pursuit, the time for proselytizing is not now.[56]

Spirituality is intensely personal. Even those who are atheist or agnostic are intense in their beliefs. It is your job to respect and support the beliefs of the patient. Remember that if a patient and their family are in need of spiritual guidance, *they* will be the ones to seek it. If your spiritual support is needed, believe me, you will be sought out.

No matter how well-intentioned, forcing your beliefs on someone who is terminally ill and not in a position to tell you what you need to hear (which may well be along the lines of "Shut up and get out") is taking advantage of someone at their most vulnerable. It is not okay and you will only serve to upset everyone intimately involved with the situation.

- **Don't discuss financial end-of-life matters:** *"Am I in your will?";* *"Who gets the life insurance?"; "Can I have your* [items, assets, belongings, valuables] *after you're gone?"; "I know a great* [estate] *lawyer."*

  The fact that this even has to be addressed is disgusting; however, the reason that it must be addressed is because these words (and worse) have actually been spoken to terminally ill patients and/or their families. Get into that hospital bed or into that wheelchair for just a moment. How would *you* feel if someone—*anyone*—began inquiring as to who gets your car, and how much money you are leaving, and to whom the checks are being written?

  Whether you are an immediate family member or not, questions such as these are almost macabre in nature. If you are a

---

56 I am not entirely sure that there is ever a "good time" for proselytizing, but I do know that there are really wrong times for it. This would be one of them.

family member who is genuinely concerned about the whereabouts of paperwork or the existence of necessary legal documents at all, by all means, speak up—to the caregiver or another close family member...*not* to the patient.

Let me also be very clear: Regardless of with whom you are speaking, rendering legal advice or direction or, even worse, submitting a "wish list" consisting of what you want after the patient is no longer here is reprehensible. You will be thought of as the metaphorical vulture whose behavior you are imitating.

When my father was diagnosed with liver cancer and his condition was declared terminal, the first thing that I asked after was the whereabouts of his will. When he sheepishly admitted that he did not have an updated will prepared, I scurried to put together a standard will in accordance with the laws of the state; a task that my legal degree enabled me to do. As both his daughter and someone who is fluent in the language of legalese, it was appropriate for me to ask these questions and act accordingly in order to protect my entire family—and I was legally qualified to do so.

However, even as his daughter, I never asked who got what, or what was "in it" for me, or when I could plunder his household for valuables. I instead let him do the talking and rightfully allowed him to control the disposition of his modest estate in the manner that he saw fit.

If you are genuinely concerned about legal documents, and/or if financial or legal matters might potentially cause complications later on, speak *privately* to a family member about the situation. Otherwise, these subjects are off limits.

From Bad Thing to Brighter Days Ahead

There is no gentle way to say it. When dealing with terminal illness, things are going to get worse before they get better. However, you also have the opportunity to line up resources so that when the time comes, you will have a sense of guidance, direction and the knowledge that you do not have to cope alone. When you surround yourself with healing tools (books, CDs, etc.); a support system (either online or in-person); education (wherever and however you can get it) and community (of those who understand what you have been through), you are taking proactive measures in preparing your Healing Journey, and you are taking as much control over the situation as humanly possible.

As I previously expressed in *Happily Even After,*[57] you will want to do the very best you can to take care of yourself health-wise—and do *not* be shy about asking for help if you need it. As previously shared, I mistakenly felt that asking for help was akin to being a failure or incapable of taking care of my family—a mistake that it took me a full year (and a few loving but firm threats from several family members) to rectify. In other words, if you receive offers from people to stay with your loved one while you get some badly needed rest or take a couple of hours away from the house or hospital, accept the offer...if for no other reason than the sake of your own health,

I wish you as much peace as is possible as you continue on this most challenging journey, knowing that when the time arrives, help and support is close at hand.

---

57 *Happily Even After: A Guide to Getting Through (and Beyond) the Grief of Widowhood* (Viva Editions). All rights reserved.

Chapter Thirteen

BEYOND THE VEIL AND ACROSS THE BRIDGE

> *"Grief is the tremendous price that we pay when we love*
> *fully, passionately, joyfully and unconditionally;*
> *with abandon and without measure or limits.*
> *It is an admittedly painful and difficult cost…*
> *…but how empty life would be*
> *if we chose against paying that price*
> *and instead kept our love locked away*
> *forever in our hearts."*

DEATH IS INDEED THE GREAT EQUALIZER. REGARDLESS OF WHO WE ARE, THE walk of life from which we hail or what we have achieved during our lifetime, death is the inevitability from which no one escapes. It is something by which all of us will be touched and forever changed as a result. Further, not only are we guaranteed to be touched by the loss of loved ones of all manner and relationship, we will also be called upon to console and provide sympathy to those who are suffering the greatest of all pain.

While news of a death is supposed to bring out the absolute best, most compassionate side of the human spirit, through many years, hundreds of thousands of letters and listening to thousands of stories, I have sadly learned that death also has the capability of bringing out the absolute worst in people—or at the very least, abject stupidity and ignorance.

Not very diplomatic…but a truth nonetheless.

Welcome to what I believe to be vitally important "loss etiquette" education: how to provide comfort to those suffering from devastating loss at a time when they perhaps have never needed comfort more.

We begin with the basics—meant to help anyone that is mourning the loss of a loved one.

Definite Do's

- **Express genuine sympathy:** *"I am so sorry; there really aren't any words at a time like this"; "I can't even imagine the pain you're in right now"; "We're going to get you through this."*

  Your goal is to provide immediate comfort and a sense of strength and security to someone whose world has been rocked, as well as reinforcement that they are not facing this bleakest of seasons alone. Remember to resist the urge to say, "I know how you feel," because as you learned in Chapter One ("How Can I Help?"), this is not about you or your experiences—not right now.

- **Create an environment where talking is encouraged and your willingness to listen is at the ready:** *"You might not be ready to talk about it right now, but when you're ready, I'm here and I want to listen."*

  Most who have experienced loss really *do* want to discuss it—maybe not on the same day as the loss itself, but eventually, they will want to talk to someone who actually cares. The aftereffects of loss linger long after the funeral is over and one of the best healing tools in the world is a kind ear. Choose to be that kind ear by letting someone know that you are there for them and that you will continue to be there to listen, to hold a hand and to wipe away a tear. Do not be one of those people who plays "Loss Over = Gloss Over", for it is when everyone else has "gone home and gone on" that you will be needed the most.

Without a Doubt…Don't

Though you will see a number of "Don'ts" in this chapter, the biggest "Don't" that I can possibly convey is:

Don't use clichés.

Ever.

The one complaint most prevalent in the bereaved community concerns those who try to provide comfort through the use of worn-out, canned, contrived, trite, heard-it-a-million-times clichés. You have seen a number of them already—here are a few more of the most often used (and despised) clichés that need to be disposed of immediately:

- *"He/She lived a long life"*: The fact that someone was on earth for decades does not make the loss easier. It also sends the subliminal message that because someone reached their golden years prior to passing away, you have no business mourning the loss.

- *"He/She was so young"*: The death of a young person is indeed tragic. There is no reason to hold a magnifying glass over that tragedy by emphasizing someone's youth.

- *You should be celebrating/rejoicing"*: Usually said in a religious context, it has been my experience that even among the most faithful, "celebrating" or "rejoicing" is the furthest thing from anyone's mind during the most immediate time of loss. The time may come where celebrating and rejoicing will occur. Now is not it.

- *"Death is part of life"*: Everyone over the age of five years knows that. What no one has yet been able to explain to me is why any adult would actually believe this to be an expression of sympathy.

And let us not forget everyone's favorite, the one cliché that everyone seems to get told and, accordingly, seems to provoke an understandable amount of ire:

"Everything Happens for a Reason"

You have seen this phrase included a number of times throughout the "Don'ts" in the book and the reason is obvious. It is used *way* too often and *way* too unsuccessfully.

Again, if a bereaved person looks at you and says in all earnest, "I believe that everything happens for a reason," by all means, get behind her belief system. However, if your idea of comforting someone is using this phrase, you need to work on your originality and compassion skills. After stifling the very strong desire to step on your foot while wearing heels, she will walk away from you thinking, "What possible reason could there be for my having to endure this pain?"

Now that the basic rules are behind us, you are about to meet a number of incredibly courageous women, all of whom have faced painfully difficult losses. Get ready for a growth experience like none other.

Here Today, Gone Later Today:
Sudden Loss

A husband and wife kiss goodbye in the morning and one of the two is widowed by evening. A teenage athlete in seemingly perfect health collapses on a playing field. A grandparent had a minor illness that took an abrupt and tragic turn.

A sudden death levies an incredible shock to the human condition. It is a quake of the soul that cannot be measured on any Richter scale. It also calls for swift action on the part of those most closely involved, for they have been catapulted into a situation for which they were likely completely unprepared.

Following is the story of Nicole*, who shares her story of the sudden loss of her husband at a very young age, and how she went on to find a new life after unimaginable tragedy.

Nicole's story

I met Lee* at my old job and soon after I left, we started dating and fell in love quickly. We built a life together, got married and had a son shortly afterward. As he was on his way to work one day, Lee was killed [in an automobile accident]. No warnings, no goodbyes, no preparation…just gone. Our entire life together shredded in the blink of an eye. I didn't get to say "I love you" one more time. I didn't get to kiss him goodbye in his last moments. I didn't get to ask him what to do, how to prepare or how to raise our child without him. We were both only in our twenties, and we hadn't even reached our fifth wedding anniversary.

HIDING AWAY FROM THE NIGHTMARE

The police came to my work [to inform me what happened] and in that moment, I felt sucked into a vacuum. I couldn't hear, I couldn't think and my brain was screaming at me to wake up because it had to be a nightmare.

I spent hours replaying our final conversation, trying to figure out the "What ifs." What if I'd called him and sent him back to the house? What if he'd taken the van instead of the car? I drove myself crazy trying to change the outcome of that day. We'd just begun our lives together and it wasn't fair. Most days I spent crying and hiding because I simply didn't know how to function.

MAJOR CHANGE LED TO MAJOR SUPPORT

After time passed, I knew that I needed to start moving forward. I sought out counseling. I journaled my feelings. I met other widows through the Widows Wear Stilettos website, and I have those friends to this day. I moved in with my mother to make ends meet (Lee made almost twice as much as I did).

I had people saying the stupidest things to me like "Oh, you'll marry again" and "I don't understand why you've changed." No one but other widows seemed to understand. It was a time of major change in my life.

I Found Purpose and Accomplishment

I was having a talk with a cousin who is a college professor. I mentioned that I'd wanted to go back to school but I couldn't figure out what I wanted to pursue. She asked what it was that I liked the best in the schooling I'd already taken, to which I responded psychology and law. She quickly replied, "Why not criminal justice?"…and that was my answer. I enrolled in classes and as time went on, I found focus through school. It gave me purpose, forced me to follow a schedule, and gave me a feeling of accomplishment.

You Are Not Isolated on Your Journey

I still have moments where Lee's sudden death hits me as hard and as fast as a tidal wave. I still write in my journal when the need arises. I spent a good amount of time reevaluating my relationships and got rid of those that were of no help to me and made some new friendships through school. I learned that it is okay to feel sad because we had an amazing love. I'm allowed to grieve, regardless of what anyone else thinks.

Sudden death is something for which none of us can prepare. It steals our breath. It's as if someone hit the "reset" button on your life. Your slate is wiped clean and you have to figure out how to move again. However, there are better days to be had. You can move forward and feel again.

Cherish your memories and take them forward with you. Never forget that life is precious, and don't waste what's left of yours on things not worth your time. Find something that reminds you how to smile.

HOW YOU CAN HELP

People who are coping with sudden death are in a condition of total shock, trying to move through the fog that takes over mind, body, spirit and soul— and they generally don't know what to do first. Though you may be in a place of shock yourself, you can still be a source of support from the outset.

Definite Do's

- **Determine what needs taking care of immediately:** *"I'm on my way to pick up the kids from school"; "Give me a contact list of people to call (or email)"; "I'm bringing dinner over; how many people are there right now?"*

  It is not at all uncommon to actually forget about children in school or daycare, lose sight of the fact that their house either is or will be full of people or forget that there are people to be called and arrangements to be made. Be their "lookout" by volunteering to do things that you know will need doing and might inadvertently be overlooked.

- **Tell them what you will be doing for them during the next few days:** *"I'll take/pick up the kids from school"; "I'll contact your boss at work"; "Don't worry about dinner on Wednesday."*

  Nobody expects you to move in and take care of an entire household; however, you can still be of help by anticipating what the household will need in the coming days and assume a duty here and there.

Without a Doubt…Don't

- **Ask for explicit details of the loss:** *"What happened exactly?"; "Tell me everything"; "Don't you have more details?"*

  People who are coming to grips with sudden loss will reveal to you exactly what they are comfortable with revealing. To compel someone to disclose any details beyond what you are being told is intrusive at best and horribly insensitive at worst. When you also consider that many situations involving sudden death are not through natural causes, the details involved can be downright gruesome. Depending upon the specific circumstances, and out of respect, even survivors themselves are not made privy to all of the particulars. Why would anyone force a survivor to recount such circumstances?

- **Ask about immediate plans to pursue legal action or give legal advice:** *"Are you going to sue?"*; *"I know a great lawyer"*; *"You should definitely…"* [followed by some kind of legal advice].

  Many sudden losses do have potential legal ramifications, e.g., personal injury, wrongful death, medical malpractice, criminal charges and so on. Unless you are a family member or a lawyer who suspects that a statute of limitations might be in jeopardy, it is not your place to get involved. If she broaches the subject, be the willing ear, but asking about taking legal action in connection with a death is akin to asking about finances—it is personal, it is private and unless you are either a legal expert or a family member who is looking out for best interests, it is not your place.

- **Magnify the tragedy:** *"But I just talked to him/her last night"*; *"He/She seemed just fine"*; *"They looked like the picture of health."*

  The fact that someone "seemed just fine" is not helpful at all. It just serves to amplify the tragic fact that the person who was in their life mere hours before is no longer here.

- **Attempt to offer a "bright side":** *"At least he/she didn't suffer"*; *"You'll find someone else"*; *"You still have other children"*; *"What doesn't kill you makes you stronger."*

  I fully understand that in pointing out that someone did not suffer, an attempt is being made to make someone feel better; no one wants to think in terms of their loved ones suffering in any way. However, the fact that someone did not suffer makes things easier on *them*, not on those left behind. Further, no matter the relationship perspective, no survivor is capable of acting as "replacements" for those who are lost. Please do not suggest otherwise by reminding that there are still other children at home or suggesting that going on a hunt for a partner is a fix-all.

  Finally, I will go on record and say that when people hear "What doesn't kill you makes you stronger," it actually *does* make them strong...strong enough to want to hit the person saying it. This is yet *another* worn-out cliché that does not serve any positive purpose.

There is no bright side here. There is no silver lining. There is only loss, and the grief that accompanies loss must be both acknowledged and respected.

The Longest Sunset:
Loss After Long-Term or Terminal Illness

Yet Another True Story

Whether he was in his police uniform or in his preferred "uniform" of Wrangler jeans, triple-starched Western shirt, cowboy boots and Stetson hat, Mike Fleet was a presence. He did not just enter a room, he commanded it. He was 6'3" and 210 pounds of physicality, whether he was chasing bad guys, training police dogs, riding mounted duty or happily tearing up a dance floor.

Exactly one week after he'd been thrown while training his horse for mounted duty, Mike began having spasms in his left arm. When the spasms worsened, he began treating with a chiropractor and acupuncturist, all to no avail. Thinking that the accident might have exacerbated a decades-old work injury, Mike underwent cervical spine surgery. His neurosurgeon—along with the rest of us—expected the spasms to disappear after recovery from surgery was complete.

A perfect plan...except that the spasms did not go away. In fact, the spasms worsened.

Frustrated, the neurosurgeon sent him to a neurologist, who began the first of what became months of painfully invasive testing. After an initial EMG[58] (which he insisted on attending by himself), Mike returned home with a look on his face that I had never before seen—a look of raw, organic fear. When I

---

58 An EMG (electromyogram) is a test that is used to detect abnormal electrical activity of muscles that occurs in many diseases, including ALS. The test is neither easy nor painless.

asked him what was wrong, he said that the doctor had told him to come back the following day and to "bring your wife." I smiled confidently, gave Mike a lingering hug and handed him a cold beer, while cheerfully reassuring him that of *course* everything was going to be okay.

On the inside, my blood ran cold.

Following what eventually totaled over one year of testing, Mike and I found ourselves sitting in the office of a neuromuscular specialist. After sitting in silence for what felt like an eternity while the doctor carefully re-consulted test results, various doctors' dissertations and the worsening symptoms that had been occurring before his very eyes, the doctor rose from his chair, came around the desk, perched on the edge and placed a sympathetic hand on Mike's shoulder. He then woefully looked into Mike's eyes, started his sentence with, "I'm so sorry..." and then delivered his diagnosis of amyotrophic lateral sclerosis.

ALS.

At that very moment, the entire world stopped.

Let me tell you about ALS. It's a neuromuscular disease that falls under the umbrella of muscular dystrophy. The ubiquitous "they" have no idea what causes this disease, and there is unfortunately yet to be a cure or any treatment that will even slow the progression of the disease.

To put it bluntly, and as you have learned in Chapter 12 ("When 'Get Well Soon' Takes a Sad Turn..."), ALS is indeed a terminal diagnosis.

Although ALS progresses differently in patients, it is nonetheless a disease that slowly robs the patient of the ability to function independently. They generally lose the use of extremities. Their speech can become compromised to the point that they lose the ability to speak altogether. Swallowing is also affected and if eating becomes dangerous, a feeding tube is placed.

In sum, even the most basic abilities and pleasures—bathing, dressing, walking, speaking, eating, drinking and so much more—are stolen away.

Slowly.

Relentlessly.

Torturously.

Eventually, the disease attacks the respiratory system. Some patients choose to undergo a tracheotomy and have ventilation placed. Others like

Mike, choose against this sort of intervention. It is an intensely personal decision that, like it or not, those who surround the patient must respect.

Note that I used the word "respect," not "like." More on that later.

Possibly most cruelly, the disease does not at all affect the patient's mental faculties. The patient is one hundred percent mentally razor sharp and aware of exactly what is happening to them—and they are also 100-percent helpless to stop it. They are ultimately jailed in the "prison" that their body eventually becomes; a prison from which there is only one release...

Death.

Given the fact that Mike absolutely thrived on physical activity, the irony that he was diagnosed with an insidious, evil disease that would rob him of every physical capability imaginable was not lost on any of us.

It just could not be possible.

In my head, ALS happened to the proverbial "someone else."

In the world of disease, ALS was considered to be "rare."[59]

Rare things *always* happen to "someone else"...right?

As have you and likely millions of people around the world, I grew up watching the telethons supporting the Muscular Dystrophy Association. We had telethon-watching parties. We donated to the cause every year. I wiped away tears at the numerous and tragic stories of loss and hope, never once dreaming that *this* kind of "rare" could ever touch our family.

That it *would* touch Mike.

That it would eventually *take* Mike.

ALS.

I knew exactly what those three letters meant.

Mike was going to die.

And it was going to be soon.

---

59 According to The National ALS Association, it is estimated that as many as 30,000 Americans have the disease at any given time; however, due to its difficulty to diagnose, the number is likely much higher. In other countries (including Canada, Great Britain and Australia), the illness is known as Motor Neurone (sic) Disease, or MND.

A New Journey Begins

A new journey began for Mike and all of us who surrounded him—because terminal illness obviously does not affect the patient alone.

The proverbial clock had begun ticking. Or so it felt.

Literally the day after Mike was diagnosed, he made the unilateral decision that he would not permit any extraordinary intervention to sustain his life. In other words, he would permit no life support—a decision from which he never once wavered throughout his over two years of battling. Mind you, at that moment in time, I wanted to hook him into anything that would keep his chest moving up and down, and I'll admit that we had a "lively discussion" on the subject.

At the conclusion of this very loud argument (um, I mean, "lively discussion"), Mike naturally got his way—after all, it was *his* life. He did very magnanimously offer a compromise by permitting the placement of a feeding tube if it became necessary. While cold comfort to me, it offered some solace. Albeit a selfish sentiment, I felt that a feeding tube would keep him around for a longer period of time.

The New Journey continued…and not one of us liked it. At all.

"Why him?"

"Why *us*?"

"Why does he have to suffer?"

"Why are we having conversations about life support and feeding tubes and burial plans? We're supposed to be living our life, not planning an imminent death."

Our lives transformed instantly. Our days became exercises in survival; our nights were fraught with fear and anxiety. We tried to keep Kendall's life as normal as possible. We desperately tried to remain husband-and-wife, while life insisted that we become patient-and-nurse. There was no denying that all of us lived in a constant state of waiting for the other shoe to drop.

Nevertheless, we pursued as normal a life as the illness would allow, for as long as it would allow us to do so.

That stinking clock was ticking louder and louder…and Mike continued to worsen.

Less than one year after the diagnosis, Mike lost the use of his arms and was unable to bathe, dress or feed himself. He went into a wheelchair, as his legs could no longer support him. Six months later, he went from chronic to acute, as the disease viciously attacked his respiratory system.

Tick...tock...tick...tock...

Two years after diagnosis, Mike could no longer speak and be understood. He became dependent on oxygen and nebulizers. Paramedics were regular visitors to our home, and emergency room personnel knew us on sight and by name.

Tick...tock...tick...tock...

After having to perform the Heimlich maneuver[60] twice, it was apparent that eating and swallowing had become extremely dangerous, and solid food was now a serious hazard. The feeding tube to which Mike had previously agreed was surgically placed.

Tick...tock...tick...tock...

Two months later, his lungs began to collapse and fill. His vital organs and functions began to quickly shut down, one by one.

Tick...tock...tick...

Time stopped.

December 19, 2000 at 7:56 p.m.

The moment that we had been dreading with our entire beings had arrived.

The proverbial shoe dropped.

Except that it wasn't a "shoe"... it was a sledgehammer.

And that sledgehammer did not just "drop."

It chopped souls in two.

I had known that Mike's death was inevitable.

I had known that it was coming.

Mike died.

Peacefully.

At home, as was his wish.

---

60 If you do not know how to perform this maneuver, learn it. It really does save lives.

Surrounded by those whom he loved and who loved him in return.

His over-two-year battle had come to its tragically inevitable end.

Leaving us behind…

…and like it or not, at that very moment, our New Journey evolved into one simple question:

"What Now?"

I had absolutely no idea.

If you were to have gauged our immediate reactions after Mike died, you might have thought that we'd had no idea Mike's death was imminent. However, the evening of Mike's death was also the night I learned that knowing death is imminent makes it no less of a shock.

As if losing Mike was not enough—and setting that gargantuan loss aside for just a moment—there were actually several losses going on of which we were not even aware. We first suffered from a loss of purpose. From the moment that Mike was diagnosed, ALS took over the entire household and dictated every move we made. ALS governed our very existence. Everyone's lives were put on hold because the illness *became* our life.

When Mike left us on that most horrible day, the "purpose" (i.e., the illness) was gone as well. The one thing that ruled every single decision in our lives was no longer there. I was waking up and asking myself, "Who the hell am I now, and what do I *do* with myself and this eighty-seven-hour day that I'm facing?" It was almost impossible to remember what life was like before that bastard illness took over.

We also felt a loss of positive expectancy. Understanding that a diagnosis of ALS is essentially a death sentence, whenever Mike would hit a rough patch, we expected to go to the hospital, deal with the situation, return home and pick up with life where we had left it. While we knew that we could not cure Mike, we had the *expectation* of a much longer period of time with him than the two years that we actually had.

We needed time to absorb *all* of the losses, as well as the shock of our new reality: the fact that Mike's life had come to an end.

BEING KNOCKED DOWN DOES NOT MEAN *STAYING* DOWN

Contrary to what seems to be disturbingly popular belief, the long-term or terminal illness that precedes the death of a loved one does not constitute a prep course in Grieving 101. It is instead laden with layers of complexity, combined with uncertainty, bewilderment and mourning. Further, the mourning period does not begin at the moment of death. It begins at the moment of diagnosis.

As Kendall and I began our Healing Journey after Mike's death, we were met with a level of surprise on the part of a number of people, many of whom I assumed would have known better. People seemed to be genuinely taken aback at the fact that even though we'd known that Mike's death had been all-too-rapidly approaching, we were experiencing overwhelming grief. I was constantly told, "Well, you knew it was coming," "At least you had time to prepare for him dying," or my personal favorite, "You're so lucky." Each time I was clucked at with one of these gems, I felt as though something were wrong with me. I mean, everyone was right—I *did* know "it" was coming. Did I have a *right* to be in mourning? And why wasn't I feeling particularly "lucky"?

It took only a short while to work out that even though we knew that Mike was going to die, we were still entitled to be in shock and to mourn our horrible loss. You see, Mike's impending death was only a concept until the very moment that he left us, after which we were catapulted from "concept" headlong into "reality"—and the difference between concept and reality is huge. The knowledge that death is approaching sooner rather than later does not even remotely lessen the pain and shock of the *reality* of death.

In rebuttal to the previous observations:

- Knowing that "it [death] was coming" made no difference whatsoever.

- There is *no such thing* as being emotionally or mentally "prepared" for a loved one's death. The only thing that you can possibly be prepared with is paperwork.

- Though I have tried to understand someone telling a brand-new, wet-behind-the-ears widow how "lucky" she is (and assuming that by "lucky" the person meant that we were fortunate to have had time together prior to his death), I can assure you that in no way does any new widow feel lucky. Mike suffered unbearably for just over two years at the hands of an evil illness and lost his life. Kendall lost her daddy, a great deal of her childhood and the wide-eyed innocence that childhood is supposed to represent.

I was simply lost…period.

No one felt "lucky," either during Mike's illness or after he died. All we felt…was alone.

However, I quickly realized that in the midst of mourning, I also had an opportunity to model healthy grief recovery for a young girl who was watching me closely. I could take this awful situation and teach Kendall how we were going to get better, even while I was learning myself. I knew that the most important lessons that our children learn from us are "caught," not "taught." More than anything, I wanted Kendall to understand that it was always going to be okay…to cry, be quiet, be angry, to talk about Daddy or to feel however she was genuinely feeling at that moment in time. I always created an environment where she knew that whatever she was feeling was going to be validated—an environment that I continue to create for her to this day.

Mike's illness and his subsequent death knocked us down hard in every way possible: financially, physically, mentally and emotionally…but we were not going to *stay* down. Yes, there were good days and there were challenging days, but we were determined to continue forward. Mike had made it very clear that he wanted us to go on; Kendall was to study hard, go after her goals and grow into the woman that she ultimately became. I was to live my life just as largely and loudly as he had, carrying forward the legacies of love and service to others that he had left to us. It was in that spirit that we took our first tentative steps forward into our new life—timidly cautious steps at first, and then bigger steps as time and determination moved us forward.

A Time of Rediscovery

If you have lost a loved one after long-term illness, you must embrace that having this supposed "time to prepare" or having the knowledge that death is approaching does not lessen the shock of the experience. You are *going* to feel shock. You are *going* to feel numb. You are *going* to grieve. Allow yourself to feel that way, and let *no one* deprive you of the grieving process in any measure.

This will also be a time of rediscovery. As you have already learned, you are not the same person that you were prior to your loss experience, and getting to know who you are as a person *now*—after everything that you have been through—is a process. Take the time to get to know *you*. Be proactive in designing your Healing Journey in the ways that you wish it to unfold. I promise that you will discover both new purposes and reasons to smile again.

In other words, it really *will* get better.

HOW YOU CAN HELP

Someone experiencing loss after long-term or terminal illness is truly adrift right now. She is coping with the loss itself, but she is also at a loss as to what to do first and what to do next. Even though she may have been prepared in the practical sense (funeral arrangements, pertinent paperwork, etc.), emotional readiness is a myth. She is no more emotionally "prepared" than someone who has survived the sudden death of a loved one.

Definite Do's

- **Assist her with immediate needs:** Have a quick look at the situation, assess what she needs immediately and to the extent that you are able, do whatever you can that will help her in the first few days after her loss.

    As the majority of Mike's care (as well as his death) took place in our home, most of the house had been transformed into a mini-hospital. Immediately after Mike's death, Kendall and I had gone to my mother's house because it was too difficult to be in our home at that very sad moment in time. In the meantime, one of my lifelong friends, Nanci, had flown in from Colorado less than twenty-four hours after Mike's death in order to both support us and help with the immediate logistics of what was a very large funeral.

Unbeknownst to me, Nanci then corralled several other friends and work colleagues of mine, returned to my house the day after the funeral and together, they contacted the appropriate vendors and organizations to clear our home of the hospital equipment and medical supplies that had been left behind in the wake of Mike's death. This most incredible gesture of kindness on Nanci's part ensured that when Kendall and I returned home (on Christmas Eve no less), we were not walking into what was essentially a death scene—we were instead simply coming home. The kindness of Nanci and those who helped her is a kindness that I will never be able to repay.

This is just one example of the many generosities that we were shown. Other friends and colleagues of mine organized a "Tupperware Brigade," where every other day, someone in the Brigade dropped off a meal or side dish. After about a week, I actually had to call the organizer of this loving project to tell her that we literally had no more space for food. We also received gift cards for coffee houses, grocery stores and even for a bed and bath store so that we could have fresh new sheets for our beds.

These are just a few great ideas that helped us during those first few difficult weeks. You can assess what your friend/loved one needs and help her out to the best of your ability. It does not even have to involve spending any money—something as simple as volunteering to take or pick up children from school is a huge help, as is running errands, organizing thank-you note lists or grabbing her grocery list and going to the store for her. There are innumerable ways that you can be a positive and productive part of the beginnings of her Healing Journey.

- **Be there after everyone "goes away":** One of the biggest complaints that I receive from survivors is that everyone "disappears" after the funeral. While I am quick to remind immediate survivors that no one else is going to feel the loss as acutely, and that it is perfectly normal for people to "go home and go on," it is so wonderful when even one person calls and says, "So, how are you *really* doing?" and listens, wipes tears, shares laughter or gives in spirit however they can. Choose to be that person—your kindness will not be forgotten.

- **Keep an eye on her:** Grief is the most raw and painful emotion that we experience. Unfortunately, many people do not have a ready support system that ensures that the person who has suffered the loss is grieving in a healthy way.

  If you remotely suspect that she is in any kind of physical or emotional trouble, e.g., serious loss of or unusual increase in appetite, sudden or rapid weight loss or gain, inability to sleep, headaches, hair loss, serious fatigue (to the point she is unable to work or otherwise function normally) or feelings of hopelessness, despair or any suggestion of suicidal ideation—do everything you are able to get her help. If she will not listen to words of encouragement, get her to someone she will listen to—another friend or family member, her doctor or even an emergency hotline or website that can immediately offer assistance. If you feel that the situation is urgent, do not hesitate to call 911 (in the United States; outside of the United States, contact your local emergency services) or take her to the nearest emergency room for assessment.

Without a Doubt…Don't

- **Don't present an expectation of emotional preparedness:** *"You had time to prepare"; "You should've been ready for this"; "Why are you so sad? You knew it was coming."*

When someone makes statements such as these, what the surviving loved one thinks is, "You're right...I knew it was coming. I should've been 'prepared,' but I'm not 'prepared'—I'm devastated. Obviously, something is wrong with me."

Is that honestly the message that you want to convey?

The truth is that expecting death does not make the *reality* of death any easier. Up until her loved one drew their final breath, death was conceptual—and you have learned about the difference between concept and reality. Statements like these deny survivors of fundamental rights—the right to be in shock. The right to mourn. The right to grieve. No one has the right to deny anyone these very real needs.

- **Don't use the "c" word—*ever*:** You will read more about the hated "c" word later – and that hated word is "closure." The short response is that there is no such thing as the "c" word, and unless we are talking about freeways during construction, we need to get rid of this word immediately.

- **Don't imply that someone's death is a relief to their loved ones:** *"I bet you're happy not to be a caregiver anymore"; "This is a good thing, he must've been such a burden"; "You finally have your life back."*

  No one is "happy" when someone passes away. There is a measure of relief when *suffering* comes to an end for everyone concerned, but to imply that somebody's loved one had become burdensome, or that it is time to rejoice because the caregiving portion of the program has come to its heartbreaking end...is frankly sickening.

  You must *always* ask yourself what the person on the receiving end of your sentiments is actually hearing—and in this case, what they are hearing is your implication that they were actually wishing for their loved one to die.

From Two Becoming One…to Only One:
The Loss of a Husband

As discussed earlier in Chapter Eight ("I Did, Now I Don't…"), losing a husband is never anything that anyone thinks is really possible. The words "Till death do us part"—or words to that effect—may have come out of your mouth, but no one is honestly standing up on that altar thinking, "Wow, I could really wind up a widow."

Laura is one of those women that you cannot help but love upon meeting. She is super-active both at work and at play, and she absolutely revels in her role as mother to a beautiful daughter. Laura became widowed at a young age, her husband suddenly taken from her without warning. Learn how she reached amazing new potential that she never knew she had, and how she has gone on to help women just like her.

Laura's story

I was widowed suddenly. My forty-three-year-old husband had been feeling flu-like symptoms for three days and went to the doctor at my insistence because we had a vacation planned the next week. The doctor noticed bruising on his abdomen, decided to draw blood and sent him home with nasal spray and antibiotics for an infection.

That night, Greg fell asleep on the couch and woke up at 2:00 a.m. shouting as he was experiencing massive head pain and couldn't feel the right side of his body. I called 911, and while trying to help him get dressed, he collapsed to the floor and was unable to speak. An ambulance and helicopter ride later, I was told that he'd had a brain hemorrhage due to undiagnosed Acute Mylogeneous Leukemia (AML), and he had hours to live.

My world came crashing down with the shock of the news. I was somehow able to make last-minute end-of-life decisions in those hours between the devastating news and his death, yet remained calm for my five-year-old daughter and my family.

GETTING TO THE OTHER SIDE

Greg and I had been working through three challenging years of marriage that included infertility issues, a separation and near-divorce. Through counseling, we were getting to the other side of our challenges and really understanding how best to relate to one another. I didn't understand how this could happen after all the work we had put into our marriage.

I admit that I went through a period of feeling that God was mad at us. I also thought that the Hepatitis B vaccine that Greg had gotten less than one month earlier could have triggered the AML. Since his death was so sudden, all possible theories were running through my mind.

A NEW PERSPECTIVE AND A HEALING PATH

I took a leave of absence from my job as a pharmaceutical sales representative, as I couldn't imagine having the strength to talk in an upbeat tone to all of my accounts. I spent time reading books on Heaven and the afterlife for spiritual guidance, to satisfy my need to learn more about where Greg was. I attended a grief support group through hospice for both my daughter and myself and also found strength in a support group through my church. These avenues helped provide the comfort and validation that I needed. I felt that I couldn't relate to my friends who complained about their husbands.

The time off also gave me the chance to soul search. It changed my perspective on life's purpose and what matters. I knew that I wanted to keep my husband's memory alive and make a difference in the lives of others, and I participated in my first fundraiser for the Leukemia & Lymphoma Society in Greg's memory.

I SET MY MIND TO ACCOMPLISHMENT

I was laid off from my job and it was a blessing in disguise. I had time to devote to grieving and be the support to my daughter that I needed to be. I signed up for the LLS Team in Training program and decided that if I was going to commit to training, I was going to go the distance and run the full marathon. I completed my first marathon and raised over six thousand dollars for LLS, providing me the purpose that I needed to keep moving through grief. I'm now "addicted" to running and have many half-marathons and endurance events under my belt.

Running and raising money for a cause was the most healing therapy that I could've done for myself. I'm fortunate to have been the group leader for our Widows Wear Stilettos Bay Area group for the past few years, and I know that the "Widows and Kiddos" group that we established has helped many widows find support when they were feeling lost.

My Future is Bright Again

Being an only parent and seeing my daughter going through her developmental grief stages is challenging; however, through hard work, self-reflection and finding ways to reach out to others, I know that we have a bright future.

My widowed friends are my beacons of hope and I wouldn't be where I am without them. Seek out other widows who can give you the support and encouragement you need as you travel through grief; your feelings will be validated and you won't feel like you are going crazy. Find a community you feel safe with and know that you are not alone in this journey—and the same goes for your children, as well.

HOW YOU CAN HELP

"I don't know what to say."

"I'm afraid of saying the wrong thing."

The number of times that I have heard these sentiments expressed by those who surround the bereaved are literally countless. Because I started out in Book World by writing for the widowed community in its very large entirety, and as someone who has personally traveled the widowhood path, we are going to spend some publishing real estate on these Dos and Don'ts, in the hopes that those who surround the widowed will be well equipped to assist on what can be a very lonely Healing Journey.

Definite Do's

- **Be a proactive part of her process:** Like anyone else who has lost a spouse, there is much to be done in terms of legal and financial transition. Help her make lists of who needs to be called (reminding her that the top priority is notification of entities that will provide income to her household), what documents she will need to organize, etc.

- **Remind her who is in charge of her Healing Journey:** At least one person is going to say "Aren't you over it?" or "Get on with it" or similar nonsense. Remind her that she is moving forward in her way and in her time—and as long as she is not hurting herself or anyone else, however she sees fit to travel her Healing Journey is entirely up to her.

Without a Doubt...Don't

Unfortunately, many people seem to have lost sight of the fact that the words "I'm so sorry" can be the most comforting words of all. Even though it may be in an attempt to console, people can instead wind up saying pretty ridiculous things. Having been at the receiving end of some of these comments (and worse), I continue to be amazed at what some say in the guise of sympathy.

In addition to comments like *"At least you were prepared"* or *"At least he didn't suffer"* (both of which have made appearances in this chapter), following are a few other "please-just-don't" comments:

- When someone says: "You were just meant to be alone," what the widowed are thinking is "If I were 'meant' to be alone, I wouldn't have gotten married in the first place."

- When someone says: "You'll find someone else," what the widowed are thinking is "What makes you think I'm *looking* for someone else right now?"

- When someone says: "You should be over it already," what the widowed are thinking is "I'm not 'over it,' I am never going to be 'over it' and I'm sorry if my healing timeline doesn't fit *your* timeline."

- When someone says: "Now you'll have closure," what the widowed are thinking is "I don't want to 'close' any part of my life. What does that even mean?" You will learn more about the "c" word in Chapter Eighteen ("A Word About the 'C' Word").

- When someone says: "He's in a better place," what the widowed are thinking is, "Better than here with me?"

- When someone says: "You can always get a pet to replace him," what the widowed are thinking is, "Did you *really* just say that to me?"

- When someone says: "I'm divorced, and divorce is the same," what the widowed are thinking is, "It's *not* the same. I understand you've experienced the 'death' of a relationship. But in your case, someone made a choice. No one chose to leave my marriage."

- When someone says: "You were married for so many years and he lived a long life," what the widowed are thinking is "It will never be long enough."

- When someone says: "You're not really a widow because you were only married for [a short time]," what the widowed are thinking is "I missed the part of the wedding ceremony that said how long we had to be married before it 'counted' toward widowhood."

- When someone says: "You weren't married so you're not widowed," what the widowed are thinking is "My heart doesn't understand technicalities. My heart only knows that the person with whom I planned to spend the rest of my life is gone."

- When someone says: "He was my brother/sister/other relative. You weren't technically related," what the widowed are thinking is "Please make sure I'm standing there when you tell our children that Mommy and Daddy weren't technically related."

One more very important Don't:

- **Do not refer to a deceased spouse or partner as an "ex"...** *ever*: *"Why do you still have pictures of your ex-husband on the wall?" "I'll bet you miss your ex"; "Your ex would want you to go on with your life."*
  Whether on health forms in hospitals or people talking in general, I have seen and heard this error made many times. However, when I hear this reference made on popular television shows and in the media, I figure that it is time to start making some noise.
  As defined by virtually every dictionary in every language, the prefix "ex" means *former*. The death of a spouse or partner does not nullify a marriage or relationship—that nullification takes a divorce or a breakup. I can assure you that when it comes to widowhood, no one left the marriage willingly.[61] No one filed any papers or either gave or sat through the "uncomfortable breakup speech." Widows were ripped apart by death and catapulted into lives that were neither planned nor chosen. Can you then imagine how it feels when a late spouse is referred to as an "ex-husband," an "ex-fiancé(e)" or an "ex-partner"? In using that reference, you not only insult the widowed, you have impugned the life that was shared and the Healing Journey on which they have since embarked.

---

61 And yes, that includes those who died by their own hand.

The correct terminology for a deceased spouse is "late." Admittedly, this term isn't the best in the world as I don't remember Mike being late for anything, but it is certainly better than "ex." "Ex" refers to someone with whom we are no longer involved, and that someone somewhere made a choice in ending a relationship. Further, widows are not "single," as that status refers to someone who has never married.

If you know someone who is widowed, do not *ever* refer to their late spouse as an "ex." They have suffered enough daggers to the heart, and they do not need one more from people who are supposed to care. I realize that making such a stink over a two-letter reference may sound trivial; however, I care deeply about the millions of widowed who are constantly subjected to this insensitivity. You can help correct that with a proper reference to a departed spouse. They are not "ex." They are not "former."

Quite simply, "ex" does *not* mark a sadly vacant spot.

A Loss with No Name:
The "Unmarried Widowed"

Many make the mistaken assumption that experiencing the loss of a fiancé or life partner is somehow easier because of the lack of a marriage certificate. In reality, being unmarried at a time of loss can oftentimes make things even *more* difficult, both practically and emotionally.

Although certainly not a sought-after title, when a married spouse dies, the surviving spouse is immediately recognized as widowed and is referred to as such. Accordingly, widows generally have access to numerous resources. They can avail themselves of any and all kinds of support (financial, emotional and spiritual) without opinion or reproach. There is instant societal recognition of the surviving spouse as a widow, along with appropriate sympathies expressed and respect paid.

It is not the same for those who were unmarried at the time of loss.

There are not any titles, except for being roundly dismissed with the word "only" (i.e., *"They were 'only' your fiancé(e)/boyfriend/life partner"*). Unmarried widowed are often turned away from support groups due to their lack of "technical" marriage. They are routinely brushed aside by the families of their late beloved (and in what is a sickeningly large amount of cases, even barred from participating in the final decision-making processes). They are frequently left with bills to pay (because they shared a life with someone and usually assumed at least half of the financial responsibilities), yet rarely have financial recourse afforded to them.

In short, most unmarried widowed are penalized practically, emotionally and by society, simply because they did not have the opportunity to walk down an aisle wearing fancy, one-time-only ensembles. Does that *really* make their losses any easier? Is love and loss *truly* measured only by ceremonies, certificates, puffy dresses and penguin suits?

Loss of a Fiancé

The two women you are about to meet both rightly identify as widowed and are models of courage, strength and perseverance. Meagan shares the story of losing her fiancé only eight days after they celebrated their engagement, and Karen shares her story of losing her fiancé on their wedding day, mere hours prior to the ceremony.

Meagan's story

My story began and ended with tragedy. I met my late fiancé, KC, at a funeral for the father of my dear friend, who was KC's uncle. We clicked immediately and felt completely at ease with each other. Three days later, I called him and we set up a time for me to visit. I knew I loved him right away, and KC always said the same thing about me.

Two months after returning from a summer Alaskan adventure, KC took me to one of our favorite coastal escapes. I was sitting in the bay window, wrapped in a blanket. KC walked over to me and was looking out the window but not saying anything. He took a deep breath, and then said "Babe, you know I'm going to love you forever, right?" I said, "Yes." [He continued],

"And you know that as long as we're together, we'll be okay, and we can do anything. And that no one can ever love you like I love you, right?" I said, "Yes." He dropped to one knee and held out a little heart-shaped box with a bow on it. He looked at me and said, "Babe, will you marry me?" I held out my left hand, he put the ring on my finger and I kissed him. He said "You never answered me," and I screamed *"Yes!"*

Eight days after he proposed, KC went lobster diving with his father and a friend. Around sundown, I got a call from KC's father. He asked me if I was alone, and I instantly knew that something was wrong. I asked if everything was okay and his father said "No." He went on to tell me that KC went down for his first dive and he didn't come back up.

KC was missing for thirty hours. His body was found on the front side of Santa Cruz Island. Two days before my twenty-seventh birthday and eight days after getting engaged, my world had come to an end.

How Can I Help Myself Feel Better?

KC had so much planned for the future, both for what he wanted to do with his life and for our future together. So much of what he wanted to do involved helping his community and the people in it. I was feeling, "Why would the world take KC of all people?" and "Why would the ocean take its number one fan?"

Much later, I wondered what I'd done to deserve this pain. There are many variables, but ultimately I know in my heart that this happened. I hate it, but I cannot change it. Now, I try to change those unhelpful thoughts into "How can I help myself feel better?"

Learning How to Make Choices…Alone

I had a horrible time making decisions after KC died. I left it to my loved ones to help me make the decisions I faced. Eventually I was able to start making my own choices again.

I'm lucky to have an amazing, supportive family and group of friends who rarely shared judgments or told me what they thought I *should* do. I was able to talk things through, and for the most part, the people in my life who matter held their opinions until I asked. I feel much more comfortable making decisions independently about the path of my life without KC. There are still struggles of course, but my future is bright and that feels good.

Learning to Love Again

What's next for me is learning to love again. I desperately want to have a family, and if I never date again, I will lose my chance. I want to become the very best version of myself so I will be open to a new relationship. I am doing a lot of work on myself physically, mentally, emotionally and even professionally to put myself in the best mindset possible before I invite someone into my life.

Loss at such a young age reminds us how short life can be. Knowing that I will settle for nothing short of true love gives me confidence in my choices and helps me to know that KC would be proud of the way I am living my life.

Allow Yourself to Feel Joy

Widowhood is a "club" that no one wants to join, and widowed do not wish to welcome any new members. However, should you find yourself widowed, know that you're still here and you have the right to live a happy and abundant life. Even in the face of grief, allow yourself to feel any amount of joy, no matter how fleeting it is.

With time, effort and guidance, you can feel sustainable joy again. The most important affirmation I have utilized is "I accept my feelings as the inner truth of the moment." I say this to myself in times of weakness, heartache, anxiety, joy, happiness or numbness. This affirmation is powerful because it gives permission to feel whatever emotion one might be experiencing.

You'll never be the same, because you have loved and lost. But you do have the choice to allow yourself to transform. My most humble words of advice are to find a therapist you trust and do the hard work of grieving. Remember the things that give you peace and joy and *do* those things. More than anything, remember that there is no wrong way to grieve as long as you do so safely.

Karen's story

I met Chris at a friend's birthday party and it was an instant connection.

He was outgoing, charismatic and had a zest for life. He was one of those people that knew no stranger. He seldom had bad days—not because there weren't bad things that happened to him, he just chose to make the best out of any given situation. He woke up every morning with confidence, ready to attack the day.

We [eventually] decided to get an apartment together. We lived together for a year and one morning, Chris prepared a candlelit pancake breakfast and proposed. We spent the following year planning our wedding and honeymoon.

The night before the wedding, we rehearsed at the church and had a rehearsal dinner where all of his groomsmen stood up and told stories about Chris. I cherish that memory to this day, knowing that they were all able to let him know how much he meant to them. Chris's parents [also] spoke loving words to me and to their only son.

On the morning of the wedding, I had my hair done and Chris was going to have breakfast with his groomsmen. When I returned to the hotel, Chris's mom called me and told me there had been a car accident.[62] She didn't know the details but told me they were going to the hospital. I was in shock and called the hospital to get more information. They wouldn't give me answers, and I remember saying in the firmest voice, "I am standing here in my wedding veil…should I be standing here or do I need to come to the hospital?" Her voice was very soft as she replied, "Get to the hospital."

I hung up and ran out of the hotel room. Along with my family and brides-maids, we rushed to the hospital. I ended up in a room with Chris's parents and a couple of the groomsmen, where Chris's mom told me, "He didn't make it." I fell to my knees shaking. I remember his parents hugging, and one of his groomsmen knelt down and hugged me. I remember Chris's mom leading us in a prayer. How she had the strength to do that is beyond me, but she triggered what would happen later that morning for me at the church.

The wedding was supposed to be at 11:00 a.m. and by this time, it was 10:00 a.m. We decided that it would be best to go to the church. I arrived at

---

62 The car accident was caused by another driver running a red light and hitting the car in which Chris was a passenger. The driver of the car who ran the red light was eventually charged with "death by motor vehicle."

the church at the same time as the guests were arriving for the ceremony. No one knew.

The church was transformed from a wedding into a memorial in a matter of minutes. The songs of joy became songs of sorrow. The bible verses full of love became verses full of sorrow. At the end of the memorial, the priest came to my pew and I asked if I could speak. I felt the need to be strong. I walked down the aisle and told everyone how special the night before was, with everyone telling him how much they loved him…he died knowing how much he was loved. I remember being very passionate and strong, as if Chris's presence was still with me, cheering me on.

After the memorial, everyone went to the "reception." Looking back, I wonder how anyone did anything that day, but we were all in shock. About twenty minutes into the reception, everything hit me and I had to leave.

So Many Questions…and No Answers

After Chris died, I often thought about the "why" question. Why did the accident happen on the morning of our wedding? Why did all the scenarios lead to Chris and his groomsmen being in the car at that particular time of day? Why wasn't it me instead of him? Why do his parents have to go through this?

The Transition from "We" to "Me"

I was teaching first grade and was scheduled to go back to work a week after our wedding. I didn't want to go back, but my parents and loved ones encouraged me to return. Within the first thirty minutes of being at school, a previous student came to my classroom and casually said, "Heard your husband died before you got married, sorry," and went off to class. She was seven years old and obviously didn't know any better, but it was a knife to the heart. She knew, the whole school knew and I just wanted to curl up into a ball.

I didn't know who I was anymore. I went from "we" to "I," and even though those words are so simple, it was mind-boggling to me. All tasks became huge challenges. Going to the grocery store took emotional strength, as that was something that Chris and I loved doing together. Cooking was always an event for Chris—great music played and creative dishes made. How could I possibly cook without him?

I Grew into New Life and New Love

A few days after the accident, my mom contacted a counselor for me. I didn't want to go, but I'm now so thankful I did. My counselor was one of the main reasons that I learned how to grieve and grow. I will be eternally grateful for her weekly meetings.

After a couple months of teaching, I decided that I would look into FMLA[63] and take a few months off from teaching. It was the best decision I ever made. I took a couple of trips by myself, and it was liberating to feel in charge of my life. I went skydiving, started new hobbies, got a new haircut, started running half and full marathons. I allowed myself to have really good days and really bad days.

Eventually, my friends talked me into trying online dating. Sometimes, the dates were just what I needed to feel alive again and sometimes the dates threw me into a downward spiral, making me miss Chris so bad I could hardly breathe. I eventually met Tom on a dating site, and we had an instant connection. We met in person a couple of months later, went out on a date and it was very nice…but I wasn't looking for anything more.

We ended up going out a few more times. Tom was a great combination of masculine and sensitive at the same time. He had lost his father the year before we met, and we shared many tears exchanging stories. Tom made me feel ecstatic about my possible future, and I hadn't felt that in a long time.

Tom proposed a few months after we got pregnant. I'd hoped to find love again, but couldn't imagine planning a wedding or having a marriage, as I associated the words "wedding" and "marriage" with death. Tom knew this was very overwhelming for me and was there for me from the beginning.

We decided to get married in the Virgin Islands and had only a few family members there. The hotel organized the wedding, I ordered my wedding dress

---

63 The Family and Medical Leave Act. For more information, visit www.dol.gov/whd/fmla.

online and it was perfect. I'm sure Tom would've loved to have had a huge wedding, but he never pushed me into something that he knew I couldn't handle. Now we have a beautiful little girl, and our love grows stronger every day. We try not to take one another for granted because we know how easily everything can be ripped away.

LET YOUR LIFE SHINE

While grieving, I believe it's important to immerse yourself in books, quotes and groups with fellow widows to remind yourself that you are not alone. The saying "There is comfort in misery" is often viewed as a negative, but not when it comes to being surrounded by others who truly get where you've been.

Sometimes we spend so much time trying to "keep it together" that it eventually backfires. Allow yourself to fall apart and break down. Don't worry about what others feel like you should or shouldn't be doing; allow yourself to grow and change any way you wish. Challenge yourself to do things that you've always dreamed of or never imagined doing.

Life is different after you lose your loved one. Instead of making it a dreadfully different life, turn it into a beautifully different life. If life leads you to love again, allow it. If life leads you to find success in another workplace, let it. If life leads you to do something that seems scary and new, let it. This is your chance to let your life shine.

Loss of a Same-Sex Spouse

If the unmarried widowed population has a difficult time achieving validation, societal recognition or even respect, members of the LGBT[64] community who are the widowed of same-sex spouses have it much worse, for a number of reasons:

---

64 Lesbian, Gay, Bisexual and Transgender.

a. Though laws in the United States now ensure that same-sex part-
    ners enjoy the right to marry, the fact remains that there are coun-
    tries where it is not only against the law, it is "illegal" to be same-sex
    anything. You can actually endanger your own life if you acknowl-
    edge a homosexual relationship or know someone who is engaged
    in a homosexual relationship and refuse to report them to authori-
    ties.

b. While same-sex marriage is now the law of the land in the United
    States, there are still and sadly, the political and pseudo-religious
    ramifications that rear ugly heads in so many ways. In other words,
    if someone does not "approve" of same-sex unions (or same-sex
    orientation), they do not approve of *you*. Period. This also means
    that any sympathy or compassion for your loss will likely be non-
    existent.

c. In addition to all of the above, if you were unmarried at the time
    that you lost your beloved, you also get to endure the same kind of
    nonsense as other unmarried widowed (i.e., you weren't married
    so it doesn't "count"; it should be easier for you to "get over", etc.).
    Simply put, you do not get any free passes from the Idiot Patrol.

Leigh Ann* is the widowed survivor of her beloved Bonni. She shares what
it is like to be a same-sex widow, as well as the bittersweet victory she feels
today that—while too late for her and Bonni—nonetheless gives her hope for
a bright future.

Leigh Ann's story

I met Bonni through friends at a Pride Festival and was immediately
attracted to her. A group of us went out for dinner after the festival, and I
felt myself falling for her. She was very outgoing and funny and I'm more
reserved. Bonni was everything I always wished I could be. We started dating
a week later.

Almost a year after we met, we bought a house and moved in together, and another year after that, we had a commitment ceremony. We were both lucky that most of our relatives were very accepting of us—and the ones who weren't accepting weren't invited. We didn't want to worry about anything that would take away from our special day.

Bonni and I were together for almost twenty years and were still having a good time and madly in love. We traveled a lot, we had a great group of friends and we also loved to have parties at home. One day, Bonni said that she wasn't feeling right, and she hadn't been feeling well for a couple of weeks. We both thought she was just tired from our recent vacation. We went to the doctor and because of her different symptoms, he sent her for more tests. Bonni was diagnosed with advanced ovarian cancer and only given six months to live. Bonni wasn't going to listen to that. She lived for about a year and a half, and she passed away in hospice.

Laughing through Despair

I didn't want to imagine my life without Bonni, and now I had to accept it was going to happen. I wished that the cancer was happening to me but whenever I said that, Bonni got mad…she didn't like negative attitudes around her. She would say things like, "Why would it be better if it was you instead? It would be better if it wasn't either of us." Even as bad as things were, she still made me laugh.

I Allowed My Support System to Help

After Bonni died, I didn't know what to do with myself. I was with her for so long and she was the outgoing, strong one. I was left alone to figure out what to do.

I was lucky that we had so many good friends and family who volunteered to do different things. Two of our best friends went with me to take care of the funeral arrangements, and I stayed with family for the first few days after Bonni's death. Other friends had a gathering after the funeral and provided all the food and drinks. They even made a picture collage of Bonni to display.

I waited almost a year after Bonni died to go through her things. I had help [from friends and relatives] with that too, and I'm so grateful for the help. I don't think I would have managed to get through everything without the support I had.

EMBRACING THE PAST AND LOOKING TO THE FUTURE

It's been [several] years since Bonni's death, and I still think of her every day. When our state legalized same-sex marriage it brought up a lot of feelings. I'm happy because it means that we have the right to marry, but I'm also sad because it's too late for Bonni and me.

I've gone to a grief support group through our local community center. I've also been on a few dates and even though I haven't found anyone special yet, I still have hope. Bonni always said that she wanted me to find someone, and she'd be the first one to say, "You need to get married." Now that same-sex marriage is legal, I have hope that marriage can happen for me one day. I'll never stop loving Bonni, but I believe I can love someone else too.

LIFE IS TOO SHORT TO BE UNHAPPY

The best thing you can do is to find support. Check your community center or other places that have support groups where you're welcome. It's okay to call yourself a widow—because that's what you are. Don't let other people put their judgment on you, especially people who aren't part of a widowed and gay community. They don't understand.

Bonni always said, "Life is too short to be unhappy," and that's how she lived. I don't want to be unhappy for the rest of my life, and even though I will always miss her every day, I know that she wants me to be happy. That's what I plan to keep doing.

HOW YOU CAN HELP

There are a number of ways that you can be helpful to someone who has lost a fiancé(e) or life partner; many of which will not only support her emotionally and mentally, but will also help ease potential burdens that she may be feeling.

Definite Do's

- **Treat the loss appropriately:** This was the person with whom she planned to spend the rest of her life and right now, she feels rightfully cheated out of her future. Dignify her loss in the ways that she deserves…because sadly, there may be those in her life who won't afford her the same respect.

- **If a wedding was being planned or was imminent, offer to help with the logistics of cancellation:** Can you even imagine the pain that one surviving fiancée endured when she had to return to her florist to cancel previously-ordered wedding flowers and instead order funeral arrangements? Rather than posing with a bridal bouquet in a beautiful white gown, she was instead selecting coffin sprays and picking up her black dress from the cleaners.

  You can help alleviate the burden of the logistics that cancelling a wedding involves. Help her contact those who were invited who may not know about the death (many people make travel arrangements for weddings). Ask for a list of vendors and wedding service providers that need to be contacted. Be sure that she indicates with whom (if anyone) she has deposited money, in the hopes that the money can be recovered. Once the circumstances surrounding the cancellation are explained, vendors may issue partial or even full refunds.

- **Support her decisions going forward:** As with conventional widowhood, this magnitude of loss leaves the surviving fiancée adrift. While most of us can easily decide to go out to dinner with friends, book a vacation or update a resumé, sound decision making doesn't come easily. As she takes her first steps forward into a new life—without the person to whom she was going to say "I do"—she is a feeling a little shaky and a lot unsure. Things like socializing, moving, taking a vacation, changing jobs and so much more are all huge deals to her, and each decision needs to be acknowledged and celebrated in positive ways. She needs to be reassured, and her positive decisions need to be reinforced.

Without a Doubt...Don't

- **Don't minimize her relationship and the gravity of what has happened:** *"He/she was only your fiancé(e) (or life partner)"; "It will be so much easier for you to get over it because you weren't married"; "Just think how much worse it would be if you were married."*

  Someone who has lost a fiancé(e) or life partner may not be a widow in "technical" terms, but since when is love governed by technicalities? Karen says, "I heard all the typical 'wrong comments.' In the beginning, the comments were like stabs to the heart. As I matured in my grief, I had an epiphany. I started being thankful for the naïveté. If they'd been through tragedy, they would never say something without thinking about how the other person would feel."

  Meagan shares, "I honor KC every day by embodying the values and core tenets of who he was in life, and that makes me feel proud. I push myself to be brave because I deserve to have all of the things I want in my life—and that will be a tribute to the man who wanted to give me all of those things."

  I have long taught that devoted and committed love is love, regardless of what is or is not on paper. It naturally follows that if love is love, then loss is loss. In her heart, an unmarried widow's loss is no less devastating than for anyone else who has lost a spouse. Her loss should not be trivialized due to the lack of a marriage license. Furthermore, no one gets to dictate how anyone "should" feel, or how much "easier" her recovery should or will be.

- **Do not discuss the "politics" of her widowhood:** *"You're not really a widow"; "It's not technically widowhood because you weren't married"; "Why are you calling yourself a widow?" "Lesbians can't be widows."*

It doesn't matter if the country in which a surviving spouse lives does not recognize same-sex marriage. Just as it is with unmarried heterosexual widows, survivors of same-sex partnerships and same-sex marriages should absolutely be referred to as widowed—for the simple reason that they are, in fact, *widowed.*

Leigh Ann says, "It was so easy for [certain people in the heterosexual community] to just dismiss [my widowhood] or even my entire relationship with Bonni. It was cruel. Just because some people don't like lesbians, I got swept under the carpet. I felt like I didn't matter. Even the funeral director asked if I was 'allowed' to be in charge of Bonni's arrangements. I had to show them her will [to prove legal standing as Executor]."

The arguments surrounding the "technicalities" of widowhood has gone on for years, and I expect it will for years to come. Be they a heterosexual or gay survivor, if in your opinion, your surviving friend/loved one is not widowed, you are entitled to your opinion. However, it is also an opinion that will cause further heartache—and while you may be entitled to your opinion, you are *not* entitled to cause additional grief to someone who is already in overwhelming pain.

- **Don't imply that a fiancé(e) or life partner is replaceable:** *"You're young/smart/pretty/well off/secure* [or other similar adjectives]*; you'll find someone else in no time"; "You'll have no trouble getting back out there"; "Let's get your mind off of it."*

Get her mind off of it? Seriously? We're not talking about a bad day at work that can be washed away with a couple of martinis and a new pair of shoes. Her beloved has *died*—and while comments like these are unfortunately common during spousal loss, they show up more often in conjunction with unmarried widows.

The implication that a person—*any* person—is simply and quickly replaceable is revolting. I can also assure you that no one who has just lost the love of their life is thinking about auditioning candidates to "take their place." Just like her technically married counterparts, she needs to take her time in finding her way forward into a new life. If she chooses, love can again be a part of her new life—but not as a "replacement" for who was lost.

Unfortunately, hers is a "loss with no name." There are no titles for a woman who has lost someone to whom they were not technically married. We therefore use the term "unmarried widow" as a way of acknowledging her hardly envious position and as a way of paying respect to her profound loss.

Loss of a Parent

Mom.

Dad.

They are the problem-solvers and fixers of challenges large and small. They are the ones who drove the carpool and cheered us on at countless school and extracurricular activities. They played Santa Claus and Easter Bunny and stole stealthily into darkened bedrooms in their roles as the Tooth Fairy. They instigated practical jokes, planned birthday parties and delivered forgotten lunch boxes and school projects. They are the ones who nursed bumps and bruises and fussed over us in doctors' offices, convinced that they knew so much more about our well-being than any doctor could (and were usually right). They taught us to drive and embarrassed us with the endless taking of pre-prom pictures. They walked us down the aisle and watched us with a mixture of pride and bemusement as we navigated parenthood. They are the ones who lifted us up when we were down and celebrated with us when we crossed each exciting milestone throughout our lives.

And then…they are gone.

"Everyone Has a Daddy Except Me": A Child's Loss

Losing a parent is difficult, no matter the circumstances or where we are in our lives when this sad event occurs. However, there is quite a difference in moving forward from a parent's death that depends largely on our age when this loss occurs.

I made this particular discovery when I lost my own father. In her loving attempts to console me on the night that my father died, an eleven-year-old Kendall shared that now I better understood what she was going through in coping with the loss of her daddy because I'd lost my daddy as well.

While a sweet sentiment, it was not exactly true.

As I explained to Kendall on that terrible night, my father was there for me throughout my growing up and for all of the milestones that I had achieved throughout the forty-one years of my life for which he was present. My father sat proudly on the altar at my Bat Mitzvah, and dabbed at tears when I was "kidnapped" by the incumbent cheerleaders when I made the squad in high school. He snapped those embarrassing prom pictures, walked me down the aisle on my wedding day and stood firmly by my side while holding fast to my arm, as we stared disbelievingly at a flag-draped coffin and bade goodbye to my husband—his son-in-law—four months earlier.

Daddy was there—for everything.

Conversely, Kendall would know none of these experiences while growing up. She never got to go to a father-daughter dance at school, and there was a memorial table at her Bat Mitzvah, where *her* dad should have been proudly standing. He was not here for proms or graduations, and he was not the one who taught her to drive.[65]

Even though as an adult, Kendall still struggles with Mike's absence and has come to the realization that she always will, she nonetheless overcame the huge loss (and several other major obstacles) that overshadowed her teen years, to realize a happy and healthy adulthood—and she did so without turning to destructive coping methods that are all too readily available.

With more pride than I can put into words—and knowing that her daddy is smiling proudly—I am pleased to introduce Kendall Brody Fleet's story.

---

65 And I am not sure that I have ever forgiven him for leaving me with *that* particular task.

Kendall's story

When I was nine years old, my father was diagnosed with ALS. His battle with ALS lasted shortly over two years, and in that time, our family saw hardships in the form of ambulance trips to emergency rooms, my dad falling and hurting himself and the stress that comes with putting a dying individual before anything…twenty-four hours a day, seven days a week.

But the illness also gave me the chance to bond with my dad in a way that most children will never experience. Every word from his mouth became much more important. Even if we were just watching television, every moment we spent together became much more memorable.

I was eleven years old when Daddy passed away in my arms and surrounded by family. I consider helping to care for him one of my greatest honors and accomplishments in life thus far, giving me the nurturing qualities on which I pride myself.

IT'S OKAY TO QUESTION

When I first learned of the diagnosis, I was eager to take part in the caregiving duties. Being so young, I wasn't able to fully wrap my head around the enormity of what would happen. For me, it was a chance to be there for my dad in a way that not many others could be, and I took pride in that. This reaction saved me from wasting time being angry or in denial about the disease taking him from me.

I didn't start questioning why all of this happened to us until five years after Dad's death, when teenagers begin experiencing the first school dance, the first dates. Later, the "firsts" included learning how to drive, winning state and national cheerleading championships and my graduation. As I moved into adulthood, more milestones arrived—the beginning of my career, my first serious relationship, moving out and living on my own. Throughout *all* these experiences, I found myself periodically asking God "Why?" Why didn't I have my dad here to guide me, celebrate with me and console me like everyone else does? It's a battle that I still fight to this day.

It's true that I won't have my dad here to walk me down the aisle or hold his grandchild when that time comes but I've learned that it's okay to feel that way. It's okay to question why something bad happened to you because it means that you care enough to miss it.

COPING THE BEST WAY I KNEW HOW

My mother was finalizing funeral arrangements, and I was home alone watching episodes of *Friends* from the video box set that we'd gotten as a Christmas gift for my dad. His hospital bed was still in our living room. I could still smell him throughout the house, and his slippers were still sitting next to the hospital bed.

I sat in the recliner next to his bed, watching episodes of the show that we'd enjoyed together for years. When the first tape ended, I muted the television and went to get the second tape. I looked at the muted television and suddenly the silence that had been absent from the house for so long was back again. You know the phrase, "Silence is deafening"? Silence can also bring you to your knees.

I don't remember crying a lot after Dad passed away. There were plenty of tears shed, but I hadn't experienced my first "ugly cry" until the silence of the muted television; that gut-wrenching scream-cry. I realized then that I had entered the next phase of my life...a life without my dad.

After about twenty minutes of crying, I realized something else. I wasn't the only person entering this phase. I had a widowed mother who, despite putting on her bravest face, had no clue where to go from there. I promised myself that while I would cope the best way I knew how, I'd be my mother's strength as well. I wanted her to know I was there to help through *her* struggle as well as go through my own grief. Being there for her helped me because I realized that I wasn't alone. In turn, her strength saved me from going down roads that a lot of young people choose in order to numb their pain.

TRUST THE PROCESS

Some days, I believe that I've healed as much as can be expected and that I've moved forward with my life in a way that would make Daddy proud... other days, I realize that I have *much* more work to do. I know that [healing] is an ongoing process and will be until the day that I see my dad again.

The process must continue. There must always be a process during which you come to terms with loss, learn from it and use the experience to better the life ahead of you. I was incredibly lucky to have had friends who were always trying to help me smile.

I also have a family who banded together and made sure that I had the freedom to talk, scream, cry or ask questions, and who made themselves available whenever I needed, without hesitation. To this day, I consider myself beyond blessed to have these people when I need them, because I still do, and I always will.

Someone once said to me, "Trust the process." I will never quit my journey of healing. I will never quit "moving through."

THEY ARE NEVER REALLY GONE

Life for me now is great. I feel my dad's absence every single day; however, I get to live my life with the lessons that I learned from that journey. I have a wonderful relationship with my mother. I have an incredible sister and blended family whom I love. I have a thriving career, I have friends who are gems and I have the pleasure of telling my story and hopefully helping others.

If you lost a parent when you were still a child, "tween" or teen and are still grieving, you're *not* alone. You must continue to trust that those around you will be there for you every step of the way. I made the mistake of bottling up my feelings after my dad's death, and as soon as I realized how many people wanted to help me, things became easier. Talk to someone, write down how you feel, sit at a park and talk to your lost parent. Allow yourself to feel whatever you need to feel and talk about whatever needs talking about.

I read a book[66] entitled *Tuesdays with Morrie* and in the book, Morrie says, "Death ends a life, not a relationship." Know that the parent you have lost will never truly be gone from your life, as long as you keep their memory alive.

---

66 *Tuesdays with Morrie* by Mitch Albom (Broadway Books). All rights reserved.

"Who Will Love Me Now?":
Losing a Parent After Reaching Adulthood

How does losing a parent as an adult differ from losing a parent while still a child? Meet Nancy, both a leader in her profession and a firecracker of a personality. She is fabulously outspoken and wonderfully strong in every way. She also beautifully teaches that no matter how old we are, and no matter the rationale that teaches us that as we age, so then do our parents, this is nonetheless a loss that cuts deeply and for which no length of adulthood truly prepares us.

Nancy's story

When I was forty-five years old, my mother, who was the picture of health and vigor, died very suddenly. Six months later, my father had a catastrophic stroke and spent the next three years completely disabled and dependent, though totally aware of what happened to him. He spent every minute wishing to end his life, and as soon as he had the opportunity by refusing a feeding tube, he did just that.

For many people, forty-five years of age is old enough to be sanguine about the loss of one's parents, but I felt like my tether to the planet had been severed. For months after my mother's death I was inconsolable and only marginally functional.

THE ISOLATION THAT SHOCK BRINGS

I felt like "What the f**k?" I was shocked, angry, disoriented and felt ripped off. I don't really remember much of that time; I cried and isolated myself.

I LEARNED HOW TO LOVE UNCONDITIONALLY THROUGH THE PAIN

It hadn't occurred to me that my mother would ever die. When she did, I was left rudderless. She'd been my navigator and intimate advisor; I was paralyzed with grief and unable to share my pain. I didn't want to move forward. I somehow felt that healing and finding a new equilibrium would diminish her memory and make her less present.

When my father had his stroke, I was alienated from him. I was angry that he couldn't be more supportive as I grieved for my mother. As the extent of his disability became clear, my brother and I realized it was up to us to care for the man who'd had such difficulty caring for us.

My first instinct was to throw money at the problem—put him in a nursing facility and stay detached. However, I realized that caring for my father was the final important thing I could do for my mother. I knew she would have wanted him to be loved and nurtured through the end of his life. I also knew that if I didn't participate, the entire responsibility for his care would fall on my brother, with whom my father had a more loving relationship.

My father stayed in his home, and my brother and I managed his round-the-clock care. As time went on, my love and compassion for my father grew. I struggled to get him into the car and took him to the beach. I pushed his wheelchair on walks around his neighborhood and invited his friends to visit. Caring for my father allowed me to crack through the paralysis of grieving for my mother. What began as service to my mother and my brother became amazing growth and revelation. I learned that I could unconditionally love him, and my father and I healed our lifelong rift, which I'm not sure could have happened any other way.

PUSHED BACK INTO LIFE

My father's stroke jolted me out of the malaise that followed my mother's death. Until then, I'd been a shell, unable to process what was happening around me and sleeping whenever possible. Knowing that others needed me pushed me back into my life.

TRANSFORMATIONAL GRIEF

There is never a time when they aren't with me. I hear their voices so much more clearly now than I did when they were alive. My grief has transformed from a black void to a security and recognition of all the gifts they gave me. If I could get through the enormity of that loss, there's really nothing I cannot endure.

HOW YOU CAN HELP

No matter your age, the loss of a parent is devastating. It is grief mixed with a feeling of surrealism. The people that have always been there for us are no longer physically present. It is also a loss that most of us will deal with at some point in our lives.

Definite Do's

- **Be willing to be "there":** Kendall shares, "I'm a big believer in actions speaking louder than words—and the most comforting thing that anyone did was simply be there. A friend of mine even asked her parents to let her stay home from school one day so that she could help me feel better. This simple act of being there meant the world to me. My friends also honored my grief process—making me comfortable enough to not mask my emotions—and taught me how to help others cope with loss."

- **Offer to have a non-funeral related get-together:** Ideally, this should be a couple of months after the funeral to give everyone a chance to catch their breath. You'll find that the mood is lighter, and you'll be able to enjoy swapping funny stories and remembrances in ways that you simply cannot immediately after the funeral. My family had a gathering shortly after my uncle's death, and my aunt and cousins were able to relax, enjoy themselves and even join in with fun stories, rather than dwell entirely on the loss itself.

- **Make sure that she is taking care of herself:** People tend to check in on those who have lost their parents on a less frequent basis. Remember that even though losing parents may be what is considered the natural order of things, it does not make the loss any easier. Make certain that she is eating, sleeping and coping with her grief in one of the many healthy ways that we have previously discussed.

Without a Doubt…Don't

- **Don't behave like everything is "business as usual":** *"Aren't you better yet?"; "Okay, it's time to quit being sad"; "Are you still moping around over your mom?"*

  Nancy recalls, "After the death of my mother, I took two weeks [off work] to mourn. When I went back to work, my boss said, 'You're entitled to three days of bereavement time. How would you like to handle the other seven days? Do you want to call it vacation time, or would you prefer to take it unpaid?' I was stunned by the lack of compassion. He never acknowledged my loss."

  I do not know why some people believe that losing a parent is somehow "easier" or does not warrant appropriate attention to grief. Whatever the reason, it is not okay. This is the loss of a person who brought someone you care about into the world. Their loss is monumental and should be treated accordingly.

- **Don't look for gratitude during a time of mourning:** *"Be happy; they lived a long life"; "They were with you for so long, you should be grateful"; "Aren't you glad they aren't suffering anymore?"*

  If we all stipulate to being grateful for long lives and the end of suffering, can we *please* get these phrases out of the water supply for good?

  Yes, we are grateful that our parents lived "long" lives. But what exactly qualifies as a "long" life? What is the age cutoff and who makes that determination?

  Mike was fifty-five years old when he died. When someone remarked to Kendall that she should be happy that her daddy had lived a "long life," she looked absolutely gobsmacked. My father was seventy-eight years old when he passed and though later along in years than Mike had been, I still did not want to hear about his longevity—because to me, it was not nearly long enough. Even if it had been "long enough" or if their lives had been "full enough," who on *earth* is going to be happy about a parent's passing?

- **Don't point out the obvious:** *"This is the natural way of things"*; *"It's supposed to happen this way"*; *"Children are supposed to bury their parents."*

  We all know that there is an order to things and that we are likely going to be the ones holding our parents' hands when it is their time to depart this earth. However, those natural events do not make the *reality* any easier.

  Natural courses and hierarchical order be damned—it still hurts.

A (Huge) Bonus "Don't"

- **If you're consoling a younger child who has lost a parent, don't trivialize the loss because you feel that a child cannot experience the same depth of feelings—and *never* present an expectation of responsibility for their parent:** *"No time for tears, you're the man of the house now"*; *"You have to be a big girl for your mommy"*; *"Your mother/father/grandmother/etc. hurts much more than you do."*

  You have no doubt heard the phrase "puppy love." I have never understood that expression and I never will. It is a phrase that immediately trivializes strong feelings for another human being. It is reductive. It is minimizing. Regardless of our age, if we feel love for someone, we feel love…period. Age does not enter into it. I was always grateful to my parents for never making light of my feelings whenever my heart was broken by any number of suitors throughout my adolescent and teen years.

  Now, let's multiply that heartbreak by a million. This is the approximate number of pieces into which a child's heart shatters after they have lost a parent.

  Just because someone is chronologically younger, does that automatically lessen their love for another? I certainly do not think so.

Why would anyone attempt to reduce a child's grief simply because they are young? Additionally, knowing how literal children can be, why would *anyone* tell a child that their parent's death has promoted them to a head-of-household position?

Again, if love is love, then loss is loss. Experiencing loss while in the younger age groups is not equivalent to a free pass on grief. In fact, if a child does not appear to be grieving at all, it can be a sign that something is wrong and that they may be processing their grief in a potentially destructive way.

Kendall says, "One of the most important things I encourage people to do is never downplay a child's loss. Children understand loss. Children are acutely aware of what goes on around them. Respect a child's loss as much as you would your own. When we do this, we're telling children that it's okay to feel sad, cry and feel that void just as adults do. Depending on age, the struggle varies, but the struggle is still there. The realization that they'll never see their parent again is still there. The void is still there."

Friends, Buddies and Pals:
Loss of a Sibling

You picked on each other mercilessly. You played pranks. You blamed one another for the missing cookies just out of the oven or the broken whatchamacallit that your parents warned you not to touch. You shared secrets. You cheered one another on and stuck up for one another when outsiders invaded your personal world.

They are your siblings.

And when you lose a sibling, it is like losing a piece of yourself.

Lisa Salberg is the founder and CEO of the Hypertrophic Cardiomyopathy Association.[67] In addition to running an international organization, Lisa

---

[67] To find out more about Lisa and the Hypertrophic Cardiomyopathy Association, visit www.4hcm.org.

also lives with the disease. Having already overcome tremendous obstacles that this illness presents, Lisa was faced with the ultimate devastation when she lost her beloved sister Lori to the same disease.

Lisa's story

Diagnosed at twelve years of age with HCM[68] and surviving a stroke at twenty-one years old wasn't the challenge—it was the death of my sister when I was twenty-six years old and pregnant that was the biggest challenge of my life. Taking my sister's two children into my home and starting a nonprofit organization to help others dealing with the same illness, while raising an infant and working a full-time job, was also a challenge and remains so years later.

I'm Too Busy to Die

I can go back over one hundred years of HCM killing members of my family, yet I never saw the universe as "having it in for us." I did wonder "Why not me?" many times. Lori was the sweet one. I was the tough one. I experienced a great deal of survivor's guilt. I was angry that she was taken, and I was angry that I was the one left to "clean up" the aftermath, including one ex-husband/deadbeat dad, one husband of six months who attempted to steal everything from her children—and then raising her children myself. I was also helping my parents cope with the loss of a child.

My attitude was survival instinct—I had to be okay and had to make sure others were too. I was too busy to die. I took an optimist's point of view. One in five hundred people are living with HCM, and I fought back with more than my heart—I fought back with my brain. I empowered others to not fall victim to HCM as my family did.

Using My Power to Stay Healthy

There were logistical issues that had to be worked out, including moving closer to where my niece and nephew were in school. Preparing one home for

---

68 Hypertrophic cardiomyopathy (HCM) is a disease in which the heart muscle becomes abnormally thick. The thickened muscle can make it harder for the heart to pump blood and, sadly, the disease can be fatal.

sale and shopping for a new home with three kids in tow was an adventure in itself. I knew one thing—I had to do everything in my power to stay healthy and alive in order to care for the children.

I researched this condition that had stalked our family since at least 1906 (the first death that I could trace). Once I found information, I started to organize data. Within months of my sister's death, I programmed my first website to share information about HCM.

I have missed my sister every day since she passed away. Not a day goes by that I don't wonder what she'd think of a situation, if she would be proud of what I have built in her memory and many other things.

My Life Path Became Clear

In 2008, my father passed away as a result of HCM. He had end-stage heart failure and passed away at the age of seventy-three years, at home with everyone he loved around him. A few months after my dad's passing, I could think of him and smile. I was honored to be a part of helping him leave this world on his own terms. Then, an event occurred that you simply can't predict; a woman in her mid-thirties was in ICU fighting HCM at the same hospital where my sister [was hospitalized and eventually died] and her family had reached out to my non-profit organization for information. This young lady looked like my sister…and was dying much like her too.

It was as if I was pulled back fifteen years in time and was sitting at Lori's bedside as the ventilator breathed for her. It was then I realized that I was so busy after my sister's death, I'd never really grieved her loss. I took a step back from life and with the help of friends, I really processed her loss. I gave myself permission to grieve and let her go. Once that was accomplished, my life's path became clearer, as well as the mission of the organization that honors her and others lost to HCM.

Leaving the World a Nicer Place

Time brings clarity. Coping with this event and living with a chronic genetic condition that is capable of killing you is a constant struggle. It taunts you daily, you try in vain to control it and in the end, you know it will win.

But there are ways *I* can win and that's what helps me cope. My sister died, but she did not die in vain and she will never be forgotten. Others lived because of her death. I survived, and I have used my life well.

If I had a wish for others it is simply this: Wake up every day and do something to leave this world a little nicer than it was the day before. I've lived with this in my heart, and in my part of the world, things are a little better every day.

HOW YOU CAN HELP

How can you best help someone who has lost their sibling? The same way you would support survivors of other kinds of familial loss, with a few additions:

Definite Do's

- **Remember them out loud:** Lisa shares, "Those who acknowledged Lori's loss shared stories of how my sister impacted their lives; they still remember and speak of her. This brings me joy." By acknowledging the impact that a departed sibling had on your life and sharing funny memories or sweet stories, you've just let their survivors know that their loved one is not forgotten.

- **Encourage dialogue:** Siblings are oftentimes the very best of friends, even during the very worst of times. A surviving sister may feel completely isolated after loss of her sibling. Encourage her to talk about her loss—her pain, her grief, her anger—whatever she is feeling in the moment.

Without a Doubt...Don't

- **Don't imply that surviving siblings replace the missing sibling:** *"At least your parents still have you"; "Your parents are so lucky to have had more than one child"; "You'll still have a full house at the holidays."*

232

On the chance that the following seemingly obvious statement must continue to be made, please remember that people cannot replace other people...and the presence of additional children does not, cannot and will never replace the child who is missing. Yes, it is nice for parents to have the comfort of others—but nothing will replace who has been lost.

- **Don't insinuate that a sibling's passing post-illness was somehow their fault or due to their own neglect:** *"Didn't they know they were sick?"*; *"Couldn't they have done something more?"*; *"Weren't they taking care of themselves?"*

  People who have been diagnosed with a serious illness are generally well aware of that illness. Placing blame on someone who is no longer here is not only useless, it is hurtful. To what possible advantage is saying anything along this line? Does it bring the person back? Does it bring comfort to the person to whom you are speaking? In other words, whatever you are planning to say to a survivor—*please* say it to yourself first.

The Greatest Pain of All: Loss of a Child

It is *not* in the natural order of things.

It is a place in the deepest recesses in your soul that you dare not visit.

It is a vision that you cannot bring yourself to imagine; the very thought is sick-making in every way.

It is the loss of a child.

When we become parents, we experience love on a level we never imagined possible. We experience a bond that is unbreakable and unshakable. We create dreams and visions of our children's future—watching them grow up, go to college, establish careers, marry, have children...and watching our families continue to happily expand.

Then one day your life shatters into a million irreparable pieces. Your child—that wonderful person that you brought into the world—is gone.

It is *not* supposed to be this way.

Paula Stephens[69] is a certified wellness coach and author of a forthcoming book on how to use exercise, nutrition and wellness as important healing tools post-loss. Paula herself survived the very nightmare that every parent on the planet fears and she is now on a mission to help others do the same.

Paula's story

My fifteen-year-old middle son Daniel had run away. When he showed up late at night on day ten, he was, dirty, hungry and clearly on drugs. In a frantic three-week education of what our options were, we sent Daniel to Wilderness Therapy. This was the beginning of a very long healing process. He came home a wise young man with passion for his strengths and direction for his future. We all breathed a sigh of relief and felt that life could begin to take on a sense of normalcy.

[A few years later], my oldest son, Brandon, who had recently joined the Army, came home on leave. Brandon was the happiest I'd ever seen him — beaming with pride, physically strong and looking forward to his military career. I said goodbye to Brandon as he left to go out with friends and watched him, still in uniform, bear hug and jostle with his friends as they climbed into a truck.

Brandon would die that night in his sleep after taking one-half of a prescription pain pill. The coroner later reported that he'd never seen a death like this and that there were no other substances in his system; nor was his death the result of an undiagnosed health issue.

I'd Already "Paid My Dues"

I felt like I'd already paid my dues when going through Daniel's treatment. I gave everything I had. I thought that would be the hardest thing that I'd ever do. Never once did I back down from the "hard stuff." I hadn't slept through the night in years, worried I was going to get the call that Daniel

---

69 To learn more about Paula, visit www.paulastephenswellness.com.

had run away again—or worse, that he'd given up [on recovery]. I'd already grieved the loss of the 'perfect family' when I got divorced, then again when Daniel was in therapy. Why more loss? Why more grief? Why did I have to go through losing Brandon? Why would my other boys have to suffer losing the brother they'd looked up to their entire lives?

I didn't want to learn anything else about death or grief. I felt as though I was paying for some horrible crime and for which I'd already paid the price.

My Search for Resources and Direction

Although my heart felt like what I'd lost had to be unlike any loss anyone had ever suffered, I knew others had lost children. I went on a frantic search to find resources—anything that would get me through. I was overwhelmed with my own grief—how was I going to support my boys as *they* tried to manage this tragedy?

In the months that followed, I began to feel like "Why bother?" It didn't matter how hard I tried to be a good mother—nothing would bring Brandon back. I sank into a deep depression. I'd exhaust myself pretending to be functional at work and then retreating into my room or drinking a bottle of wine after work. I had no direction or desire to have a direction.

Mending a Broken Heart with "Expansion Joints"

Shortly before I quit my job, I received a call from the mother of one of my childhood friends who'd lost a son. She talked about how broken a mother's heart feels after the loss of a child, and she understood how I felt. However, it was her next sentence that struck me. She said that I had an opportunity to be able to love more and step into something bigger. She suggested that I pick up all the pieces of my broken heart and put them back together with "expansion joints." It was the first time that I had the smallest sliver of hope that I might not just survive, but thrive in a way that felt like a way to start moving forward.

Building something out of my broken heart started small, and there were days that I still couldn't do it…but it eventually became the cornerstone of my healing. I began to catch myself when I wanted to use "superglue" on my broken heart and shut myself off from living. I slowly replaced the superglue with expansion joints made of love, openness and compassion. It's the perfect way for me to honor the love for my son, while allowing myself big spaces to grow.

Be Present in Your Process

Unlike losing a spouse or a parent where there are words like "widow" or "orphan" to identify these life events, there is no word to define someone who has lost a child. Our culture doesn't allow for such a horrible event. We're free to find or create our own word to describe how we'll carry this experience, and we're free to change this word as we work through the process. While I am the mother to three living boys, I will always be the mother of four amazing boys.

Regardless of the type, we are all equipped to deal with loss, and we have the ability and the power to choose how we do it. Be present in the process, knowing that each day gives us strength for the days ahead as we evolve our definition of this experience. Every day, I decide if I want to use superglue or expansion joints to define myself. I choose expansion joints!

HOW YOU CAN HELP

As impossibly difficult as it seems to be able to afford any comfort to a mother who has lost a child, there are still things you can do that will let her know you care deeply and that no matter what, you will be there for her.

Definite Do's

- **Talk about her child:** My cousin lost his daughter when she was in her mid-teens. Since her birth, she had suffered tremendously from numerous serious health problems and had battled mightily all of her life. She was sunshine and a delight and it was a terrible loss for my cousins, her older sister and the entire family.

  A couple of years after her death, we were at a family function and I was talking to my cousin about her—I even pulled out a few pictures from years gone by. My cousin wiped at his moist eyes and said, "Thank you." When I asked him what he was thanking me for, he quietly replied, "No one talks about her anymore."

As with every other loss, there is a fear of discussing a departed loved one, for fear of upsetting people. You know what upsets people? Thinking that their loved one has been completely forgotten because *no one is talking about them!*

If it is true about everyone else, it is especially true about a child: Not talking about them does not make parents forget. Not talking about them simply makes people think that you either do not care or do not remember. Assuming that neither is the case, *please* talk about her child. Ask to hear stories. Ask how siblings (if any) are adjusting. If Mom begins to cry, it does not necessarily mean that she's upset—it can be that, as with my cousin, she is grateful that someone is talking about her sweet angel.

- **Offer to help create memories**: Many parents are at a loss as to what to do to help keep their child's memory alive. You can offer to help in the ways that you feel Mom will be best comforted. Some great suggestions include collecting meaningful poetry and verses and putting them into a journal (themes that refer to always being a parent no matter what are favorites) or creating a large, multi-mat picture frame that includes both individual and group pictures. This not only reminds Mom that it is always going to be okay to remember, it also means that they are always going to be Mom, even though their baby is no longer here.

Without a Doubt...Don't

- **Don't imply that her other children are either replacement or diversion**: *"You have other children to worry about"; "You're so lucky that you have other kids"; "Why don't you and the kids take a vacation?"; "You can always have more children."*

Not only are the surviving siblings never going to be able to "replace" their absent sibling, but be it consciously or otherwise, they are likely to try to do so in order to make Mom feel better.

It does not work.

Children cannot replace absent children. The surviving children need to grieve their loss, Mom needs to grieve her loss and everyone needs to realize that there is always going to be an angel-sized hole in their hearts that only an angel will fill.

Further, a change of scenery does not erase a person's passing—it simply changes scenery. There may come a time when Mom and siblings want to take a getaway together, but that has to come from them. If and when Mom broaches the idea, support it wholeheartedly—but do not suggest it as some kind of half-hearted diversion or distraction from the tragedy that has occurred. Aside from being inappropriate, it also suggests that leaving town will help Mom "forget," which is the worst implication in the world to a grieving parent.

Lastly, the very notion that having another child will replace the child that has been lost borders on the disgusting. Do you really envision a bereaved mother and father saying to one another, "Okay, Junior has passed away—let's go make another one to take their place"?

Just as we discussed in Chapter Nine ("Hope Interrupted"), the decision to have more children is deeply personal and not an appropriate suggestion for anyone outside of a bereaved couple to make.

- **Don't suggest a path of "creative avoidance":** *"You should probably stay away from schools and parks"; "Just avoid children's departments in stores"; "Change their bedroom into another type of room/get rid of their things/take pictures down/etc."*

I cannot bear the fact that there are mothers (and fathers) out there who have to listen to this tripe.[70]

---

70 Tripe: Technically speaking, the stomach of a cow, bull or ox. It sounded better to me than another reference to bull that I could have used instead.

Think about it. A mother has lost her child—her "baby." How to feel better? Just take the long way around parks and avoid places where children's clothes are sold. Or better yet, turn their bedroom into a gym.

How do you write a sound effect? Because that is exactly what I need here—a forehead slap.

There may come a time when Mom will want to do something with her lost child's bedroom and their personal belongings. However, that time is far into the future. More importantly, and just as with the decision to have another child, the choice to convert a bedroom and go through personal belongings is so incredibly personal, to suggest any action even five minutes ahead of Mom is wholly inappropriate.

Of course, if she mentions wanting to redo the bedroom, you should absolutely support her, as this is a terribly painful decision to make. You can even offer to help (remembering to accept any decline of help graciously as she may want to do this alone). However, to suggest that a makeover of a bedroom will make her feel better is just not okay.

And avoiding parks, schools and children's departments in stores?[71] Come on.

While the World Watches: Loss in the Spotlight

When most people suffer a bad thing, they generally have the "luxury" of experiencing it in private. They can cry, rail and be angry. They can mourn, grieve and begin the arduous process of healing as a civilian. Most people experiencing bad things are not subject to media scrutiny, public opinion or repeated broadcast accounts of their tragedy in minute detail.

---

71 Please see Chapter Nine ("Hope Interrupted"). Same rules apply.

So what happens when the news of the day—or perhaps the news of the year—is *you?*

These nightmare scenarios became real life bad-thing experiences for two women who each had to deal with their bad things under the white-hot glare of the media spotlight, all the while persevering toward healing with both dignity and sanity intact.

Loss Through a High Profile Event

Whether you are celebrity or "civilian," when you experience a loss that involves a high profile event,[72] the tragedy catapults you into a spotlight that you neither asked for nor want. In these situations, you are not only dealing with all of the feelings that loss brings, you are also likely dealing with the media, be it locally, regionally, nationally or even internationally. You may feel as though the entire world has set up camp on your front lawn. The eyes of the world are constantly trained on you. Your bad thing is not only about you and your family, it is now being broadcast everywhere and is being magnified, dissected, discussed and rehashed in pictures, on social media and in commentary over and over again.

And inevitably, at least one less-than-enlightened reporter has asked you, "How are you feeling right now?"

Tanya Villanueva Tepper[73] is a writer and founding member of Fiancés and Domestic Partners of 9/11. She is also one of the five participants featured in the Peabody award-winning documentary *Rebirth*, which premiered at the Sundance Film Festival and was broadcast on Showtime Television Networks.

Once upon a time, Tanya was a woman in love with her Sergio. They started a business together and were happily planning their future—when September 11, 2001 dawned, bright and sunny…

---

72 A high-profile event includes events such as September 11, 2001; the Oklahoma City and Boston bombings; mass shootings; aviation, cruise-ship or railroad accidents; or any event that garners widespread attention on local, regional, national and/or international levels.

73 For more information about Tanya, please visit tanyavillanuevatepper.com and projectrebirth.org.

Tanya's story

My whirlwind romance with Sergio began with a kiss at a club in Miami Beach. He [thereafter] returned to New York, where he was working as a police officer for the NYPD [New York Police Department]. We fell in love and nearly a year later, I drove a seventeen-foot-long U-Haul [truck] packed with all of my belongings to New York. Shortly thereafter, we moved in together.

Sergio was by my side during some of the most pivotal times of my life. He was there when I went to Germany to learn the truth behind my biological mother's suicide, and he held me up as I grieved the loss of my beloved dad. He stood by me as I fulfilled my dream of opening our gift shop, Inner Peace, and in 2000, he left his career as a detective to become a firefighter for the FDNY [Fire Department, City of New York] so that he would have more time to dedicate to growing our business. We [then] celebrated the purchase of our first home, a pre-war garden apartment blocks away from the store. With a solid foundation in place, Sergio proposed to me on the seventh anniversary of our first kiss.

On the morning of September 11, 2001, Sergio was supposed to come home from his twenty-four-hour shift at his firehouse, Ladder 132 in Brooklyn. Instead, he answered the call to the World Trade Center with five other men. The six men never came home—and to this day, their remains have not been identified.

I FOUND COMFORT IN THE STRENGTH OF COMMUNITY

It was very easy to get sucked into a vortex, having experienced such profound loss just a few years earlier with the passing of my father, and the feelings of abandonment that came with learning about my mother's suicide. But in spite of my shock and needing to feel sorry for myself, being part of a very large community who were experiencing the loss of their loved ones helped me keep things in perspective. In particular, there were two men on the truck with Sergio who also lost brothers; seeing their families push forward gave me strength to keep going.

COUNSELING ENABLES HEALING

I had the "unfortunate" good luck of being a part of the September 11 community, and the added bonus of being a part of the FDNY and NYPD families. The men of Sergio's firehouse and precinct were unwavering in their support of our families, ensuring that our immediate needs were met, from bringing food by to helping plan memorials, to taking care of "honey-do" lists and transporting us to therapies.

The FDNY set up a counseling unit for one-on-one grief counseling and peer support groups, which I sat in for two years. They were essential for my ability to move forward and heal.

I TOOK TIME FOR MYSELF

Besides my therapy sessions where I leaned into the pain of my journey, I took regular breaks by seeking sanctuary in Miami. I crossed many things off of my "bucket list," including traveling to Europe, hiking to Machu Picchu and volunteering in Peru, skydiving and buying a motorcycle.

HOLD YOUR SORROW GENTLY

My motorcycle was one of the biggest tools of my healing. In 2003, I rode into a gas station in Ft. Lauderdale, Florida, and met Ray, whom I later married. We are now living "happily even after" with our two daughters in Miami.

Being with others who have gone through similar loss and having your feelings validated by others who truly get it will make all the difference in your ability to move forward and heal. Grief is a marathon, not a sprint, and it is lifelong because love is lifelong. Hold your sorrow gently, seek loving support, and trust that time and change will carry you through.

Loss as a Public Figure

We live in a celebrity-driven culture. Where fashion magazines once limited their cover subjects to professional models ("super" and otherwise), these same publications now almost exclusively feature celebrities on their glossy covers. There are more television programs and publications revolving around celebrities (real and imagined) than ever before. Their every word is subject to broadcast and scrutiny. People want to know what they wear, what they eat (or *don't* eat) and who they date. Their lavish lifestyles are envied, and many fantasize what life might be like in their rarified world.

From all appearances, celebrities lead "perfect" lives. It then must certainly follow that celebrities are untouched by the bad things in life that befall mere mortals like us.

Except for one small problem.

Celebrities are human beings—and bad things happen to them too.

Lisa Kline is not just a presence—she is a force. She is a good friend—a metaphorical uncorked bottle of champagne that has been shaken first, and a bundle of seemingly limitless energy. Known as one of the visionaries at the forefront of what eventually became the "Robertson Boulevard" fashion scene in Beverly Hills, Lisa is a designer, stylist and fashion industry icon.[74] Her eponymous stores were the places to see, be seen and shop the latest styles and trends. Uniquely, if there was a celebrity in the store, the staff would press a button and electronically drop a paparazzi-proof screen over the windows, offering a modicum of privacy in an otherwise crazed atmosphere.

Off the grid, Lisa lives and loves just as hard as she works. Mother to two beautiful children, loving wife to Robert and friend to so very many, Lisa was one of those women who really seemed to have it all.

Until she seemed to have everything taken away.

However, if the universe thought that knocking Lisa down was going to keep her down, the universe was in for a huge surprise.

---

74 To learn more about Lisa, please visit www.lisakline.com.

Lisa's story

On January 22, 2009 at 1:20 a.m., everything that I once knew changed instantly, and my life would be different forever. I also knew it was the start of a very dark journey.

I'd found Robert lying under the table on our deck after falling twelve feet from the bedroom balcony. When six ambulances and six police cars arrived, I knew it would be the beginning of a lot of scrutiny from the public. In fact, the coroner called me and asked, "Who are you?" When I asked him why, he said, "I am receiving over eighty calls a day from the press, trying to find out what happened to Robert Bryson."

Robert's death was reported on several morning news shows, who all said something to the effect of, "The husband of fashion designer and stylist to the stars, Lisa Kline, passed away last night. They suspect it was sleepwalking."

I Was Meant to Help Others

I didn't walk around in despair. I believed that this life-changing event happened to me because I was meant to help others. I've always been a trailblazer, not a follower, and I knew that I had a greater purpose.

I tried to be as positive as I could. I walked around for about a year-and-a-half saying to myself, "Is *this* my life?" because it was so hard to believe that it had happened. I asked this question more as a comic relief for myself; I tried to use humor to ease the pain of my reality.

Grace in the Face of Losing Everything

Since I began my business in 1995, it was magical. I owned and operated five retail locations, an online store and a huge corporate warehouse. After the [economic] crash of 2008, I was dealing with the downsizing of the stores, laying off staff and trying to sell one of the homes against Robert's wishes. It also happened to be the house where Robert had died at the height of the recession.

The loss of my company was very painful, as I'd built it from scratch when I was twenty-five years old. I was closing down stores one by one, and I was losing everything [in addition to Robert's loss].

At that point, all I could control was how I looked. I could shower, put on makeup, do my hair and work out. I had no clue what was going to happen, but I *did* know that the world was looking at me. Staying put together was a good thing for me.

I became a warrior, and every day and night I'd say "Bring it on" out loud. It was years of torture. I had to be on my game and adjust to being a single mother of two small children [daughter Dylan and son Colt], a widow and [to the loss of] my business. I was also in the middle of two major lawsuits.

I worried about money, and I was furious that Robert died and left me with a mess to clean up alone. But I knew I had a choice to make, and my choice was to survive and keep moving forward—I had a lot to do. I was gracious in my exit from the stores, in my new widow-life and single motherhood. It was powerful, and I'm happy with my choice and determination.

CHANGING SCENERY CHANGED MY LIFE'S VISION

I was in a continual process of resolving my feelings. I did a television show [Bravo TV's, *Launch My Line*] a few weeks after Robert died, which was a nice diversion from what was happening.

After the "clean up," I decided to take what I called my "hard reset"; a life-changing trip. I needed to snap out of the fog. I couldn't find my passion or my imagination. It was inside of me but it was dormant. The trip did its job—it was time for my true reinvention.

There was something interesting about dealing with all of my losses in the public eye. I actually found it to be very supportive. My fans cheered me on; wanting to help, wanting to hug me and looking at me as a woman of strength. Being in the public eye helped me stay positive, strong, focused on the end goal and able to receive and give love. I was definitely in an abyss, but I was also connecting to my friends, fans and colleagues who were so helpful in getting me through the darkness.

I HAVE CHOSEN TO BE IN A GOOD PLACE

The only positive thing about grief is that no one can tell you what to do. Use that to your advantage. Use this time to reach into the depths of your soul and map how you're going to get through what may be the worst time of your life. You have control in your grief, your choices, and your life. Become a visionary. Take care of your needs and make decisions based upon that.

I am an optimist, which goes along with being an entrepreneur. I looked at this experience for me as a way to help others. I looked at these losses as an opportunity to start over. Nothing was easy, and it still isn't always easy, but I always keep a smile on my face and grace in my heart. I am in a good place because I have *chosen* to be in a good place. I have an entire new exciting life ahead of me. Why? Because, as I tell my children, we didn't die! We are alive, and we need to be happy and live this life the best way we know how...because that's what Daddy would want us to do.

HOW YOU CAN HELP

People sometimes forget that those who are in the public eye (either by choice or through high-profile bad-thing circumstances) are still human beings, with the same feelings and frailties as everyone else. Keeping this in mind:

Definite Do's

- **Make offers that include staying in:** Whether someone is already in the public eye because of their celebrity status or is catapulted into the public eye though a high-profile event, the last thing that she may want to do is go to a public place. Have suitable ideas prepared that do not involve places where crowds are likely to be. Lunch, dinner or cocktails...any kind of quiet activity will likely be welcomed.

- **Declare a media-free zone:** Public losses are covered in a public way. Add in that we have become a twenty-four-hour, instant-news-cycle society and it is very easy to be stricken with a severe case of information overload—and that is as a "civilian."
  Now imagine that you are at the epicenter of all the attention.

If you are staying in, make sure that your time and space with her is media-free. She does not need to see a loop of her tragedy playing continuously. Do her a huge favor—turn off the television and limit exposure to any media coverage while you are together. Enough is enough.

- **Be yourself and allow her to be herself as well:** Someone who has been thrust into the spotlight by tragedy needs a time and a place where she can let her hair down and her feelings out. Create the atmosphere where she will feel safe in doing so. Whether she needs to laugh, cry, be quiet or do something as simple as have a decent meal, be the island of normalcy in a sea of turmoil.

- **Reach out:** If you see or read of someone (public figure or otherwise) who has suffered a tragedy and you are moved to action, it is a lovely gesture to write a note or send an email through a website or social media page. They may not be able to respond, but many times, these letters, emails and notes of sympathy and encouragement are read, appreciated and treasured.

Without a Doubt...Don't

- **Don't ask after intimate or "gory" details:** *"What really happened?; "Okay, now tell me the 'real' story"; "Let's dish the dirt."*
  She is already dealing with enough inquiry and curiosity, and some of it downright morbid. She will reveal as many or as few details as she feels is appropriate. Respect her boundaries. Do not press her for details that she hasn't voluntarily revealed, and definitely do not approach her in a gossip-y "Come on, you can tell *me*" sort of way—you can easily destroy a relationship.
  A few years ago, a very good friend of mine suffered a very public loss that sadly became tabloid fodder. A couple of months after this tragedy, an acquaintance took me off to one side at a party and

conspiratorially whispered, "So, what *really* happened?" I could not believe the dying-for-juicy-details undertone of her question and felt like I had been slapped. After all, we are supposed to be adults, not a gaggle of high schoolers, huddling during a Friday night dance for the purposes of sharing "dirt."

How did I react? I looked at her with utter disgust and replied, "I know exactly what you know, and if I knew more, I would not be discussing it with you"...and then I turned and walked away. Happily, I have not seen that acquaintance since.

- **Don't betray confidences—for *any* reason:** As illustrated above, people ranging from friends and acquaintances to the media may approach you in an attempt to obtain information ranging from a personal email address to those "juicy details" to which the public may not be privy. You may even have money or other inducements thrown at you.

  This is called "selling out"...and it is despicable.

  Regardless of what the bad thing may be (divorce, death, break up, betrayal, loss, financial challenge, etc.), this is not "juice." This is not "gossip." This is someone's life and their personal tragedy should not serve as entertainment. Moreover, breaching the confidence of anyone who has entrusted you with personal information (or thoughts, feelings and emotions) is the very definition of betrayal. Choose instead to close ranks around your buddy, and refuse to disclose any information whatsoever. This is what friendship is all about.

- **Don't be intrusive:** If you recognize someone who has publicly suffered a tragedy, there is nothing wrong with briefly and appropriately expressing condolences and support. However, use good judgment—timing is everything. Do not approach someone when they are eating or, worse, when they are using the restroom (and yes, it does happen—a lot). Further, asking for an autograph or asking them to take a picture with you while they are in the midst of tragedy or mourning is entirely improper.

FROM BAD THING TO BRIGHTER DAYS AHEAD

If you find yourself dealing with a bad thing in a public forum, there are two things that I strongly recommend. First, appoint a family spokesperson to deal with media inquiry. This can be a relative, a close friend, a cleric, your attorney or someone from a governmental authority, such as a representative from law enforcement, if applicable. You should not have to be appearing in the media right now if you do not want to—and at least initially, most who are mid-bad-thing generally do not want to be in front of microphones.

Also make every effort to keep your Internet exposure to a minimum—in other words, stay off of social media. Remember too, that you do not have to participate any activities that make you uncomfortable (e.g., interviews, appearances, vigils, public memorials, etc.)…and you certainly are not obligated to answer any questions that you do not wish to answer.

The second thing I recommend is that you turn off the television and limit your exposure to all media coverage. You do not need to see your personal tragedy replayed over and over again and neither do your children. Most importantly, if you need help (either practically or emotionally), reach out for help. There is a lot of it out there, and all of it can be gotten confidentially.

Thinking back over her experiences after September 11, Tanya shares, "I embraced the public aspect of the loss by using the platform to bring attention to the senselessness of the terrorist attacks; I made sure that people had a personal connection to September 11 through sharing Sergio's life story and the journey through grief. There were times that it felt overwhelming to be under the constant barrage of news stories, as well as under the scrutiny of others who had judgments about how a widow 'should' behave. Peer support made an enormous difference in having my feelings validated and assuring me that I was not alone."

Lisa adds, "I am very happy with the decisions I made after the sudden loss of my husband. I had no idea if what I was doing was correct because the truth is there are no 'right' answers. All of the decisions I made were methodically thought out and made on my own. I choose not to be hard on myself. My life has been like a game board—this part of the game was very dark, and I did my best to get out of it. I'm proud of that girl."

Suffering a bad thing as a public figure or in a public way is an added challenge that most do not experience—and that can also invite its fair share of idiots and insensitivity. However, there is an upside; the reality that for every idiot or insensitive remark, there are millions of people who are in your corner. They are genuinely concerned and are rooting for your complete healing. Allow that support and compassion to buoy you and carry you forward.

By Their Own Hand: Suicide Survival

I wish to first make something very clear concerning suicide, especially for those of you who are suicide survivors. Please take careful note: Although their death may have been by their own hand, I fervently believe that your loved one did not "choose" to leave. Generally speaking, a suicide victim sees no other way out of their own personal pain. In other words, it is not that they wanted to leave...they felt that there was no way for them to stay.

Jan Andersen is the founder of the non-profit Child Suicide[75] and the author of *Chasing Death: Losing a Child to Suicide.* Lisa Schenke is the author of *Without Tim: A Son's Fall to Suicide, A Mother's Rise from Grief.*[76] Both women are suicide survivors, left behind to ponder the eternal question of "How could this happen?" However, each is determined to continue moving forward, keeping alive the legacies of love while teaching others to do the same.

Jan's story

My life took a dramatic turn following the suicide of my twenty-year-old son, Kristian, via an intentional heroin overdose. He left two notes—one to his girlfriend and another to everyone else saying, "Tell my mum and my

---

75 To learn more about Jan and *Chasing Death* (Perfect Publishers, Ltd.), please visit www.childsuicide.org.
76 To learn more about Lisa and *Without Tim* (Lisa Schenke), please visit www.withouttim.com.

family that I am sorry, but I hate myself and my life and I just could not take it anymore." Plunged into despair and trapped in a whirlpool of suffocating emotions, I knew that something positive had to emerge from such a senseless tragedy.

Even though I tortured myself by believing that there was something that I could have done to save my son, I became aware that this was a devastating situation that could strike any family. I felt driven to talk about depression and suicide in an attempt to help erase the stigma that prevents many from seeking help. I established the Child Suicide website to offer support to anyone who has experienced the loss of a loved one to suicide and to provide resources for the depressed and suicidal. I wrote *Chasing Death* to provide a voice for other survivors about the reality of grief after suicide, and to help people reassess their blinkered views on mental illness and depression.

POSITIVITY EMERGING FROM TRAGEDY

Bad things happen to everyone, irrespective of the type of person they are or the life they've led. I asked myself, "What can I learn from this?" and "How can I use this experience to help others?" Rather than be a victim, I believe that something positive has to emerge from every tragedy. The questions I asked after my son's suicide were, "Why didn't he tell me how he was feeling?" and "Why couldn't I have done something to prevent the tragedy?" There were also the "if only"s,; e.g., "If only I'd known how he was feeling," "If only he'd called," "If only I hadn't had cross words with him the last time we spoke," "If only I'd had told him I loved him more."

Immediately after Kristian's death, I felt completely detached from my body. The shock knocked me into a dreamlike state, and I was a spectator in my very worst nightmare. [But] I couldn't wake up [from it]—because this was cruel reality. I performed routine functions on autopilot, existing rather than living. There were many moments when I thought grief and guilt would kill me. All the threads and knots that had formed the tapestry of my life became unraveled, leaving a heap from which I could make no sense.

Initially, I could focus on little other than the manner that Kristian's life had ended. I grappled with the heartbreaking realization that death was the most favorable option to him, that killing himself was preferable to enduring whatever circumstances had caused him to slide into the dark, slippery depths of an emotional pit. My conversations with family and friends revolved around the suicide, rather than the person he was or the life that he'd led. I was supposed to protect him—but when he made the decision to end his life, I realized that I was unable to protect him from his own mind.

Becoming a Voice for Others

I knew what I had to do within an hour of the police officer delivering the news. In fact, when [the officer] was driving me to the hospital where my son had passed away, I told him, "I'm going to write about this until I'm blue in the face." I had to be a voice for families who were unable to articulate their complicated emotions, yet still wanted others to understand that this is a tragedy that can strike anyone regardless of background, family circumstances, personal circumstances or socioeconomic status. It made me uncomfortably aware of the fragility of life, and I developed a degree of paranoia about the safety of my other children, to the degree where I became overprotective.

Families of suicide victims often hide the truth from people, as they may believe it reflects badly on their relationship with the victim, or that suicide is equivalent to murder. They think about suicide bombers or convicted murderers who have taken their own lives in prison as a way of escaping their sentences, and fear their loved one being compared. This callous judgment would be too much to handle [and as a result], many suicide survivors endure the pain of isolation from a society that is largely ignorant about depression and suicidal behavior.

I swayed between determination to do something worthwhile and wondering how I was going to continue living without my son, experiencing the whole gamut of emotions. When I had to identify Kristian's body, I wanted to curl up beside him and die myself. What kept me going was knowing that I could never inflict the same misery on my family. I had other children and a loving partner, all of whom would be devastated.

The brief respite from the most intense phases of grief came in writing

Chasing Death. I sought comfort from online forums for parents who had lost a child and [connected] with other bereaved parents around the world. Being able to share our innermost feelings without fear of judgment was a great release.

THE FORCE OF REALITY

When the numbness and shock began to wear off, there was nothing to soften the pain—just the full force of cruel reality. When others expected me to be feeling better, I actually felt worse. They assumed that the pain had diminished and that I should be emerging from my cocoon of wretchedness to assume their interpretation of "normal." I felt unable to talk honestly to those close to me about the depth of my pain, because I didn't wish to cause them further discomfort. I coped the only way I knew how—by writing about what happened and communicating with other families who had experienced a similar tragedy, since they were the only ones who could truly understand my pain.

I also realized that despite his untimely death, Kristian still had a purpose. Were it not for his suicide, I would've never established the Child Suicide website, I wouldn't have written my book, I wouldn't have campaigned for suicide awareness and I wouldn't be helping other bereaved parents or depressed youth. I believe that Kristian has helped to save the lives of others.

At no point does one ever return to "normal." It will never again be the same normal that we knew when our child was alive. The "normal" that follows the loss of a loved one to suicide will be very different. While it will never again be the same, it's a normal that doesn't have to be perpetual misery. It encompasses an acceptance of life with a valuable part missing, and where phases of intense, resurfacing grief become customary.

I HONOR MY SON BY LIVING MY LIFE

Although the loss of a child is not something that you "get over," you eventually reach a point where joy and sadness coexist. Many people feel guilty when they experience pleasurable moments, almost as though they're insulting their loved one who has passed. However, our loved ones would never wish us to stop living. If they could speak to us, they'd want us to be happy and would hate the thought that their absence was causing so much pain. When I enjoy myself now, I think of it as honoring my son. It doesn't mean that I've forgotten him or that I'm no longer missing him.

Lisa's story

My oldest son, Tim, died by suicide at the age of eighteen, seven weeks short of his high school graduation. Tim was a scholar, athlete and sensitive boy with a wonderful smile; however, he also suffered from low self-esteem.

Tim had been evaluated throughout childhood and adolescence for depression and ADHD, but wasn't diagnosed or medicated. The hyperactive/impulsive characteristics were disregarded because Tim suffered no academic or social consequences. After Tim admitted to me (only once) that he wanted to take his life, he was treated for depression and possible bipolar [disorder]. During the three-and-a-half months between Tim's admission of feeling suicidal and his actual death, he convinced seven different professionals that he was not suicidal.

Since Tim's death, I've have reached out to many, and I'm deeply rewarded by helping others. What started out with talking to Tim's friends [eventually] grew to talking to other teens, young adults and parents in the community, then spread wider through social media, a website, and eventually the publication of *Without Tim*.

I'm proud of the progress that I've made in my grief recovery. It is a work-in-progress and I'm extremely grateful for the wonderful people I've met along the way.

How This Could Happen?

My husband and I are happily married, neither of us has ever taken drugs, we're not heavy drinkers and we lead a fairly normal life. We're not perfect [but] so many children are suffering from the challenges of living with parents who don't get along. So many others have parents who are drunk or high on drugs. Why [did this happen to] us?

MY DESIRE TO BE OPEN

I had to help my other two children survive; I worried about them night and day. I drove myself nuts trying to be available to them every time they walked in the door from school. I also obsessed over finding a specific reason for Tim's suicide—I went through his room a hundred times [and] tried to follow every Facebook communication I could.

I never planned to be proactive in suicide prevention, but my desire to communicate with others surfaced early on. My need to be approachable and as honest as possible was for the benefit of my other two sons, who were seventeen and fourteen years old at the time [of Tim's suicide]. My wish for them is to lead happy and emotionally healthy lives.

My desire to be open has allowed me to help others myself as well. I began with a letter to the editor of our local newspaper explaining that yes, Tim appeared to "have it all"; yes, Tim was self-medicating and yes, Tim was having difficulties getting over a girl. There are many factors in Tim's death, and there is not one specific cause for blame.

ALLOW YOURSELF TO FEEL GOOD AGAIN

I didn't experience shame or worry about what others were thinking. My friends were very supportive. I mainly felt sadness and guilt. I found a way to focus on modeling "embracing life." I found a fantastic grief counselor who helped me a lot. The main message I took away from working with him was, "When you feel good, you have to allow yourself those feelings. Even though it doesn't feel 'right,' the more you allow good feelings, the more natural they become."

Over time, I began to enjoy music again. I spent time with friends, spent as much time as possible in the sunshine, rode my bike, etc. These activities were not always enjoyable, but I trusted that things would get better.

MAKE THE TIME FOR LIFE'S EXPERIENCES

I deeply appreciate life. When feeling low, I remind myself that I feel good a lot of the time. I have become more compassionate; the change was gradual but I definitely feel it. Time doesn't eliminate the pain but it does help heal.

Depression will come and go. When you're feeling down, remind yourself that the feelings will pass. Grief does not end; it ebbs and flows.

I make the time for friends, fun activities and enriching life experiences. I enjoy every moment of watching my other two sons grow. My husband and I will be going to Europe for the first time [to celebrate] our thirtieth wedding anniversary. I allow myself to feel the good and the bad. I choose to live life to its fullest.

HOW YOU CAN HELP

Suicide survival is among the most sensitive, stigmatized and misunderstood types of loss. It involves so many complexities both for the person lost and the people left behind. Our family experienced two suicides within three years and though the questions by the survivors likely linger, there is still a great deal of support and comfort that you can offer.

Definite Do's

- **Act as a barrier between her and anyone who is behaving inappropriately:** Sadly, a suicide can elicit a tremendous amount of gossip and a borderline sickening amount of speculation. It is incredibly hurtful and not at all conducive to healing—and if you think that the immediate survivors do not find out about these whispers and innuendo, you are mistaken.

  If you come upon or are directly in the line of gossip surrounding a suicide, be a true friend and shut it down. Understanding that diplomacy has never been a strong suit of mine and for that reason, I personally do not see any problem with a rude shutdown; however, if you prefer to be diplomatic, you can say something like, "We don't have all of the facts, and I don't think that it's right to be talking about this."[77]

---

77 Actually, you can say that even if you *do* have all of the facts. Gossip is gossip, and it is just plain wrong.

- **Reassure her that there was nothing that she could do to prevent the situation:** One of the most common, baked-right-in sources of guilt for the survivor is the absolute conviction that there was something that she could have/should have done to prevent the suicide. She must understand that the suicide had very little to do with her and everything to do with the victim—that sometimes there simply are no signs or warnings.

  Help her understand that whatever her relationship to the victim, she was a loving, giving part of their life. Help her to reflect on a life lived, rather than a death planned. Lastly, get her to a source of support for suicide survivors so that she doesn't feel alone in her struggle to understand.[78]

- **Listen:** I bring up listening a lot and there is a good reason for it—it remains one of the kindest things that you can do for anyone who is suffering, and one of the things that oddly enough, not enough people are willing to do. When it comes to suicide, the pity is that many people are so uncomfortable with the subject, they shy away from discussing it altogether.

  Do not be afraid to bring up what happened. You can start by saying something like, "How are you *really* doing?" Putting the emphasis on the word "really" sends the message that it is OK to talk about whatever is on her mind...because you care.

Without a Doubt...Don't

- **Don't express negative opinion to a survivor:** *"I'm not at all surprised this happened"*; *"He/She was headed in that direction"*; *"Only cowards commit suicide"*; *"How selfish can you be* [to commit suicide]*?"*

---

78 For suicide survivor support, resources and information, visit The Alliance of Hope for Suicide Survivors at www.allianceofhope.org and the American Foundation for Suicide Prevention at www.afsp.org.

When I asked Jan about her reaction to others' opinions and the less-than-sensitive observations that people can make at such a difficult time, she replied, "Other people's opinions do not have to be my reality. What other people say is their responsibility, but how I react is mine."

This is without a doubt one of the most brilliant responses that I have ever heard (and took immediately into my heart). Suicide survivors shouldn't have to worry about negative opinions, conjecture or speculation. Are you entitled to an opinion? Yes. What you are not entitled to do is pile onto pain. Comments such as these only serve to hurt—keep your opinions away from suicide survivors and to yourself.

- **Don't say anything that will cause her to question herself:** *"Didn't you see any warning signs?"; "If only you hadn't left them alone..."; "Just think, if you'd have gotten home just ten minutes sooner..."*

   I can save everyone a whole lot of time here. Throughout my many years of experience working with the widowed community (which includes its fair share of suicide survivors), I can assure you that without exception, *every single suicide survivor* has these thoughts (and worse) playing in their already-troubled minds. If that were not enough, they have also likely encountered someone who is blaming them for not preventing another human being from doing that which they were determined to do. You really needn't point out the "If only"s and "Why did/didn't you"s of the situation—she is already doing it herself.

   She is also playing a very troubled loop of possible missed "warning signs" over and over in her head. The fact is that sometimes, there *aren't* any warning signs. As Lisa pointed out, sometimes there is absolutely *no* indication that anything is amiss...because someone who is seriously contemplating suicide can be quite capable of disguising what is going on inside.

Further, it is physically and logistically impossible to be with another human being twenty-four hours a day, seven days a week, 365 days a year. Unless there is a maximum security prison involved, human beings are not meant to be guardsmen or gatekeepers over one another, nor are they responsible for another's actions. Do not make her feel like she should never have left the house—believe me, if she thought on any level that her going to work or the grocery store would mean that she would return to an unimaginable tragedy, she never would have left in the first place.

- **Don't involve your personal religious beliefs:** *"You know God views suicide as murder, so they committed a sin against God"; "They won't go to Heaven because it was a suicide"; "Now you can't bury them in a* [insert faith here] *cemetery because they took their own life"; "Only God can take a life."*

  Yes, this happens. A lot.

  Now, I too hail from a religion that takes a dim view of suicide—most religions do. That said, I also recognize two very important points:

  1. My spiritual point of view is not necessarily everyone else's spiritual point of view.

  2. Why in the name of common sense would I *ever* deliberately and painstakingly paint a picture of eternal damnation and condemnation for someone who is already suffering beyond comprehension?

If a suicide survivor brings up the matter of religion and God to me, I will *listen.* I will listen to *their* concerns, *their* beliefs and *their* worries. I will encourage them to seek guidance from *their* cleric and from *their* church, synagogue, mosque or any other house of worship or organization that I have inadvertently omitted. What I will *never* do is arrogantly determine the spiritual destiny of another person based on my beliefs. As stated earlier, to my mind, there is only one judge who has that privilege and that judge is not anyone who is currently walking the earth.

- **Do not make jokes about the suicide—*ever*:** Normally, I would include quotes as examples, but the very idea of giving any paper to attempts at levity surrounding such a horrible event makes me ill.

    Suffice it to say, joking about a suicide is disgusting and beneath contempt. Don't do it…and loudly refuse to tolerate it from anyone who does.

More Than a "Just": Saying GoodBye to a Pet

It might seem silly to include the loss of a pet in a book of this ilk; however those who now own or have ever owned pets will undoubtedly nod along when I say that the death of a pet can certainly be considered both a bad thing and a most difficult event. As the owner of quite a few pets throughout most of my life, I can affirm that when the awful day comes that you must say good-bye to a little personality with its own idiosyncrasies, routines and infinite ways of making you laugh out loud or feel better when you need it most, when this adorable creature has loved you unconditionally and asked for nothing more than your love in return…it is a difficult and sad day indeed.

A Final True Story

My Aunt Betty was a "broad" in the most fabulous sense. She loved to gamble, she loved her Scotch on the rocks, she swore like a sailor and made no apologies for smoking. She had an opinion and she was not afraid to use it; nor was she afraid of standing up to anyone or anything. She was one tough bird.

Except when it came to Princess.

Princess was Aunt Betty's cat…and her entire world. She loved Princess as one would love a child—especially because Aunt Betty never had any children. She talked about, proudly showed pictures of and doted on Princess constantly.

Gift-giving was always easy when it came to Aunt Betty—either something for Princess or something that had anything whatsoever to do with cats.

Princess lived to be eighteen years old and passed peacefully in her sleep. After her passing, I noticed a distinct change in Aunt Betty, almost as if the light in her eyes and the spark in her spirit had dimmed. She was quieter and far less boisterous at family functions. There was a haunting sorrow about her. When another family member asked if she was going to get another cat, she would shake her head and change the subject. One could tell that losing Princess was every bit as profound for Aunt Betty as the loss of a human being would have been.

Not long after Princess's death, Aunt Betty too passed away.

I will always quickly reassure anyone mourning the loss of a pet that going through all of the grief processes is completely normal. Unfortunately, there will likely be at least one person in your midst that will say something to the effect of "It was 'just' a dog" or "It was 'only' a cat." We will be discussing that later—but for now, please hold on to the reminder that if love is love…then loss is loss. Grief cannot be measured by who or what was lost.

Bottom line: Do not deny yourself the right to mourn the loss of your pet, even if others would try to diminish or eliminate that right.

ALLOW YOUR PROCESS TO UNFOLD WITHOUT BLAME

A grieving process is quite common, particularly if your pet was very young, became suddenly ill or was lost soon after it became part of your family. Allow yourself to go through this process thoroughly, despite what others around you may be encouraging you to do (e.g., getting a "replacement" pet, etc.). If your pet did pass away at a younger age, do not automatically assume that it was something that you did or didn't do. Most of the time, when pets die at a young age, it was either due to an accident or something was not physically right to begin with. Please do not blame yourself.

FREEDOM TO LOVINGLY REMEMBER

Anyone who has pets also has a routine that goes along with the pets…and oftentimes, that routine is established by the pet. For example, our cat Sassy has a specific time of day that she designated as "Love-Me Time." Unfortunately, that time generally occurs somewhere between 4:00 a.m. and 5:00 a.m. She has been this way since she was eight weeks old and woe to the soul who doesn't respond to her requests for affection. I do not know where she hides her watch, but danged if that cat doesn't know exactly what time it is and goes loudly hunting for one of her (sleeping) two-legged family members.

Beyond routines set by pets, there are also the other daily routines: the times to go for a walk, play, eat, explore, cuddle…the list goes on. There are also those wonderful "little things"—being greeted at the door after returning home from a long day, that special place on the couch or on the bed that belonged to them (at least in their minds), the birdcage in the kitchen from where happy songs and chatter emerged.

When your pet is no longer here, the routine is jarringly eliminated, leaving a huge hole in both your daily life and your heart. As with any grieving process, you must let the immediate aftermath unfold on its own, according to your time frame and comfort level. Take your time in putting away or disposing of the vestiges of your pet (food dishes, beds, toys, cages, etc.). There is no rule that says it all has to be done immediately.

You might also include ways to honor the memory of your pet. For example, it has become quite common for pet owners to have a small memorial. You may wish to light a candle and place a small picture next to it or put together a collage of pictures for display. You can do whatever it is that brings you comfort and a measure of peace, regardless of what anyone else may say or think.

The Most Common Dilemma: Getting a "Replacement"

I am one of those people who believe that pets cannot be "replaced." You cannot simply slot another pet into the place that the last pet held in the household and in your heart. Every single pet that I have ever owned came with their own personalities, habits, charms—and irritations. Using our own Three (Feline) Amigas as examples:

- Pepper's primary residence is on my home office desk. She lounges happily on top while I work alongside her, and when she decides that it is time to quit working, she will stop me from typing by placing her paw on my hand. She turns up her nose at virtually all cat food, yet descends from the heavens if she smells bread in the toaster. Paper clips are her "prey" and if she gets hold of one, she will howl as if she had caught a vulture.

- Bandit is a full-figured twenty-two pounds and would rather teethe on a plastic bag than visit her food dish. She gladly approaches visitors and displays her back end, begging for it to be scratched (eliciting many confused looks from the aforementioned visitors). She also has a distinct talent for effecting the most balefully sorrowful look, while softly stroking you with her paw. I believe she stole this move directly from Oliver Twist (i.e., "Please sir, can I have some more?").

- Solid black with huge green eyes, Sassy (whom you met earlier) is a breed unto herself. She believes herself to be a dog: she comes when called, wags her tail in excitement and plays fetch. She is afraid of no one and intimidated by absolutely nothing. Our cats have always been indoor cats as we live in an area where coyotes reside and roam… and Pepper and Bandit are perfectly content to remain indoors. In stark contrast, Sassy's singular mission is to get out and run rampant. When she has escaped, she has led us on merry chases through the neighborhood—and I am quite confident that if she ever did happen upon a coyote, she would march up and hit him in the nose.

You may now have a better idea of why I rail against the notion that a pet can be easily replaced by another animal. For that reason, I highly recommend giving yourself as much time as you need to mourn your loss prior to making decisions concerning another pet.

ACKNOWLEDGE YOUR LOSS AS IMPORTANT

The kindest thing you can do for yourself after the loss of your pet is acknowledging that this is a huge loss. It seems counterintuitive to have to say something this obvious; however, there are people in the world (most of whom do not own or like animals) who do not understand how animals infiltrate our hearts and affect our lives. Consequently these people also do not understand the grief involved when a pet passes away. Sadly, people experiencing this loss are made to feel foolish for feeling the loss so profoundly.

Do not feel foolish, silly or childish. You have experienced a loss, pure and simple. If others do not understand your loss or the gravity that this loss carries for you—find those who *do* understand. Believe me, there are plenty of us out there.

HOW YOU CAN HELP

People are pet owners because they love animals and animals enrich their lives. No one who dislikes animals owns an animal. Is it wrong not to love animals? Of course not. However, it is incumbent upon you to understand that a love for animals naturally implies that losing a beloved pet is extremely traumatic and will evoke feelings of deep sorrow.

Am I equating the loss of an animal to the loss of a human being? Absolutely not. However—and this is important—there are people who *do* make that equation. I may not agree, but I will not impose that opinion on others. As with any loss, I never tell anyone else how they should or should not be feeling, and the loss of a pet is no different.

How can you best support someone who has just lost a pet? Quite simply.

Definite Do's

- **Send them a sympathy card:** Greeting card companies have gotten wise to the fact that the loss of a pet is a loss that should elicit sympathy. As a result, there are many wonderful cards on the market that speak specifically to pet loss. It is so inexpensive to purchase and mail a card to someone who has lost a pet and is trying to reconcile that loss. Not only have you shown them that you care, you have also sent the message that you take their grief seriously.

- **Encourage dialogue:** Ask to hear funny "remember when" stories about the pet (trust me, we all have those stories). Look at cute pictures. Dialogue helps the grieving to process their loss and this loss is no different. You can help alleviate the pain, and you will be one of the "good guys" who takes her loss seriously.

Without a Doubt…Don't

- **Don't reduce the gravity of the loss:** *"It was only a dog/cat/fish/ bird"; "All animals do is make a mess and drain your wallet"; "For Heaven's sake, it was just a _____, they're a dime a dozen."*

  To you? Perhaps. To the bereft owner? It was a family member. It brought smiles, laughter and gave unconditional love. It was company on lonely nights. What a pet *wasn't* was a "just."

  Mike was an award-winning canine (K9) handler on the police department for most of his career. The dog who helped put "award-winning" in that title was Carlos, a Belgian Malinois. Together, he and Mike were responsible for setting national records in the seizure of drugs and drug money.

  One day, Carlos suddenly stopped eating. He could not stand. Mike needed help from other officers in loading Carlos into the van to take him to the veterinarian (who cared for many of the police dogs throughout the county). After an undergoing a series of tests, the vet determined that Carlos had lung cancer (attributed to the years of sniffing out enormous quantities of drugs) and that his lungs were filling. In other words, Carlos was dying and would suffer tremendously in the process.

  The decision was clear—and it was a heartbreaking decision for Mike to make.

  For Carlos was not just Mike's partner. He was also a pet.

  Within the hour, all officers in the K9 unit who were not on duty arrived at the vet's office and joined other officers, all of whom were there to provide support. We crowded into a small examining room and waited while Mike took Carlos out on a nearby greenbelt for one last time. They returned and tears streamed down Mike's face as he and Carlos entered the room.

The silence in the room was deafening, broken only by sounds of our soft crying. As Mike held Carlos and the rest of us held one another, the vet helped Carlos cross the rainbow bridge into a place of peace.

As is ritual with most police departments, a memorial was held, as police canines are also considered officers (complete with official police badges). I was still working in law at the time and when I informed the attorney with whom I worked that I was leaving early to attend Carlos' memorial, I was met with:

"What's the big deal? It was only a dog."

Did I hit him? No…but I fantasized about it.

A pet is not "only a dog" or "just a cat" or "that noisy bird." A pet is a living being who brought love into a home and made a difference in people's lives. If you think that a pet is a "just" or an "only," that is fine and certainly your prerogative. What is *not* fine is expressing that sentiment to someone who has experienced this loss.

- **Don't make someone feel foolish:** *"Don't you think you're overreacting?"; "It wasn't a person"; "Come on, it's just not that big of a deal."*

  I never understood people who felt that they could dictate feelings to other people. It would be like saying "You need to be right-handed" if you are left-handed. You are who you are. How you feel is how you feel. I would never tell someone to quit crying or quit being angry or quit feeling what they are feeling—because you cannot "quit" a feeling, anymore than you can quit being left-handed.

  Instead of making someone feel silly for grieving, get behind their eyes and into their heart for a moment. Would *you* want to be told how to grieve or how to feel? Probably not.

  In short, their reaction is *their* reaction and is not subject to ridicule.

- **Don't imply that a pet is easily replaceable:** *"You can always get another* _____*";* *"Let's go to the animal shelter/pet store and get another* _____*";* *"When you get another* _____ *you won't miss* [the pet who has passed] *so much."*

  While you may be acting in what you believe to be her best interests with a hurry-up attempt to replace her pet, grieving takes time. Accepting that a pet is no longer part of the household takes time. Can she easily obtain another animal? Of course—but is it wise to do so immediately? Not necessarily.

  The decision to get a new pet *must* come from the person who is grieving the lost pet—and it must come in their time. It may be a matter of days, it may be years—or it may never happen at all. You cannot circumvent a mourning process by attempting to replace what is lost—and that includes the loss of a pet.

- **Don't surprise them with a new pet:** It is a kind gesture; however, as pointed out above, the decision to get another pet must be made on the part of the person who has just experienced the loss. If *she* begins talking about another pet or appears eager to do so, this may be a surprise to consider. Make absolutely sure that those hints are being dropped and that she really wants a new pet—otherwise and despite the kindness intended, you may instead create a very awkward situation.

FROM BAD THING TO BRIGHTER DAYS AHEAD

Owning pets automatically means that at some point, we will be bidding goodbye to them. It is both a heartbreaking thought and a huge responsibility. I know that the day will come when I will have to say goodbye to those three precious little furry faces you met earlier, and after having owned each of them since the age of eight weeks (all of them are in their mid-teen years now), I know that it will be an awful experience. However, I would not trade in one moment of the comfort, love, laughter or peace that each one of those crazies have brought to our family. Furthermore, I would be happy to again welcome a fabulous feline into our home…but only when the time is right.

Do not hesitate to keep the memories of your pet alive. Remember them and the love that they gave you without condition—and if and when the time is right for you, do not think twice about welcoming another precious pet into your home and into your heart.

A Final Word Concerning Death and Bereavement

Death of a loved one—no matter the relationship perspective—is the biggest bad thing and greatest grief that one can experience. It is vital that you remember to:

1. **Grieve each loss individually, regardless of the relationship or the proximities of the loss one to the other.** For example, I lost my husband and my father within four months of one another. I was spouse to one and the child of the other. Even though both are devastating losses, the loss perspectives are entirely different and must be recognized as such.

2. **Recognize that there is no statute of limitations with loss.** If you feel stuck in a place of sorrow and need help moving forward, seek out help immediately. However, do not feel as though you have to hurry through your grief—not for anyone or for anything.

3. **You *can* be the first avenue of comfort to someone who is bereaved**. If someone you know has experienced or is facing the death of a loved one, you now know how you can best be a source of support and comfort. Even though not your original intent, you may truly be a heroine to someone who is suffering.

Hopefully I have also counteracted the whole "I Don't Know What to Say/What to Do" syndrome that seems to afflict far too many who surround the bereaved. No longer are the excuses "I don't know what to say" or "I'm afraid of saying/doing the wrong thing" acceptable. While I am not sure that I ever bought into the cliché that "Ignorance is bliss," this I know for certain:

When it comes to consoling the bereaved, ignorance is not "bliss."

It is instead a gigantic *miss.*

Chapter Fourteen

VICTIMIZED...BUT NOT A VICTIM

MANY PEOPLE SPEND A GREAT DEAL OF TIME TALKING ABOUT THE "GOOD OL' days" that are the decades of yesteryear—but rarely do people speak of some of the things that comprise part of the flip side of those particular days.

You see, in those decades gone by, women had little in the way of basic rights. Most did not have any kind of personal financial security; most banks would not even grant a loan to a woman. Husbands could not be accused of criminal acts like raping their wives because wives were considered "property" and sex was considered a husband's "right," regardless of how his wife felt or what was going on in the marriage. Stalking was not considered a criminal act until or unless the offender "moved" against his victim[79]...and good luck pressing a domestic violence charge resulting in anything beyond a police officer saying, "Can't you just talk it out?"

To coin a once-popular phrase, we have indeed come a long way.

---

79 Tragically, the first indication of such "movement" against a victim was generally the victim being killed by their stalker.

However, as far as women have come, many laws (particularly those involving the Internet) are taking time to catch up. Meanwhile, the statistics for women victimized by criminal behavior are sobering and crimes against women still happen with alarming frequency. The good news is that with time and the advancement of the legal system, there are now stricter laws in place, harsher punishments for criminals and numerous resources available to anyone who is a crime victim.[80]

You are about to meet some incredibly inspiring women, all of whom have suffered unbearable pain on virtually every level and in every way possible. Yet all of these women refused to be defined as "victims." They did not let their perpetrators determine their destinies, and they are all resolute in their goal to teach others to do the same.

Fighting for Your Life:
Surviving Domestic Violence

Founder of the nonprofit organization Strength Against Violence[81] and a public speaker and advocate who appears in national and international media, Holly McCrary had it together at what many consider to be a young age. Where her contemporaries were living the storied lives of single girls in their twenties, Holly was the mother of a young son and a homeowner, enjoying an already-successful career that was poised to take her to even greater heights.

Not only did Holly almost lose everything that she held dear, she almost lost her life in a shockingly horrific act of domestic violence. However, the perpetrator underestimated the strength of Holly's spirit and determination by a long shot.

While Holly's attacker inflicted life-threatening wounds from which she is still recovering, her will and her spirit are both stronger than his heinous act

---

80 A comprehensive list of resources and contact information is included at the conclusion of this chapter.
81 To learn more about Holly, her story of survival and the non-profit organization Strength Against Violence, please visit www.strengthagainstviolence.org and www.hollymccrary.com.

of violence. Holly refused to be taken, both from her son and the life that she built and loves so much.

Holly's story

I was living a normal, happy life. I was twenty-five years old and raising a wonderful five-year-old boy. My circumstances were not the easiest, but despite the hardships, I was able to overcome the odds and provide for my son. I purchased a small condominium, I worked a regular schedule and I was home every night for my son.

Fifteen days before Christmas and ten days before my son's sixth birthday, M* took all of that away. He showed up at our home in the middle of the night, tried to kill me and very nearly succeeded. I was stabbed over twenty-two times in the heart, lungs, chest, neck, face, back and arms.

I got away and I climbed a flight of stairs to a neighbor's house. The neighbor let me in and, just when I thought I was safe, M burst into her house and began attacking me again. With over twenty-two stab wounds, broken bones and an extreme amount of blood loss, I tried to hold on to life. It took everything I had to stay conscious because I knew if I closed my eyes, it would be over.

The officers arrived prior to the paramedics. One of them tried really hard to keep me awake. He yelled at me to stay with him, to keep my eyes open. At that point, I realized that I might not make it. I needed to tell [the police officer] who did this so that if I died they could hold him accountable. The only thing that kept me from dying was the thought of my little boy being left alone and finding out that his mom died ten days before his birthday and right before Christmas.

When I finally left the hospital, I stayed with family. I couldn't walk. I couldn't care for my son, and I had to be cared for day and night. I couldn't take a shower on my own; I couldn't even use the bathroom on my own. If I lay down all the way, I couldn't breathe. I could not eat or drink on my own, and I had no use of my arms.

I am still in the recovery process. The doctors say that it's a miracle that I am alive today. I still have a hole in my heart and liver, and it's still unknown if they'll operate on those areas. I still have no feeling or use of most of my left hand, no feeling in parts of both of my arms, my jaw and chin, parts of my neck and back, and most of my chest. Forcing myself to get up in the morning sometimes seems impossible. But despite all that has happened, I refuse to give up. I will keep fighting. I refuse to let him win.

I Refused to Blame Myself

The first question I asked myself was, "What did I do to cause this?" This is something that is horribly wrong with the way our culture views victims of violent crimes. We have a habit of "victim-blaming," from rape victims who are blamed for wearing revealing clothing, to the murder victims who are blamed for choosing bad guys. In my case, I was "the stabbing victim who probably did something to upset or to anger her ex-boyfriend."

I look back now and I see how wrong he was and how wrong *I* was for thinking that I was to blame or that I could have or should have done something differently. I never felt sorry for myself and I always stayed strong, especially for my son.

I Worried About Our Future

Many victims of domestic violence have serious injuries. I was lucky enough to make it, but because of these life-threatening injuries, I spent a very long time in the hospital. The entire time that I was [hospitalized], I wasn't working, so one of the first difficulties I faced was guilt. Who was going to throw the birthday party for my son? Who was going to take him to hockey practice? Who was going to sing to him at night and read him a story? What if he needed me and I wasn't there? These were the only things I could think about…it was so hard.

I Will Not Succumb to Depression

I thought that fighting for my life would be the hardest obstacle I would have to face. I thought, "Just stay alive. Keep fighting so the doctors can fix you." I didn't know that when I woke up, I'd still be fighting for my life and that more surgeries were in store. This was a recurring theme for two years.

Every time I thought that I'd overcome something, there was another battle.

Leaving the hospital did not mean going home. I had to go back to the hospital several times a week to learn to sit up, eat and drink on my own, and eventually [learn] to stand and walk. When I was able to do the basics on my own, I was able to go home. This was such an accomplishment, but of course new challenges arose. My home is where [the attack] happened, and I was weak and helpless. What if M got out on bail and came back to "finish the job"? What if I couldn't protect my son?

I still visit doctors regularly and recently underwent another surgery. I can see how someone in this situation might succumb to the depressing thoughts that invade your mind, but I refuse to do that, no matter the number of setbacks or how hard the obstacles.

I Am Thankful for the Life that I Have Now

I may never know what the reasoning was [behind the attack] or why he felt the need to do something so horrible. The fact remains that he chose to do what he did, and I'm not to blame for his choices.

The best advice that I can give is to keep fighting, keep living and don't give up. At times it can seem like no matter how hard you work, something always sets you back...but there will come a time that will make all the hard work worthwhile. You can get through this.

The important thing is that you keep living life. Learning to focus on even the smallest positive things can help more than you know. I'm still facing many hardships but there have also been so many things that I've overcome. If I'd given up, I would have missed all of the good things along the way. I am very thankful for the life that I have now, and I look at each day of my life as a gift.

AUTHOR NOTE: As the book goes to press, we were advised that Holly's attacker was tried and convicted on all counts with which he was charged: attempted murder; first-degree burglary with domestic violence; torture and assault.

Heart Wounds: The Abusive Relationship (emotional and verbal)

When someone uses the term, "domestic violence," we generally think of incidents that are similar to Holly's story—scenarios involving a physical attack or physical attacks taking place on a regular basis. Sadly, a great many people mistakenly think that because a physical attack or weapons or physical injuries are not involved, that a relationship is not abusive.

Think again.

Maxine Browne is the author of *Years of Tears: One Family's Journey Through Domestic Violence,*[82] which chronicles her story of abuse, her eventual recognition that she was being abused, the warning sides of abuse (physical, verbal and/or emotional) and how she emerged from her darkness as an advocate for abuse victims.

Maxine's story

Five years and two children after my divorce, I met a man who I thought was the answer to my prayers. He turned out to be my worst nightmare.

John* swept me off my feet, speaking the language of my faith. He was a minister who promised to honor and love me before God. After my disastrous first marriage to a drug addict, I couldn't believe my good fortune. John said that he was going to help me raise my two daughters. Since I was an overworked single mom, this was music to my ears. A long-distance romance ensued, followed by a nine-month engagement.

After we were married, I worked full-time and John was at home. He said he'd help me with errands. He told me he'd pick up the mail for me and I handed over the key. I didn't see the mail for the next *ten years*. He was going to make the bank deposits and then took over the banking, winding up with my credit cards. He was taking control over my life, one area after another.

John forced my children to do most of the household chores. He became their disciplinarian and cut off communications between them and myself.

---

82 To learn more about Maxine and *Years of Tears* (Bridge Communications), please visit www.maxinebrowne.com.

He kept the children locked in the basement hour after hour. Gradually, my own voice was silenced. I became the person standing in the background in silence, unable to protect my children from their stepfather.

The children finally left home to escape the abuse. Afterward, it was nearly impossible to speak with them, and seeing them was out of the question. John controlled all of the money. He rationed my time. After the children were out of the house, I rarely saw them anymore.

After ten years of abuse, I was no longer the person I once was. I became severely depressed and began to plan my suicide. I had decided to hang myself in our shed. I knew how I would kill myself and where, I just hadn't chosen the day. However, instead of going through with suicide, I chose instead to leave with only my clothing in trash bags.

Searching for God

I was a devout Christian and my belief system was that, as a woman, my role was to submit to my husband. If I submitted myself to his authority, God would defend me. God would answer my prayers and speak to change my husband's heart.

My husband called us horrific names. I did not defend myself. We bore his insults as he called us worthless, lazy, scum and much worse. I prayed about the verbal abuse. Why didn't God intervene? Where was His defense?

We all struggled under the weight of the workload that my husband piled upon us. I cried out to God, asking him for clarity. Surely, He didn't intend women to live this way. I felt bruised and battered...but John had never beaten me. Because of the lack of physical assault, was this relationship abusive? God was silent. Search as I might, I could not find my answers in the bible.

I Regained My Sense of Self

A woman [I knew] said that I could live with her until I got myself together—and I did just that. She allowed me to stay with her for fourteen months, and during that time, I figured out how to put my life back together. After ten years, my life felt like the site of an atomic bomb blast. There was nothing left of the life that I had prior to meeting John. I'd given away my power. I'd been ruined financially and had mountains of debt. My children and I were estranged, and I had to rediscover who I was.

Once I decided to leave, John became a lunatic who harassed me endlessly over the phone, showed up at the house and bounced between love notes and threats that he would destroy me. He claimed that if I came home, he would stop the abuse.

John and I had created our own company during our marriage, serving as interpreters/translators and working to bridge the communication gap between the Hispanic population and the English-speaking world. When I left the marriage, I also left the business and created an entirely different career while negotiating my divorce and custody arrangements. The practical business matters were tough to handle, but they were nothing compared to the emotional and psychological healing I faced.

At the time I left, I'd been days away from committing suicide and, needless to say, I wasn't in the best frame of mind. I began attending Adult Children of Alcoholics meetings which gave me a place to begin healing. I was able to talk about the abuse and process my feelings. These meetings also helped me begin healing from the childhood wounds of having lived in an alcoholic home. Once I'd found a full-time job, I began counseling. Shortly thereafter, I got a car, and I finalized my divorce. I purchased a mobile home. Little by little, I regained my sense of self.

A Life Free from Abuse

I worked on healing for several years. I continued attending Adult Children of Alcoholics meetings for four years, individual therapy for two years and domestic violence support group meetings for one year. I worked on a survivor's task force under our state's coalition against domestic violence for two years before becoming the chairperson of the task force; our efforts are spent increasing awareness and understanding of domestic violence. I made new friends and began a life free from abuse.

I got the idea to write a book about our family's experiences; however, I didn't want the book to be my story exclusively. The abuse in our household touched many lives, and everyone experienced the same events very differently. I decided to interview my children, and anyone else who consented to be interviewed.

GETTING AWAY FROM ABUSE

I [have since] met and married a wonderful man. He is kind, we enjoy our life together and he's my biggest fan. I travel the country, sharing the story of abuse and recovery in the hopes that I can save other families from the years of tears we suffered. I'm developing new materials with the intention of creating school programs that will teach about healthy relationships. Domestic violence is preventable through education, and together we can end abuse of all sorts.

Anyone can be a victim of domestic violence. If you are in a controlling relationship, you are not alone. Please call a domestic violence hotline *today* to find ways to plan your escape and your safety. If you're thinking about leaving the relationship, *don't* announce your plans to your abuser. It's when women are trying to leave that they are in the greatest danger.

This is a problem that surrounds us. Know how to recognize the signs. Don't turn away from abuse...you could save someone's life.

After the Unspeakable Crime: Child Molestation

Molestation is a crime that makes us shudder to even think about. It makes our skin crawl. We recoil in disgust at the perpetrators of such an evil act. While our only recourse in a civil society, we all agree that prison is too good for these beings who are beneath contempt—and an actual prison is nothing compared to the metaphorical "prison" to which many of their innocent victims are sentenced and in which many live day to day.

Unfortunately, we are so appalled and disgusted that our discomfort can unwittingly deny victims the opportunity to talk about their experiences. Worse, and in many cases, victims are denied justice or even support—someone who will look at them and say, "I believe you and I want to help."

It is for those brave survivors that this story must be told. Meet Kelly

Meister-Yetter, author of *Crazy Critter Lady*[83] and survivor of child molestation at the hands of her father.

Kelly's story

My father molested me for over ten years, starting when I was two years old. The abuse led to years of alcoholism, terrible self-esteem, dysfunctional relationships with inappropriate men and multiple suicide attempts. I was desperately unhappy and had no idea how to make a satisfying life for myself. As a result of the abuse, I suffered from depression and post-traumatic stress disorder (PTSD).

"Buying" My Silence Inhibited My Recovery

As a teenager, I made many cries for help that my family dealt with by ignoring the cause of my problems—they all turned a blind eye to the abuse. My family tried to "buy" my silence with money, gifts and after my last suicide attempt, bail-outs that financed a year-long emotional meltdown. The result was that as an adult, I had a huge sense of entitlement. Instead of trying to move forward with my life, I was stuck in a loop of feeling sorry for myself that inhibited recovery.

Life Had to Drastically Change

After my last suicide attempt, I spent two weeks in the psychiatric ward of a hospital. I made the conscious decision to rip the Band-Aid off of my emotional wounds and let healing begin. Although I'd spent years in therapy prior to my hospitalization, the real work began only after I recognized that my life needed to change drastically. It was the right decision for me but it created huge problems among family members who had been previously involved in buying my silence—because I refused to be silent any longer.

The dynamic of my familial relationships changed. I had no contact with my father, I had limited contact with my mother and I began speaking the

---

83 To learn more about Kelly and *Crazy Critter Lady* (CreateSpace Independent), please visit www.crazycritterlady.com.

truth to anyone who would listen. I refused to back away from the ugly truth that my family tried to keep hidden for so many years.

FORWARD IS THE ONLY DIRECTION WORTH MOVING IN

Almost ten years after the last suicide attempt, and after years of dedicating myself to intensive therapy sessions, I felt sufficiently clear-headed to think about writing a book. I'd amassed enough stories about the animals I'd spent years rescuing to fill a book. Those "critters"—all of whom contributed in some way to my sanity and well-being, were potent medicine for my fragile psyche, and I attribute the vast majority of my recovery to their unconditional love.

I'm writing a follow up to *Crazy Critter Lady*, as well as continuing my recovery work. I recently married the love of my life, and I continue to move forward because forward is the only direction worth moving in. And that's worth getting out of bed for!

TALKING *YOUR* TRUTH

There *is* hope for a better life! It requires you to take charge of your recovery. Start focusing on your strengths—no matter how few of them there seem to be at the outset—and shed any negative voice within; [that voice] is not your friend, and it's not looking out for your best interests. Keep going to therapy, and keep searching until you find a therapist who fits your needs.

Stop listening to the people who want to keep you silent, and start talking your truths to those who will listen. The best piece of advice I ever got was the one piece of advice I initially struggled against: Empower yourself! Having control over your feelings, your situations and yourself is the most potent medicine there is.

Every Woman's Nightmare: Sexual Assault

Without doubt or argument, it is the ultimate violation against women. The mere thought of such a thing sends a cold chill down one's spine.

Sexual assault.

Unbelievably in the twenty-first century, sexual assault remains one of the most underreported crimes. Even now, women are terrified to report sexual assault for any number of reasons—fear of recrimination (i.e., someone inferring that she was "asking for it"); fear of the judicial process; fear that what they see on television police dramas is the truth; the list is long.

Many people also make the mistake of assuming that sexual assault is a crime of sex. On the contrary, it is a crime of torture and violence. It is an attempt to render a person powerless, while empowering the criminal with a feeling of invincibility.

Happily, there is a way through the horror to a place of healing. CJ Scarlet and Jillian Bullock are two women who were each sexually assaulted, yet went on to turn their horror into hope and their personal experiences into advocacy for victims everywhere. As these women and millions more like them demonstrate, healing after sexual assault is neither quickly nor easily accomplished. However, their refusal to become lifetime victims of this horrendous set of circumstances combined with their determination to use their experiences for good by enriching lives is an inspiration to us all.

CJ's story

I was nineteen years old when [the assault] happened. I was a carefree college student dating a sheriff's deputy. I felt so safe when I was with him… after all, he was a cop.

We'd been on a couple of dates, so when my car broke down, I called him to take me home. He wanted to stop by his apartment first and invited me in. No sooner were we through the door when he lifted me into his arms and carried me to his room. I laughed and told him to put me down. He ignored me, and I suddenly read the intention on his face. Fighting panic, I demanded that he put me down and started to struggle under his grip. He threw me on the bed as I fought with all my might.

He overpowered me easily and I began to zone out, feeling dissociation creeping through my veins. The only thing I felt aware of was my head slamming violently into the headboard, over and over again. When he was done, he drove me home and gave me two hundred dollars to get my car fixed. I wondered if that made me a prostitute.

I fell into a deep depression and began failing most of my classes. I slinked home to live with my parents and sat numbly while family hubbub went on around me. My mother broke the impasse by demanding that I "snap out of it." My father suggested I enlist in the military, [saying that] some discipline would do me good.

After joining the Marine Corps, I was again raped, this time by my recruiter. The second incident was a direct result of my response to the first...I was simply too terrified in that moment to resist. I came to hate my body, my face, my bubbly personality—everything that "attracted" these men to attack me, believing it was somehow my fault.

THERE IS SOMETHING WRONG WITH ME

I believed there was something inherently wrong with me that made people do bad things [to me]. My question was not, "Why me?" but rather, "Of *course,* me."

CARRYING—AND ABANDONING—THE SHAME

For the next two decades, I carried the trauma, shame and fear with me like a black stain on my soul. I limped through those years like a wounded animal, my former confidence in myself completely shattered. Although I excelled on the outside, I lived in constant fear that people would find out about the rapes and turn away in disgust.

When I was thirty, the emotional pain became greater than my ability to contain it and I went to therapy. I spent the next ten years working through my many issues. As my courage grew, I began advocating for others who'd been victimized. I volunteered on rape crisis and domestic violence boards, ran a child advocacy center and worked as Director of Victims Issues for the North Carolina Attorney General's Office. In the process, I earned both bachelor's and master's degrees and became an international expert on crime victim issues.

Making an Impact on a Global Level

One morning, I intoned my daily affirmation to myself in the mirror: "I love you." These words usually caused me to roll my eyes, but in that moment, I realized I *meant* it! I finally appreciated that the shame was not mine to carry; it belonged to the men who had raped me. I'd escaped the hell I had created for myself and found lasting peace and joy. I was truly free.

That awareness loosed the fetters that had held me prisoner for four decades, and I suddenly had access to vast stores of energy and creativity. I made it my life's mission to use my newfound power to make an impact on a global level. Today, I am the author of *Neptune's Gift: Discovering Your Inner Ocean*[84] and the Founder/Chief Executive Officer of 10 for Humanity, which is developing ten innovative technologies to reduce acts of crime and violence by ten percent in the next decade.

Fight Your Way Back into the Light

If you have been the victim of rape, abuse or domestic violence, find a way to get help. Therapy can help you with feelings of shame and blame that are crippling you emotionally and spiritually and help you recover your precious, undamaged self.

Most importantly, keep working until you transform your trauma into joy. Deal with the trauma head-on and fight your way back into the light. Extend compassion and forgiveness (for being a victim) to yourself, and then extend it to others who have experienced pain like yours. When you do this, you'll create happiness for yourself and others, and you will have found the secret to a truly happy life.

---

84 For more information about CJ, her organization and *Neptune's Gift* (iUniverse), please visit www.10forhumanity.com.

Jillian's story

I was a young African-American girl who grew up with my mother and white stepfather. I experienced many horrific experiences, including being raped at the age of eleven years and homelessness at the age of fifteen years. When I found out that I was pregnant at sixteen years of age, I knew that I had to find a way to turn my life around for the sake of my unborn child.

ANGER AND ABANDONMENT

My mother kicked me out of the house when I was fifteen years old. I cursed both her and God. I was especially angry with God because I couldn't believe he was a loving God if he allowed misery to happen to a child.

I KNEW THINGS HAD TO CHANGE

Even after I got off the streets and delivered my baby, I was angry at the world. I felt alone, scared and empty. Over the years I accomplished many things, including graduating from college, training in martial arts and earning two black belts, becoming a reporter for the *Wall Street Journal*, and eventually working in the entertainment industry as a screenwriter and filmmaker. However, my emotional pain made it difficult for me to open my heart to love. I struggled to have warmth and compassion with my children.

Despite wonderful successes, I unfortunately continued to get involved with men who were toxic or abusive. I eventually reached the point where I knew things had to change and sought therapy for my healing process.

FORGIVENESS: THE FIRST STEP TOWARD LOVE

I realized that I couldn't learn to love a man because I didn't love myself. I had to learn how to forgive myself, and I had to forgive those who had hurt me...especially my mother. Forgiveness is the first step toward love; however, this is an ongoing process. I no longer have a "victim" mentality; instead, I surround myself with people who lift me, who are positive and loving and who want the best for me.

YOU CAN TRANSFORM YOUR LIFE

I am proud to say that I've raised three wonderful children. [My oldest son] has a master's degree and is a professor at the Department of Defense. My middle son is an actor and television/movie producer. My youngest child is in college and works as a banker. My memoir, *Here I Stand,*[85] was recently published. I'm also a life coach, fitness and wellness expert and motivational speaker through my program, Fighting Spirit Warriors, which enables all women to be victors, rather than victims.

So many people make mistakes and think that their lives are ruined for good, but that does not have to be the case. You can transform your life and attain success, happiness and purpose.

Who's Watching Me?: Stalking

The legal definition of stalking is "A course of conduct directed at a specific person that would cause a reasonable person to feel fear." While succinctly defined from a legal standpoint, the emotional definition of stalking is so much more complicated than can be put into words. At the very least, stalking results in a plurality of losses for the victims—loss of security, loss of feeling safe, loss of independence, loss of confidence, loss of trust…the list is lengthy.

At worst? We already know what the worst results of stalking can be. Further, the statistics concerning stalking incidents are sobering.[86] It is estimated that:

- Approximately 6.6 million people are stalked per year in the United States.

- One out of six women have experienced some level of stalking victimization at some point in their lives (including yours truly).

---

85 To learn more about Jillian and *Here I Stand* (Infinity Publishing), please visit www.jillianbullock.com.
86 Source: The National Center for Victims of Crime, Stalking Resource Center. Visit: www.victimsofcrime. org/our-programs/stalking-resource-center.

- Approximately sixty-six percent of female stalking victims are targeted by someone they know or with whom they are at least acquainted.

Adding to the ability to victimize is our old friend, the Internet. Reiterating again that I believe the Internet to be more of an instrument of good than evil, the painful reality is that the Internet is also one more tool available to a stalker's arsenal that can be utilized in waging terror. The Internet also added the word "cyberstalking" to both our lexicon and to law enforcement units and task forces.

Not all of the news is bad. There was once a time when police were helpless to act against stalkers until a direct physical threat presented. A stalker was free to do anything and everything that they wanted to their victims, and law enforcement had to wait until physical harm ensued—a verbal threat or even harassment tactics (phone calls, written correspondence, trespassing at a victim's workplace, repeatedly driving past a home) was not enough to legally stop a stalker.

While progress has been slow, there has nonetheless been advancement in the enactment of anti-stalking laws and legislation in the United States. California was the first state to introduce and enact anti-stalking laws, due in large part to the vicious stabbing attack on actress Theresa Saldana in 1982, and the brutal, premeditated murder of actress Rebecca Schaffer in 1989, both effected by deranged fans. While laws vary from state to state and from country to country, all fifty states now have anti-stalking legislation in effect.

However, even with anti-stalking laws and entire units in police departments and federal agencies dedicated to the capture, prosecution and conviction of stalkers, it still exists and as the numbers earlier demonstrate, it is a major problem that victimizes far too many.

Elaine* was in her mid-thirties, divorced for several years and had recently ended a long-term relationship when two friends convinced her to go with them to a New Year's Eve event that was being hosted by a five-star establishment. While unsure that she was ready for another relationship, she did not see the harm in going out with her friends. She thought it might be just the thing to get her back into the dating scene.

It was a New Year's Eve that forever changed her life.

Elaine's story

I met Greg* at a singles' event on New Year's Eve. He was very handsome and friendly, and it seemed he was exactly my type. He said he was a self-employed computer repairman, which meant that he had a lot of flexibility with his schedule. He liked to travel, dance and try new restaurants. I was excited when he asked for my phone number and email address, since there were a lot of beautiful women he could've asked out instead.

He called the very next day, which was kind of a surprise because it was New Year's Day. I was flattered he called so quickly. He asked me out to dinner for the next night and since I wasn't busy, I decided to go.

I met him at the restaurant and I was immediately weirded out by the way he was acting, like we were already boyfriend and girlfriend. He came on too strong for a first date and it made me very uncomfortable. I'm not a prude or stuck up, but I think that certain physical things shouldn't happen on a first date. He kept saying that when he saw me on New Year's Eve, it was love at first sight. I was pretty uncomfortable through the entire date, but I was still nice to him.

At the end of the evening, I thanked him and when he tried to kiss me, I told him I don't kiss on the first date. He seemed annoyed and said, "But I told you I'm in love with you." I told him I was flattered but I didn't move that fast.

I didn't want to go out with him again and that's not an unusual thing. Lots of people have one date, figure out it's not going to work and don't go out again. But starting the very next day, he started calling. He was leaving voice mails almost every hour and then the emails started. He kept asking why I wouldn't go out with him again, that he loved me and we were meant to be together. I talked to him one time and tried to let him down gently by telling him that I didn't think it would work. He wouldn't listen.

I finally emailed and asked him to stop contacting me but he didn't pay attention. After that, the messages and emails turned from nice to very nasty.

He called me a prick tease, a whore and a lot of other terrible names. I tried changing my phone number and my email address but it didn't help. He found me somehow (I guess because he's a computer repairman and knew how to get information) and said, "Do you think you can avoid me? You're even dumber than I thought."

I started keeping track of the phone calls and printing out the emails. I called the police who suggested I get a restraining order. I was in the process of getting the final restraining order [papers had been previously filed and served and a hearing date set] when Greg sent an email saying that he knew where I lived, he was going to come over so we could talk in person and I could see that he loved me. I knew I was in trouble and called 911. Sure enough, Greg pulled up in front of my house and, lucky for me, two police cars pulled up right behind him. He was arrested for stalking and violating the restraining order. The police also searched Greg's car and found a loaded gun and a knife. They told me that he had a criminal record [that included violent offenses] and later on, he was also charged with computer hacking when [law enforcement] found evidence that he hacked my computer.

I BLAMED MYSELF

I blamed myself for everything. I felt like I deserved what I got because I was the one who gave my phone number and email address to him. It was a therapist who works with crime victims who helped me understand that it wasn't my fault. He said that stalkers want their victims to believe they are the ones who created the situation and that [the stalker] isn't responsible for their own actions.

COUNSELING PUT ME ON THE RIGHT PATH

Even though he was in jail, I was still afraid of him. I was afraid to go out, even to go to work or the store, and I was convinced he could still reach me by phone or by email. He took away my freedom because I was convinced that he would somehow get out of jail and come after me.

When my family and friends saw what was happening to me, they got together and talked me into going to counseling. I went to a counselor who works with people that have PTSD after crimes like stalking, robbery, hostage situations, kidnapping and sexual assault. It changed my life and put me back on the right path. It took awhile but after [a few months] I began to feel like my old self again and like I could leave the house without being afraid.

Conquering Fear and Finding True Love

Instead of putting me through a trial, the prosecutor offered a [plea] deal which I was okay with. I didn't want to ever see him again. He pleaded guilty to [various other charges in addition to stalking and computer hacking] and received a prison sentence [in excess of ten years].

After my experience, I was afraid to go on a date again. I thought that every man in the world was like Greg and I didn't want to go through that again. My therapist reminded me that most people are good and don't mean any harm, I just got unlucky [with Greg].

About two years after Greg went to prison, I met an amazing man. He was so sweet and understanding and never tried to rush me into a new relationship. After dating for about a year, we got engaged and a year after that, we got married. We moved out of state because of my new husband's job and even though he says that as long as he is alive, I will never have to be scared again, I still feel much better that I don't live anywhere close to where Greg is.

Don't Do This Alone

A lot of people still don't take stalking seriously, but it is a serious crime. Even stalking victims don't take it seriously at first, or think they can handle it on their own. I tried to handle it on my own and didn't realize I was in over my head. Don't try to handle [stalking incidents] on your own and if no one takes you seriously, go to the police.

It was not my fault I was stalked. There's obviously something that drives people to behave this way and whatever [it was in this instance], it didn't come from me. I learned to let people into my life and trust people again. I'm so glad I did, because that's how I met my husband.

If you are ever stalked, don't blame yourself. Get help as soon as you can from the police and from counseling. There are also stalking victim support groups, and even though I didn't go to one, my therapist says that they can be very helpful for a lot of people. Don't quit living your life because you don't have to. I waited too long to figure that out.

HOW YOU CAN HELP

So much is involved in moving forward after being victimized by crime. As with any trauma, there are practical, emotional and mental aspects to tackle; however, when it comes to a criminal act, many of those aspects (most notably the practical aspects) are extremely urgent. You can help her begin her healing processes both immediately and well after the crime has been committed.

Definite Do's

- **Ensure that evidence is preserved:** I hate to sound overly clinical, but my legal-eagle instinct and training still surfaces from time to time and this is far too important not to discuss.

    If someone you know has been the victim of any kind of crime, help her preserve any and all evidence to the best of her ability. Create a checklist of to-do's so that nothing gets overlooked. For example, and if applicable, make sure that she records voice mails onto tape or otherwise digitally preserves them for evidence, making sure that preservation includes dates and times (keep a hard-copy log if necessary). Print out email communications so that there are hard copies. Take clear pictures of any physical injuries immediately. If there is a crime scene, photograph it as well, if possible.

    If the crime involves any kind of assault (sexual or not), save all clothes that she was wearing (including undergarments), and if you have been made aware soon enough, instruct her *not* to shower or bathe, and not to wash, launder or attempt to destroy her clothing. She should instead proceed to the nearest emergency room so that personal physical evidence can be gathered. If it is at all possible, go with her to the hospital or doctor to lend badly needed support.

- **Be compassionate:** CJ shares, "I shared part of my experience with a doctor to find out if he thought I was losing my mind. He touched me gently on the shoulder with a look of such deep compassion that it made me cry. He told me I was fine and that everything was going to be okay."

  A kind ear and a willingness to listen brings so much comfort to a victim who needs both so very much. Listen to her for as long as she needs to talk about her experience.

- **Encourage her to seek help:** The perpetrators of these horrendous crimes bank on the hope that their victims will be too ashamed, embarrassed or afraid to seek help or talk about what they have endured. Sadly, too many victims do just that—remain silent. Silence helps no one (except perhaps the perpetrator) and multiple studies and statistics show that offenders who are not caught and punished are likely to offend again.

  Anyone who has endured the kind of monstrosities that this chapter discusses needs support and they need it quickly. Offer to get information for her and if appropriate, you can offer to accompany her to whatever support group, one-on-one meeting or session that she chooses to attend. Elaine says, "I would've been lost without counseling but it took my family and a couple of friends awhile to convince me [to seek help]. I'm not sure I would have ever gotten over the whole experience without help."

  You will find resources at the end of this chapter to provide to anyone you know who has been the victim of domestic violence, abuse, child molestation, rape and/or stalking. Get her the help she needs as soon as you possibly can.

Without a Doubt...Don't

- **Don't *ever* blame the victim of *any* crime:** *"Maybe if you didn't dress so sexy..."; "You led him on because you* [gave him your information/went to his place/invited him to your place/kissed him, etc.]*"; "Couldn't you tell he was going to be violent?"*

  Incredibly, it is commonplace to hold the victim at least partially accountable for the horrors that they experienced at the hand of another. Holly shares, "Someone once asked me, 'What did you do to make him do that to you?' Another person said to me, 'How could you not know he was like that? You had to have seen the signs.' These were the worst things someone could say. No matter what anyone does, no one deserves what I went through, and nothing can justify what he did. Nothing he did was my fault, [and] his actions are one hundred percent his [responsibility]."

  The only thing that I can possibly add to this is...amen.

8 **Don't question her reactions in the moment:** *"Did you fight back?"; "Did you scream?"; "Why didn't you claw his eyes out?"; "If it had been me, I would have..."*

  There is *no way* that anyone is capable of predicting what actions they would take in a fight-or-flight situation. As well-informed as most of us are regarding defensive measures, when your life is on the line, your instinct is to preserve your life in any way possible. You cannot possibly judge someone else, or worse, opine as to what you think you would do, given the same set of circumstances.

  A crime victim needs to be received with relief and gratitude that she is alive. Do not question her defensive tactics or regale her with tales of the supposed superpowers that you would have engaged if you had been in her position.

- **Just as before, don't even hint at "I told you so":** *"I knew he was no good"; "I had a feeling something like this would happen"; "I wish*

293

you'd listened to me when I warned you."

Why are we still discussing "I told you so"? Because it seems to happen way too often in way too many bad-thing situations. Do people *really* need to feel superiority at a time when someone is obviously suffering? If someone has that level of need to be right—especially at a time like this—I would seriously reevaluate their place in my life.

Even if you *were* right—even if you *did* warn her ahead of time, and even if you *were* able to predict dire results, now is not the time to make that point, and a crime victim is not the person to whom the point should be made. Keep your opinions and any prior prognostications to yourself.

From Bad Thing to Brighter Days Ahead

The common denominator among all of these remarkably courageous women is that they refused to let their attackers determine their destiny. They refused to let criminal circumstances steal their spirits, their love of life and their determination to make something good happen out of a horrific experience. The bravery that each demonstrates by telling their stories shows that they are just as concerned with helping others as they are with continuing their own journeys of healing.

Remember that the women who have shared their stories aren't "other women." They are people you know. They may even be you. If you are in a position of danger or threat, please avail yourself of the resources that follow. Tell someone. Talk to everyone. Most of all, remember that be it physical, emotional or verbal, love is *never **ever*** supposed to hurt.

They got out.

They got away.

They refused to be intimated by a criminal and were determined to move forward.

They ran away from pain and toward *life*.

You can too.

FOR IMMEDIATE ASSISTANCE:

- If you and/or your children are ever in imminent danger, please call 911 immediately.

- National Domestic Violence Hotline:
  1-800-799-7233 / www.thehotline.org

- RAINN (Rape, Abuse and Incest National Network):
  1-800-656-4673 / www.rainn.org

- Adult Survivors of Child Abuse (includes molestation):
  www.ascasupport.org

- Safe Horizon stalking victims' hotline (assessment and referrals provided) 866-689-4357

- Stalking Victims Sanctuary and Solutions:
  www.stalkingvictims.com

Chapter Fifteen

THE "MISTRESS"
NO ONE TALKS ABOUT:
LIVING WITH SUBSTANCE ABUSE

WE ALL KNOW THE STORY. SUBSTANCE ABUSE IS EQUAL IN ITS OPPORTUNITY to strike. It is indiscriminate. It knows no age, gender or socioeconomic boundaries. Whether latent or blatant, oblique or obvious, nothing is more important to a substance abuser than the substance itself.

Yet we believe…

We believe that we are "different" than every single person who is, has been or will ever be in the abuser's life. We have the power to make it stop because we are more important than the substance. We believe that "it" (code for "the abuse") will "get better" (code for "magically disappear") when we move in together/get married/have a baby/have *another* baby/have more money…

Except—it *doesn't* get better.

Still…we believe.

Until it inevitably worsens.

Despite our beliefs, best efforts and thinking that we are somehow bigger, better or worth more intrinsically than whatever substance is being abused, the sad truth is that we cannot compete with a substance and win…not unless at some point, *sobriety* becomes more important to the abuser than the substance itself.

Tammye McDuff [87] is a talented writer with a lengthy list of credits and who by all appearances, had everything going for her…yet found herself living in a scary and unpredictable world with a spouse who abused alcohol. Her story is more than inspirational—it may well save lives.

Tammye's story

I met my husband at work. He was the on-site construction superinten-dent for the project for which I was hired to raise funds. Through working together, we became close and began to date. I was aware that he was a drinker but was not aware of how heavily he drank. I'd never known an alcoholic or for that matter, a heavy drinker. I confess that I was innocent to certain warning signs and "red flags."

When my husband and I began living together, I'd notice a whiskey glass in the sink in the morning. At first I thought it was from the previous night, but soon learned that he drank before he went to work in the morning. When I confronted him, he made a promise…if the drinking got in the way of our relationship, he would quit.

Over the years, his drinking increased. He would meet friends for lunch at the local bar, then have several more drinks when he'd come home. Our rela-tionship hit rock-bottom when he [started going] to bars after work and not coming home, oftentimes resulting in his friends calling me to pick him up.

My husband eventually lost his job because of his drinking. I reminded him of his promise to me that if drinking interfered with our relationship, he would quit. I told him that he had to choose between me and his drinking. He replied, "I will never stop drinking…" and that ended our relationship.

---

87 To learn more about Tammye, please visit www.tammyemcduff.moonfruit.com.

PEOPLE COME AND GO FROM OUR LIVES FOR A REASON

I've always believed that people come and go from our lives for a reason, and we never really understand some of those reasons. When I realized what a heavy drinker my husband was, I honestly thought that I would be able to help him stop. There was a point when he actually did stop drinking. He was sober for six months and during that time, his health was returning, his relationship with his parents and children began to heal and he was losing weight.

MULTIPLE LOSSES AND CHALLENGES

My husband and I lived in a beautiful home owned by his parents. I loved that house. I knew that I would not be able to stay, but I'd accumulated two dogs and five cats. I had also begun to care for my ailing parents and started working for my father's business.

When my husband "fell off the wagon," his attitude changed. Instead of being a "happy drunk," he became belligerent and defiant, with arguments raging into the wee hours of the morning. Toward the end of our relationship, he began to use hallucinogenic drugs. The people with whom he would associate were very questionable, and at one point I believe he was selling drugs himself—he carried an extra cell phone and was picked up and dropped off by men in black SUVs at all hours.

I owned a Rottweiler named Roxanne and when my husband's "acquaintances" would come to the door, Roxanne refused to let them cross the threshold. One of these men threatened her life as well as my own. I let both my husband and this gentleman know that if he ever returned to my home again, I would let Roxanne loose and call the police. The man never returned.

At the same time, my mother's hearing and eyesight was beginning to fail. She could no longer drive and there were many incidents where she would forget she was cooking and pans would catch fire. My father was still active but I began to notice that he was "dragging" his right leg and would forget driving directions to places with which he was familiar. I was spending most of my time taking care of my parents during the day. The only logical thing for me to do was to move back home—at the age of fifty.

Not only was I dealing with the loss of my relationship, the pain of my husband choosing alcohol over his family, the stress of taking over my father's business and my mother's resentment of having to rely on me for daily activities, but I also lost friends—other women who at one time I thought were my best friends.

Finding Healing Through Yoga and Writing

I cried a lot and felt alone and abandoned. My heart hurt. Years before, I'd gone through extensive therapy because of a divorce. I knew what steps needed to be taken in order to begin healing, so I wrote them down—and I just kept writing. I poured my heart into the printed page. Common sense told me that in order to be able to completely heal, I had to take control. I also set boundaries and made sure people knew what they could and could not say to me.

I began yoga class, even though my spiritual beliefs were hit hard. I questioned my faith. I questioned those who said they were my friends. I questioned everything. Yet, I kept going to yoga class. The instructor and I became good friends, and he taught me how to move through my pain, how to come to resolution with my loss and how to heal.

Take the Risk to Make a Change

I am reminded daily of a Raja Yoga quote from Swami Vivekananda: "Take up one idea. Make that one idea your life; dream of it; think of it; live on that idea. Let the brain, the body, muscles, nerves, every part of your body be full of that idea and just leave every other idea alone. This is the way to success."

Remember that whatever situation you are in, you can get out of. Nothing is permanent. Take the risk to make a change. It may be difficult at first, and you stand the chance of losing family, friends or finances. But what is your happiness worth?

Reach out. Someone will be there to take your hand and help you through.

HOW YOU CAN HELP

Substance abuse affects everyone that is connected to the abuser in any way. If someone you know is living with a substance abuser, she needs help and support as well.

Definite Do's

- **As with the prior chapter, if you suspect that she is in imminent danger or you suspect any kind of potentially dangerous situation to exist (e.g., the threat of or actual, physical violence, weapons in the home, etc.), take action immediately:** Within the boundaries of your own safety, do whatever you can to get her out of the situation and if necessary, call the authorities. Tragically, an alarming number of domestic violence incidents (including murder) occur when there is alcohol and/or drugs involved—and sadder still, this level of intoxication is still used as a defense in courtrooms today.

- **Help her locate support for loved ones of substance abusers:** Groups such as Al-Anon[88] and Nar-Anon[89] are excellent sources of support for friends and loved ones dealing with the addiction of another.

- **Remind her that the addiction is *not* her doing, it is *not* her fault and it is *not* her responsibility:** Do not allow her to accept the label of scapegoat that has likely been thrust upon her by the substance abuser. The hallmark of an addict is blaming everyone and everything around them for their lot in life, and unfortunately, too many affected loved ones are all too willing to accept the blame and the accompanying venom that is hurled at them—until they

---

88 For more information about Al-Anon, please visit www.al-anon.alateen.org.
89 For more information about Nar-Anon, please visit www.nar-anon.org.

learn that addiction has nothing to do with them and everything to do with the addict.

- **Help her to understand that an addict is an addict because of their own actions and accordingly, *they* must be the ones that choose to seek help:** An addict does not become an addict because of anyone around them, and this is one of the first realities that they must own. Further, an addict cannot and will not get help until they (a) recognize that they have a problem; (b) are willing to seek help; and (c) put that help into practice.

Without a Doubt...Don't

- **Don't assess the situation based on outward appearances:** *"But he's so nice"; "I've never seen him drunk/stoned"; "So what if he over-does it once in awhile, everyone needs to relax."*

  Having personal experience in this area (prior to my marriage to Mike), allow me to share something about addicts. They can be masters of manipulation, disguise and deception. They can put on acts in public that are worthy of Academy Awards. They can convince work colleagues, relatives and friends that they are the proverbial "life of the party" or "great guy" or "party girl" who only drinks socially or would never use drugs other than for medicinal purposes. Since most addicts are also lying to themselves about their disease, it is not a difficult act to sell.

  Let me also share a secret about an addict's loved ones—the people that have to live with addiction on a daily basis. They too can be masters of disguise. On the outside, they will pretend that everything is great, when on the inside, they are ashamed because they know better. They feel helpless because they are powerless to change the addictive behavior. Most of all, they are scared to death of the monster named Addiction that has invaded their lives...and what sort of tomorrow that monster might bring.

In other words, you have absolutely no idea that what you are seeing is someone's truth.

It takes a great deal of courage for someone to share the reality of their life as the family member of an addict. If someone chooses to share their truth with you, you must acknowledge the courage that this takes, and do not question the seriousness of what she is sharing.

- **Don't imply that the addiction situation is her fault:** *"Did you do something to provoke this?"; "Was he/she that way 'before'?"; "Maybe they're 'that way' because of your* [personal or job success/children/financial issues/other potential sources of 'blame']. *"*

  One of the most important lessons that I came to later in life (and now zealously teach) is that you cannot control other people's activity or actions—and you certainly cannot control the consequences of those actions. The reality is that the only activity that you can control is your own. Therefore, addicts need look no further than the bathroom mirror to assess blame for their situation.

  Whether blame is self-inflicted or heaped upon them by the addict (i.e., "It's your fault I'm this way"), and even though we cannot control the actions of anyone else (much less the actions of an addict), loved ones of addicts are likely already blaming themselves. Do not feed that myth.

- **Don't encourage her to stay in a situation that is not going to improve or might prove dangerous or detrimental:** *"You have children together, you have to stay for their sake"; "What about 'for better or worse' or 'in sickness and in health'?"; "You could make things worse by leaving"; "Don't you think you should stand by him?"*

  I have never understood the whole "staying together for the children" rationale. How is raising a child in an environment of addiction and abuse conducive to a healthy result? How exactly is it productive and positive for a child to see one parent living in a downward spiral (because addiction knows no other direction) and the other parent suffering in all manner possible as a direct result?

If an addict continues down the path of addiction rather than seek the help they need, that is their choice. However, it should *not* be the obligation of the person (or people) living with them to continue that life out of misplaced and unappreciated loyalty, out of guilt or because of the presence of children. If anything, these are all instead excellent reasons to leave.

From Bad Thing to Brighter Days Ahead

Loving and/or living with an addict is, at best, one of the most horrendous kinds of stress imaginable and, at worst, a potential danger to you (and your children if applicable). Be it best or worst case scenario, one thing is certain… it is no way to live.

You must first understand that any decisions an addict makes to seek help, support or change their entire lifestyle must come from *them*. Further, an addict's impetus for getting help cannot be you, your children, a job or anything other than the fact that they no longer wish to live their lives hopelessly dependent upon a substance that dictates their every decision and subsequent action in life.

Once you have reached that understanding, you must then seize control of that which you are capable of controlling—and as you have learned, you control *you*. Seek support immediately, whether that support comes from the resources listed here or from elsewhere (church, synagogue, other support groups or resources). You do not need to do this on your own, nor should you attempt to do so.

Your brighter days will arrive when addiction is no longer part of your daily worry. When that day comes (either because your loved one made the decision to get the help that they need for the right reasons, or because you have made the decision to extricate yourself from the situation), you will feel like you are breathing fresh air and enjoying sunshine on your face for the first time. The day that addiction no longer governs your life in any form is indeed your brightest day.

Chapter Sixteen

THE SECOND TIME AROUND: WHEN BAD-THING HISTORY REPEATS ITSELF

THE MOST COMMON QUESTIONS THAT I'M ASKED BY WIDOWED (BOTH MEN and women) is, "Weren't you afraid to fall in love again after being widowed? And aren't you afraid of becoming widowed again?"

The answers are yes...and *hell* yes. More on that later.

When we have lived through and recovered from any bad thing, we are naturally going to be afraid of a repeat of that bad-thing experience. To be otherwise would take superpowers of which I am not in possession.[90] However, the third question that must asked is, "Do we consciously choose to remain so afraid of what *might* happen, that we refuse to live in the present and for the future?"

You earlier met Louise (Chapter Eleven, "The Black Cloud of Uncertainty") who had experienced serious illness of a spouse two different times. We now take a closer look at the "second time around" with Natalie, who also

---

90 You know what I mean...the same superpowers that would enable me to wake up looking great, eat San Francisco sourdough bread without it showing up on my hips and magically eliminate rush-hour traffic.

experienced a second-time-around bad thing. Although it is not an enviable position in which to be, Natalie teaches us that even a double-portion of the bad-thing pie should not keep us from living again—and it should *definitely* not prevent us from loving again.

Natalie's story

I had been happily married for seventeen years when my husband Kenny was diagnosed with leukemia. He lasted a year [after he was diagnosed] and then passed away. At the time he died, he was forty-two years old and our boys were ten years old and seven years old.

About three years after Kenny's death, I met Tim through a friend at work. He was divorced but was totally understanding of my situation and really sympathized with me being widowed. We started dating and took things slowly. Tim also took it very slow with the boys so they would understand he wasn't trying to replace their dad.

After dating for almost two years, Tim asked me to marry him. I was so happy and excited for all of us. The kids loved him and I never thought I'd ever be that much in love with someone again. We had a small wedding with the kids, our families and close friends. It was such a happy day.

We'd been married for two-and-a-half years when one day, Tim started complaining about his chest hurting while we were watching TV. I told him to get dressed and I was taking him to the emergency room. While getting dressed, Tim collapsed. I screamed and called 911 while my older son ran next door to get help. I started doing CPR and the paramedics got there in less than ten minutes.

Even though the paramedics did everything they could and the emergency room worked on Tim for another twenty minutes, they couldn't save him. He died of a massive heart attack and I was a widow again.

My Happiness Was Taken Away...Again

It sounds selfish, but the first thing that went through my head is, "I can't believe this is happening to me again." I had to tell the boys that we were going through this all over again, and even though they were older this time, it was still so hard. They thought of Tim as a second dad and now they didn't have a dad again. I just couldn't understand why it felt like every time I found happiness with someone, they were taken away.

I STARTED TO BELIEVE IN MYSELF AGAIN

A lot of people around me expected me to automatically know [what to do] because of Kenny's death, but I had a hard time accepting that this was happening to me again. I felt like I was cursed or I was cursing other people [with whom I fell in love].

Even though I'd been through [spousal loss] before, it was harder to make a start [to heal] this time because I kept thinking, "What's the point?" I felt like as soon as we started feeling better and things got back to normal, something terrible was going to happen again. My kids helped me get over that. They kept saying, "Mom, it's not us." I began thinking that if my kids believed in me that much, I could believe in myself too.

I AM ABLE TO LOVE AGAIN

I needed to be there for the boys, but I also didn't want to wait as long to take care of myself as I did the first time. I thought back to the things that helped me after Kenny died, like going to the [grief] support group at church, reading books and exercising and I started those things again. I also let the boys decide when to go back to their activities and sports.

I haven't started dating yet and I'm okay with it. I've been concentrating more on work as well as my kids, and I've also started some new things. I got very involved in yoga workouts and I take classes in flower arranging. I like being creative and even though it might sound strange, it actually helps me with the grief I still feel.

Even though I'm not dating yet, I believe I'll be ready to someday. I have a lot of love to give, and I know how lucky I am to have been married to two great men. The one thing I do know now that I didn't know when Kenny died is that I'm able to love someone again just as much as I loved Kenny and Tim.

Be Open to Your Future

It's terrible going through widowhood twice, but I don't think about that as much now as I think about how lucky I was to have been married to Kenny and Tim in the first place. I don't want to concentrate on the negative. A lot of people don't get to have even one good marriage and I had two.

If you go through [a bad thing] again, just remember that you didn't do anything to bring it on and you don't deserve it. Try to look at the positive parts as best you can. Also, find something that helps you with your grief, like a hobby or an activity that helps you meet new people. Reading helps a lot too.

Don't be afraid of the future because you went through something terrible more than once. Take care of yourself and be open to what the future can bring you.

HOW YOU CAN HELP

The very prospect of a second-time-around bad thing is frightening. When someone finds herself in the situation, she needs immediate reassurance and reinforcement.

Definite Do's

- **Quickly reassure her that a second-time bad thing has nothing to do with her:** Many is the time that I have heard from second-time-around widowed that "I'm bad luck" or "I am jinxed" or "I'm a black widow."[91] Natalie shared that she too felt "cursed" or as though she was actually "cursing" anyone who spent time with her. To you and me, that may sound silly—but to someone going through a second-time experience, it is a very real feeling.

  Let her know that whatever the bad thing, it is not her doing. It is

---

91 When it comes to widowhood, let us also pledge to use the term "black widow" *only* as it pertains to black spiders with red belly marks.

not her fault. It is simply the result of living life and because of that, she is unfortunately dealing with a repeat experience of a bad thing. This alone will bring immediate comfort.

- **Encourage her to utilize her previous bad-thing experience to help her:** Take her back in time to the first time around. What did she do that was helpful? What did others do for her that she appreciated? What was successful for her and what made her feel better? This exercise encourages her proactivity. You are helping to remind her of how she coped the first time, the steps that she should be taking now and most importantly, that she *can* get through this second-time bad thing once again.

  P.S. When you ask her what others did for her the first time that were helpful, listen carefully. Then do a few of them.

Without a Doubt…Don't

- **Don't instill a sense of fear:** *"Aren't you afraid of* [losing a loved one again/getting into another car accident/getting cheated on again, etc.]*"?; "Do you really want to take a chance and go down that road again?"*

  It is time for another stipulation. Let's all agree that we are each afraid of all of these things and more, and that if we have suffered through *any* of these or any other bad-thing event, we really do not want to go through it again.

  Agreed? Good. Now a repeat of the question asked earlier. Does being afraid also mean that we should vow never to fall in love again, get into a car for any reason, take a trip, embark on a new relationship, etc., on the off-chance that we might experience a second-time-around?

  I don't think so.

  As stated at the opening of this chapter (please refer back to *"Hell* yes"), not a day goes by that I am not afraid of losing my Dave. I have hiked up Widow Mountain once and it is a hike that I neither relished nor do I recommend. The fear of losing Dave has made my heart beat funny. It has kept me up nights...and if I think he is sleeping too quietly, I admit to checking his breathing.[92]

However, when I considered the alternative so many years ago—staying inside because I was too afraid to venture out, not fully embracing life, not even thinking about loving again—that did not seem like a viable option either. ALS had already stolen so much from us—why would I choose to let that wretched disease take away any more than it already had?

There is no point to be served by instilling fear into someone who is already afraid. What is called for instead is encouragement and congratulations—that she found a new relationship, fell in love, got back into a car, took another trip or in general, refused to let her fear of a repeat bad-thing experience define her present and her future.

- **Don't foist *your* life decisions on her:** *"I've been there and I'm never going 'there' again"; "I've already* [been divorced/widowed/cheated on/lost a home, etc.].*"*

  I have seen it a million times and so have you. Someone we know goes through a bad thing, unilaterally decides that "all men are cheaters" (or liars or asshats in general) or that "all marriages end in divorce" or that owning a home again is not worth it (whatever "it" is), and because *she* has decided that way, *you* should decide the same. Who knows—maybe she wants a misery-wingman (and we have all known at least one of those); maybe she wants you to set up camp in Bittertown alongside her; perhaps deep down she does not want to see you happy. Who knows?

  To be clear, this is not to say that there is anything wrong with choosing against remarriage, buying another house, starting a new

---

92 He woke up and caught me doing that once. It was more than a little embarrassing.

business, etc., if that is indeed a *choice* that you came to on your own. If your "choice" is actually as a result of being too afraid, too bitter, too angry, settling for what life has handed to you or all four combined…it's not okay.

It is also not someone else's choice…it is *your* choice.

Do not impose your life choices on someone else. If you are happy with your choices, that is fantastic. However, if you are looking for someone to follow your choices simply because you cannot stand to be miserable and alone—look elsewhere. Someone who has just gone through a bad thing does not need to have that bad thing reinforced by anyone.

- **Don't imply that the second time around is easier or less painful:** *"It's not your first time, you have experience with this"; "Just do what you did the first time this happened"; "You're getting good at this."*

Any second-time-around bad thing is not a skill set that you practice many hours to master. It is horrific. Let's be honest, facing any of the experiences that you have read to this point is harrowing to say the least. Facing the same experience a second time (or third or fifth or tenth time) is almost beyond comprehension.

Natalie says, "I was shocked at the people who expected me to handle things without crying or being sad because I was widowed before. Some people treated me like 'You've already done this once' and [like] I was some kind of sympathy junkie."

Let there be no mistake. *No one* wants to be experienced at handling bad things. Multiple losses are tragic. Serious illness recurrence is tragic. Subsequent financial devastation is tragic. Whatever the second-time bad thing is, it is a tragedy and it is a tremendous burden on the people affected. As I said in reference to multiple surgeries (Chapter Nine, "Hope Interrupted"), this is not tennis… it isn't something that we want to practice in the hopes that we will get good at it.

FROM BAD THING TO BRIGHTER DAYS AHEAD

No matter the previous bad-thing experience, the "second time around" is the risk that we take by simply living our lives as abundantly as possible—and I believe with all my heart that it is *still* a risk worth taking.

Do not allow fears of a possible second-time-around experience to paralyze you—and get away from anyone who *does* encourage that sort of paralysis. Do not let the second time around keep you from truly living a life that you want to live, loving in the way that you wish and experiencing everything that is out there waiting for you. To do otherwise is a complete surrender of power to a beast called Fear—and fear should *never* be given that kind of power.

Above all, remember that the definition of courage is not "Don't be afraid." The *real* definition of courage is being afraid...and going forward anyway.

Chapter Seventeen

"Pancake" Tragedy

When I share the story of our family's Healing Journey with various audiences, I generally share only part of the story. Ten days prior to Mike's death, our uncle very premeditatedly committed suicide—in fact, Kendall and my mother were at his memorial service while I was with Mike in the intensive care unit at the hospital, where he lay dying. Three *weeks* after Mike's death, I was on an out-of-state business trip when I collapsed. I was flown home, taken off of the airplane in a wheelchair, rushed to the hospital and on an operating table twelve hours later, undergoing number twelve of what is now thirteen major abdominal surgeries. Six weeks later, I received a phone call from the hospital, informing me that my father had been admitted. He was diagnosed with metastatic liver cancer and passed away nine weeks post-diagnosis.

All of these events happened within four months.

I quickly coined the expression, "Pancake Tragedy"—defined as the bad things that come one on top of another in such close proximity, you scarcely have a chance to absorb the enormity of what is happening to you.

April Dawn Ricchuito[93] is a wonderful writer whose work actress Fran Drescher describes as, "a great lesson for all about following the intuition and wisdom of the body." April was faced with multiple serious health situations challenges—and as if fighting those challenges was not bad enough, she lost her job the day before undergoing major surgery. She shares her story of pancake tragedy and her determination to triumph over what certainly can seem insurmountable.

April's story

In the summer of 2009, I started to feel strange. I would get awful headaches and be exhausted to the point of falling asleep while at the computer. I had vision problems and I had little to no appetite because nothing tasted good. By the fall, my periods had become heavy and irregular. I was sent to numerous doctors who ran numerous scans, one of which showed a suspicious spot on my thyroid. When I went to my internist for the results of my brain scan, she told me that my pituitary gland was fine, but that, "You might have thyroid cancer. Come back in six months because the nodule is too small to biopsy." I was only twenty-five years old.

As soon as I heard "cancer," I automatically thought that the doctor had pronounced a death sentence. I then threw myself into my work. I'd graduated with a master's degree in social work and I was working full-time as a therapist for the state's Department of Juvenile Justice. I was also working part-time for a makeup company, hoping to fulfill my dream of being a celebrity makeup artist. I literally had no days off between the two jobs, and because of what was going on health-wise, I was extremely exhausted.

While all the doctor appointments were going on, my job was growing increasingly intolerant of my absence from the office. When my employer confronted me, I made the mistake of thinking they were concerned about me. I told them what was going on [with my health] and their attitudes towards me drastically changed. I went from being a star employee who was constantly

---

93 To learn more about April, please visit www.verbalvandalism.com.

praised for my dedication, innovative thinking and program development, to someone who was under a microscope. I was well aware they were trying to find a way to get rid of me, and I contacted the Department of Labor, who opened an investigation.

The doctors decided the only way to find out what was going on with my thyroid was to surgically remove the left half. Surgery was scheduled and to my surprise, my employer approved my medical leave. The day before my surgery, I was fired for "poor job performance."

Assuming the Worst Gave Me a Push

It was because I'd [initially] assumed the worst that pushed me to do everything I'd ever wanted to do. I was scared, confused and unsure how to deal with my feelings, which is why I went to New York. Moving a thousand miles away was irresponsible [when I knew] that I might be seriously ill [and had] no insurance, no job, and not much money. At that point, I didn't care…I felt that I'd lost what I worked for and loved. I'd just graduated and was supposed to be out in the world, not lying in a hospital bed.

Lifestyle Changes Took Me into a New Life

Since I barely knew anyone in New York, I was in complete control. I had to confront and deal with my feelings and learn how to take care of myself. I felt independent and liberated. I started meditating, yoga, juicing and made lifestyle changes that I continue to embrace to this day.

I Can Turn an Obstacle into an Opportunity

After surgery, I gained sixty pounds before I was prescribed medication. I'm losing the weight and regaining my confidence about my appearance.

I do feel confident that in the face of adversity, I can effectively advocate for myself, and that if faced with a sink-or-swim situation, I can swim. I'm confident that I can turn almost any obstacle into an opportunity, as long as I adjust my attitude as needed. I have learned to be patient with myself.

You Are the Boss of Your Life

Even when things look bleak, just hang on—better days are coming. Trust the process and trust your struggle. Trust yourself—a woman's intuition is amazing. We already know the answers; we've got it all inside of us. Win from within and you'll never go without.

Learn to see opportunities instead of obstacles, because if you're determined, you'll find at least one positive in the situation. Don't be afraid of change. I've had to [face it] a few times and I'm not afraid to do it again.

HOW YOU CAN HELP

Anyone experiencing a pancake-tragedy situation is overwhelmed, anxious, exhausted and feels that her life is in chaos. You have a wonderful opportunity to be her calm and her balance during an otherwise tumultuous season of her life.

Definite Do's

- **"One Jump at a Time":** This is a tried-and-true approach that my own mother taught me when I was up at pancake-tragedy bat. When I was completely overwhelmed by the issues with my father's estate, resolving the sale of property that Mike and I owned in another state that needed to go through a probate process, dealing with non-negotiable work deadlines and Kendall's impending Bat Mitzvah,[94] my mother sat me down, handed me a legal pad and being fluent in equine-ese, [95] asked, "Which jump is first?" I began prioritizing according to the calendar, and as I continued to list, the priorities took shape. I no longer saw everything as one "lump" that rendered me paralyzed. Instead, I could see for myself that there

---

94 An event that is akin to planning a wedding in terms of time and expense, with the added bonus of your child having to learn an extraordinary amount of Hebrew and coaching them accordingly.
95 Horse-y talk. I cannot count the number of times my mother has likened everything to horses—and she has a horsey metaphor, simile or saying for every occasion, situation or quandary.

was an order and a priority to what needed to be done, one jump at a time.

Take the same approach. Sit her down in a quiet space over a cup of coffee where there aren't going to be interruptions and ask what she needs to focus on first. What comes after that? Once she begins to see a sense of order, she will begin to relax...and the chaotic, heart-in-her-throat feeling will begin to calm.

- **Gently remind her that she has the right to grieve each situation individually:** In our society's collective desire to rush through the grieving process, people experiencing pancake tragedy tend to lump everything together into one big grief pile. Years later, they may be surprised to find themselves suddenly grieving a situation to which they did not pay sufficient attention earlier.

  Anyone suffering through pancake tragedies needs to be reminded that the challenges are individual and that they must be treated accordingly. It is easy to lose sight of that fact while in the midst of what feels like treading water as an invisible hand is pulling you underneath. You can be the reminder and the encouragement.

Without a Doubt...Don't

- **Don't treat her like an inconvenience:** *"You're such a drama queen"; "What's going on **now**?"; "It's always something with you, isn't it?"; "You're jinxed."*

  All that is missing from these comments is eye rolling.

  Before you say (or think) anything along these lines, ask yourself if the pancake situation in her life is something that she (or anyone) would actively seek. Ask yourself if perhaps there are not better ways of getting attention. Finally, ask yourself how *any* of the above statements would make anyone feel better.

- **Don't try to be funny or make light of the situations:** *"When it rains, it pours"; "At least you're getting everything out of the way all at once"; "Try to have a sense of humor."*

  Although it felt like it was metaphorically "pouring rain" at the time, I really did not see the positivity when others voiced that observation. I also guarantee that there was no advantage in "getting it all out of the way" by having Mike and my father die within months of one another, nor was my funny bone in overdrive at the time.

  Take the situation(s) just as seriously as the person directly affected. No one seeks out tragedy—and certainly not several tragedies at once. Save the jokes for professional comedians.

FROM BAD THING TO BRIGHTER DAYS AHEAD

As a pancake-tragedy alum who at one time felt like there were so many "pancakes" that the only thing missing was a bottle of syrup, I understand fears like turning on the computer and seeing the dreaded email inbox. I remember wanting to answer my telephone with "What *now?*" rather than a pleasant "Hi, this is Carole." I fully understand the challenges involved when trying to embrace, juggle and eventually triumph over multiple tragedies.

The good news is that, as April shared, it can be done.

Do your very best to keep each situation separate. You are entitled to handle each situation as the singular situations that they are—no creative avoidance allowed. Keep in mind that grief ignored is grief that comes back to bite you.

Finally, remember that regardless of your pancake situation, grieving any kind of loss, challenge or life-altering experience is a right—not a privilege. Even better is the certainty that even during the darkest seasons, the storm clouds do pass…and the "pancakes" will disappear.

Chapter Eighteen

A Word About the "C" Word

I'll just say it…I *hate* the "c" word.

Most women hate the "c" word.

I *never* use the "c" word—because there is *never* any good reason to use the "c" word.

Do *you* ever use the "c" word? If so…shame on you.

It is impossibly offensive.

And no…I'm not talking about *that* "c" word.

The "c" word to which I refer is far more damaging in terms of a Healing Journey.

What "c" word could possibly be any worse than the obvious?

CLOSURE

This "c" word is absolutely horrendous…and the "c" word would not merit repeated discussion if it did not continue to be a huge problem.

Regardless of whatever bad thing we have experienced, as used today, "closure" refers to some mysterious component that we are assumed to be frantically seeking on our Healing Journeys. "Closure" has become catch-all code for an ultimate goal for which we are supposed to be striving to achieve. This alleged goal is evidently reached when we wake up one day and *ta-da!* The pain, the sorrow, the anger, the raw grief and apparently the experience itself have collectively vanished from our psyches. After the "ta-da" moment, we then dust off our hands and say, "Okay, it's 'closed.' I'm all better. What's next?"

How many times have you been told "Now you'll have closure" (or words to that effect) since your own bad-thing experience? Have you heard it once? Twice? Eight thousand times? If so, I am going to save you a lot of frustration in the search for closure by revealing a colossal secret:

There is *no such thing* as "closure." Quit looking for it.

When news of the death of Osama Bin Laden hit the airwaves in May 2011, I too was in front of the television for hours. However, almost immediately after the President announced that the mastermind behind the worst terrorist attack in America's history (as well as other terrorist attacks around the world) was indeed dead, reporters, news anchors, pundits and worst of all, people calling themselves "experts" (and who should ostensibly know better), took to their microphones and keyboards, throwing around the "c" word in reference to the survivors of the victims of September 11, 2001; the survivors of lost military loved ones; the survivors of first responders; public safety employees; and many others who have died as a direct result of September 11.[96]

Alarmingly, the collective attitude was, "Yippee! Bin Laden is dead. Now all these poor survivors have closure."

Seriously?

Did anyone ever once stop to think that rather than some kind of mythical closure, many survivors were instead experiencing a grief-revisit? That rather than doing the Dance of Joy or popping champagne corks in celebration of closure, these brave souls were instead back in a place of horrendous pain?

---

96 Due to toxicity-borne illnesses.

That the Band-Aid precariously covering a gapingly painful wound was just ripped off to re-expose that wound? That just perhaps, this event brought terrible memories back to nightmarish life?

Did anyone ever *once* stop to consider that as a result of Osama Bin Laden's death, many survivors felt like they were literally starting from square one in their recovery?

(…And that is what *I* said on the air).

Here's a newsflash (and perhaps what should have been an *actual* newsflash): Any bad-thing experience is something from which you move *forward*. It becomes a part of you. You do not "close" it. It does not cease to exist.

I have been quacking for years about "closure" and how there is truly no such thing when it comes to bad things. Closure is something that surgeons do when they complete an operation. Closure is what happens to the fast lane on the freeway after an accident, generally during rush hour. Unfortunately and as defined by too many, "closure" apparently means that you have the desire or the capability to leave your bad thing in the past. Essentially, "closure" has become a diplomatic way of saying, "Get on with it. You're done now, it's closed," because people are either uncomfortable with or do not care to deal with what you have been through or what you may be going through right now. The Closure Crowd is dictating *your* timeline for *your* bad-thing Healing Journey…and they just do not want to hear about it anymore because in their minds it is now "closed." [97]

Now, do not confuse closure with healing. You absolutely *should* pursue healing and moving forward from your bad-thing experience in healthy ways.

But "closure"? *Never!*

First, you cannot have something that does not exist, and we know that closure does not exist. Secondly, even if you had the ability to "close" your bad-thing experience, why would anyone *want* to? Why would anybody willingly close themselves off from a huge part of their life? Have I healed and moved forward from the tragic loss and raw pain that was my husband's death and

---

97 I suppose that someone pronouncing that you now have "closure" is more diplomatic than saying *"I don't want to hear about it…shut the f**k up already."*

the over two years that led up to his death? Yes, I have. Do I have "closure"? Absolutely not.

To all of the courageous survivors of bad things, I happily repeat what I have also discussed in two other books, in countless articles and on numerous shows of varying sort. Rather than think of your Healing Journey in terms of achieving "closure," I encourage you instead to think of your bad thing as the life-altering event that it is and from which you move *forward*. Do you want to leave the horrible feelings of grief and anguish behind? Of course you do. But "slam the door" on your past? No way. You instead bring your loss experience *forward* with you as you move forward into your new life.

It is my sincerest hope that through continued education and by standing up as a sisterhood and shouting *"Stop it!"*, the word "closure" will once again be limited to surgeries and freeway shut-downs. Until then, I am going to keep right on making noise and I am going to keep reassuring millions of people with broken hearts and holes-in-souls that you do not have to "close" anything.

Not now...and not ever.

Chapter Nineteen

IS HAPPY EVEN AFTER
REALLY EVEN POSSIBLE?

THE SHORT ANSWER…IS A RESOUNDING *"YES!"*

Have you noticed one large common denominator running throughout this entire book? Every single woman who fearlessly shared their story overcame the circumstances that befell them.

They persevered.

They did not give up or give in.

They did not listen to those who were unsupportive or negative.

Every single one of these women designed and defined both their Healing Journeys and their futures.

You must remember that while your past—whatever that past may entail—will definitely *shape* you, it does not have to *define* you. If you are dealing with any bad thing whatsoever, know that the grieving process is vital to healing; however, you are not destined to live in a place of sorrow for the rest of your life. Remember what we learned earlier: You do *not* have to settle for where you are if where you are…is not where you choose to be.

Let's go back to December 22, 2000, where you and I started our journey together. Following is the second-half of the thought process that ultimately became a teaching tool to those who have or who are facing loss or life-challenge:

Healing began with a choice.

That one tiny step...

I decided then and there (and while you are reading, I want you to imagine that this is you, talking to you):

- **Although I've experienced a devastating, life-altering event or seemingly insurmountable challenge, it is *because* I am still here that makes me entitled to the life that I want to live:** I do not have to wait any specific amount of time to begin or continue my Healing Journey, and I will not question my right to live a life of happiness. Settling for less than the life that I choose to design for myself will never be an option.

- **My Healing Journey is *mine:*** It belongs to no one else. I cannot be compared to other people, and my bad thing cannot be compared to any other experiences. Even though there may be people around me who wish I would, I cannot "hurry" my Healing Journey—and for that reason, I will not try to avoid my healing processes. Healing is neither fast nor easy, and I will truthfully honor whatever I'm feeling when I am feeling it, rather than let others' opinions dictate how I "should" be feeling.

- **I recognize that I cannot avoid the grieving process, and trying to do so will only result in my grief eventually resurfacing:** I also recognize that I do not have to do this alone and I will surround myself with the support of others who understand exactly what I've been through. If I do not feel that I am making any progress, I will consult with my doctor, my cleric, a therapist, a mental health expert or anyone else who is in a position to help.

- **I am open to meeting new people, especially those who relate to and understand what I have experienced and what I am going through now:** During difficult periods of time when I feel that the faith I have in myself is wavering, I will turn to those who will breathe belief into me, rather than turn to those who might bring me down.

- **I acknowledge that not everyone will agree with what I do or how I do it; however, as long as I am not hurting myself or anyone else, I will pursue my Healing Journey in the ways that I see fit:** I further recognize that my identity and self-esteem have nothing to do with my current or future marital status, what I look like, my career path, a number on a scale, material accumulation or what anyone else's opinion might be. My identity and self-esteem come from within, and my opinion of myself remains the most important.

- **I recognize that I cannot control life circumstances and/or the activities of other people:** Bad things that are beyond my control are indeed *beyond my control.* For that reason, I will eschew humiliation, guilt, embarrassment or feeling otherwise ashamed. Further, I will not use these feelings as a way to avoid those who truly care about me and want only for my healing and happiness.

- **I recognize that my Healing Journey is not simply about my bad thing or my needs alone:** I realize there are people around me who are eager to help. I also understand that people may be hesitating to call or initiate invitations because they are afraid of intruding—and I will reassure those people that I am receptive to calls and invitations for quietly social activities. Additionally, I will strive to occasionally pick up the phone and initiate invitations as well. If applicable, I will also accept practical offers of help that fit into my comfort zone, remembering that letting others help me will help them as well.

- **I accept that I cannot control the fact that I have suffered a bad thing—but I *can* control what I am going to do as a result:** Whatever I decide to do or try, I will do so with the understanding that by exploring new opportunities and experiences, I am not casting aspersion on or disrespecting my past. I am taking control of a bad-thing situation over which I may have had little or no control by honoring my past without living in my past, welcoming today, designing my destiny and embracing a future of my choosing.

  And through my darkness, the light began to shine again.

  The uneasy quiet eventually filled with laughter and hope.

  The calm came.

  It does *not* have to hurt forever.

  It does *not* have to be dark forever.

  It does *not* have to be a life without laughter, without new possibilities...

  Or love.

  And you know what else I discovered?

  When you silently ask yourself, "Is this really *it?*"

  Your "this" doesn't have to be *"it."*

  Make your decision.

  Remembering that if you think you can, you can...

  And if you think you can't, you're right.

  Bad things *do* happen—but bad things do not have the final say.

  Bad things are only a small part of your life's journey—not your destination.

  Don't focus on "can't" or "shouldn't" or "What will they think?"

  Change your focus to "can," "will" and "What do *I* want?"

  Scream your declaration of healing to the world...and journey forward.

  Wishing that you know only blessings and "good things," now and always.

  Your journey continues...

  Starting...right...*now.*

acknowledgements

THE AUTHOR LOVINGLY AND GRATEFULLY ACKNOWLEDGES THOSE WITHOUT whom any success (let alone three books) would have been entirely impossible:

To an incredible team of visionaries and positivity personified: My agent, Dr. Sidney Harriet, and Agents Ink, from my beginnings in the world that is writing, you have believed, you have advocated and you have never once questioned either the mission or my sanity. Just as I have shared the challenges, so too I share the celebrations. I also must express my sincerest thanks to Viva Editions and everyone at Start Media Group for your dedication, commitment and patience in bringing this project to fruition—with very special thanks to Mia Amato, Susan Twum-Baah, Stephanie Lippitt, Meghan Kilduff, Karen Thomas, Gretchen Spiegel and Sid Orlando.

My "Glam Squad" is second to none and I would be lost without Teddie Tillett, Ashley Hoffman, Brandon Hyman and Anna and everyone on the "Princess Team." Thank you all for putting up with my last-minute nonsense, making everything happen the way that it needs to and for helping me to be the best "me" possible (a daunting task).

Nothing can be accomplished without those who are willing to help us reach an audience in need. I give my sincerest thanks to the many members of the media with whom I've had the privilege of working through the years, with very special thanks to: Deborah Norville, Amy Newmark and all of the editors and crew at Chicken Soup for the Soul; Arianna Huffington, James Thilman, Shelley Emling, Laura Rowley, Kristen Stenerson and everyone at the *Huffington Post;* Nancy Redd and the crew at *HuffPost Live;* Nate Berkus; David Cruz III and Nicole J. Adelman; Leslie Marcus and FOX/KSWB; Brooke Russell and CBS/KMOV; Jessika Ming-Yonekawa, Andrea Flores, Elaine Ledesma, Stacey Butler, Michael Joseph James and the wonderful team at CBS2/KCAL9 who have supported us for many years; Shawn Tempesta, Dao Vu and ABC/KTNV; Cynthia Newdel and FOX/KVVU; Kim Iverson; Amy Morin; Mary Jones and Tony Borelli; Victoria Davis; Nick Lawrence; the dynamic duo that are Stacey Gualandi and Pamela Burke; Gary Pozsik; Ben Merens; Francesca Bastarache; Tim Ridley and the team of "Jacie and Jeep" at SiriusXM; Evan Gold and Deb Goldman; Dr. Stan Frager and Kate Chawansky; Sondra Forsyth and ThirdAge and every single member of the media with whom we have worked over the years. Thank you for being so willing to deliver our messages of hope to the millions who need to hear it.

Out of tragedy, blessings can emerge in the form of earth angels. My earth angels include Senator Nina Turner, Kristen Higson-Hughes, Stacey Gualandi, Lee and Bob Woodruff, Lisa Kline, Jennifer Arches, Shannon Bell, Michelle Neff Hernandez and Michael Dare, James Alt, Randy Neece and Joe Timko, James Patrick Herman and Christopher Bahls. Thank you all for being the earth angels in my life.

I give much love to our "Ritz Family," the people who helped me stand during the darkest times and who cheer me on to this day. Special love to Beccy Rogers, Judy Simpson, Sharon Virtue, Jim Roberts, Staci Beech, Lisa Jenkins, Kim Guse, Stacey Fetterman, Taylor "Tay-Tay" Gibson, Moises Mejia, Noelle Williamson, "Uncle" Arthur Shegog and Walter "Uncle Stretchy" Yong.

To the entire Widows Wear Stilettos team: Your contributions to the community we serve are indeed without number, and to all of our hundreds of WWS volunteers and ambassadors in the United States, Canada, the United

Kingdom and Bermuda, I am deeply grateful for the love and support that you have given to so many in need. Thank you all for making Widows Wear Stilettos a pioneer and a leader in helping millions to heal.

When the people of your long-ago choose to support your present, it must be celebrated. It is with gratitude that I lovingly celebrate this moment with: Nanci (Doran) Cooley, Karen (Anderson) Cooper, Laura (Billingsley) Evink, Susan (Venuti) Hampton, Lisa Guest, Taryn Whiteleather, Kathy (Green) Schutt, Nancy (Lum) Korb, Donna (Salvitti) Nagle, Pamela (Jaques) Marches, Dr. Carla Payne (Beach Boys forever!), Dr. Mark Ivanicki, Connie Skogen, Gary and Elissa Wahlenmaier, Doug Tatom (of blessed memory), Sharla Sanders, Mark and Tina Armijo, Gary and Kathy Bruce, Gene Genisauski, Derek and Stacey (Brewsaugh) Gee, Mercy Songcayauon Cheung, Rosie "Bing Bing" Gasche, Mariellen Belen, Lyn Ramirez, Royce Ramirez, Rachelle Basso and Rhonda Okurowski, Linda (Snyder) Steward (my roomie!) and Debra Boyd (still waiting on the mezzanine for chicken enchiladas). Your love and support mean the world to me, and I do not take it or any of you for granted.

Bobby Slayton, for giving me the gifts of laughter and courage; for sharing your beautiful girls with me; for teaching me to stay true to my "inner skull"; for constantly reminding all of us that it will always be okay to laugh no matter what; and of course, for your amazing homemade Pizza Rosa, I love you. Teddie Tillett Slayton, you are my "sister," my heart and my center of gravity. I don't know what I would do or where I would be without you, and it is my prayer that everyone in the world has a Teddie in their lives to be for them what you are to me—I love you so much. Natasha Tillett Slayton, you are my forever "like-a-daughter" and as you continue to rise to the heights of success for which you have worked most of your life, I stand in both pride and awe of you. Your Mommy C loves you without end.

Joel Berman and Rob Gludt: You eased a pathway of illness and dying with compassion, love and humor and are a shining example for others to follow. Also fresh from the "Mensch Department" are Hallie Berman and Rabbi Kelley Gludt: Thank you both for sharing your boys with us and for twenty years (and countless hours) of girl-time, encouragement, hand-holding, listening, crying, praying, laughing and celebrating. I love all of you.

Without the love, support and understanding of family there can be no real success. My family regularly sacrifices so much in order to allow me to do what I do…and they do so with grace and a smile. It is with all my love that I again thank my partner in life and in love, Dave "Stanno" Stansbury; my amazing daughters, Kendall and Michelle who inspire me every day to do more, be more and try harder; and the creator of so many "Mom-isms," my mother, Eilene Clinkenbeard; as well as Kenneth "The Boss" Stansbury; Terry and Pam Stansbury and the Leeson/Gullick Families; David Clinkenbeard; Barbara Hedrick; Russell Gilbert, MD, and Kiyomi Gilbert; Max and Linda Ciampoli; Chuck Collins and Randy George; Gloria Rhodes and Jennifer Bulger; and every single member of the Berman/Spielman/Horn Families; the Gaylord/Bernstein/Nantais Families; the Williamson Families; the Zimmer Family and the Bobinsky/Fahrenkrug/Borg Families. A super-special thank you to Sue and Diane (Peaches 'n' Cream!) for so graciously allowing me to tell our tales. I love you all so very much.

Finally, to three people whom I love deeply and to whom I owe so very much. Walter Gobas (1922–2013), Rena Tarbet (1943–2013) and Bonnie Peterson (1952–2014): Your absence from this earth has left a huge hole in my heart and in the world. It is with all my love that I pray this work is to your honor and that I have done service to the many teachings that all of you gave to me over so many years. Even now, I can almost hear you saying, "Enough already Fleet, get back to work."

And so I shall.